Ethics and Selfhood

Ethics and Selfhood

Alterity and the Phenomenology of Obligation

James Richard Mensch

STATE UNIVERSITY OF NEW YORK PRESS

Published by
State University of New York Press, Albany

© 2003 State University of New York

For information, address State University of New York Press,
90 State Street, Suite 700, Albany, NY, 12207

Production by Diane Ganeles
Marketing by Jennifer Giovani

Library of Congress Cataloging-in-Publication Data

Mensch, James R.
    Ethics and selfhood : alterity and the phenomenology of obligation /
James Richard Mensch.
        p. cm.
    Includes bibliographical references and index.
    ISBN 0–7914–5751–6 (alk. paper) — ISBN 0–7914–5752–4 (pbk. : alk. paper)
    1. Ethics. 2. Phenomenology. 3. Self (Philosophy). 4. Other (Philosophy)
    I. Title.
B945.M485 E84 2003
170—dc21
                                                                    2002030482

10 9 8 7 6 5 4 3 2 1

This book is dedicated to Jessica Claire Mensch
and to the promise of her work

Contents

Acknowledgments

Some of the chapters appearing in this volume are reworked versions of previously published articles. Acknowledgment is made to the following publishing houses, periodicals and persons for their kind permission to republish all or part of the following articles: "Selfhood and Politics," *Symposium, Journal of the Canadian Society for Hermeneutics and Postmodern Thought* 6:1 (2002), "Crosscultural Understanding and Ethics," in *New Europe at the Crossroads I*, ed. U. Beitter (New York: Peter Lang Publishers, 1999), "Rescue and the Face to Face: Ethics and the Holocaust" in *New Europe at the Crossroads II*, ed. U. Beitter (New York: Peter Lang Publishers, 2001), and "Literature and Evil" in *Ethics and Literature*, ed. Dorothee Gelhard (Berlin: Galda and Wilch, 2002). I wish to express my gratitude to Dr. Mordecai Paldiel, the Director, Department for the Righteous, for permission to quote from the material at the Archives at Yad Vashem in Jerusalem. Without Dr. Paldiel's assistance and encouragement, a crucial chapter of this book could not have been written. I also wish to thank the director of the Husserl Archives in Louvain, Professor Rudolph Bernet, for extending me the hospitality of the Archives and granting me permission to quote from the *Nachlass*. Finally, grateful acknowledgment is due to the Social Sciences and Humanities Research Council of Canada for a grant supporting the research that made this volume possible.

Introduction

Ethics and the Human Framework

The experience of the past century presents a remarkable feature. Its course was punctuated by attempts to eliminate entire populations. Given this history, the very least we can ask from an ethics is that it guard against the moral collapse that accompanies genocide. This seems like a relatively straightforward demand. We all assume that our ethical sensitivities would have been outraged were we to have been, for example, contemporary witnesses to the isolation, roundup, and extermination of the Jews in Nazi-occupied Europe. Hannah Arendt, however, reminds us that these actions were legally sanctioned. As she notes in her classic study *Eichmann in Jerusalem*, they apparently enjoyed a nearly universal, if tacit, approval. Both the academic community and the religious establishment kept a prudent silence. Those seeking to oppose them had to rely on their own sense of conscience. This, however, seemed "completely at odds with what they must regard as the unanimous opinion of all those around them" (Arendt 1977, 295). The ethical sense expressed by their communities was incapable of resisting the unprecedented circumstances that obtained. The result was that when people did resist, they could not rely on this sense. In Arendt's words, they "went really only by their own judgments, and they did so freely. . . . They had to decide each instance as it arose, because no rules existed for the unprecedented" (295).[1] Most people, however, did not resist. The overwhelming majority went along with the roundups and deportations.

What is behind this failure to act? The practical reasons for not resisting the Nazis are obvious enough. The whole power of their police state, with all its ruthless brutality, was employed to prevent people from opposing their actions. Beyond this, however, the particular type of crime they committed played a role. Its nature as a "crime against humanity" was such that it exceeded the attempts to make sense of it. Its very senselessness often disabled people's judgment. This may be put in terms of Arendt's remark that a crime against humanity is not simply a war crime. It is not, for example, on a par with shooting partisans or killing hostages. It involves something more than the inhuman

1

or particularly cruel acts that are taken for "some known, though criminal purpose." The crime in which humanity itself comes to be "grievously hurt and endangered" is one where the object is "the extermination of whole ethnic groups" (Arendt 1977, 275). Eichmann, she writes, "supported and carried out a policy of not wanting to share the earth with the Jewish people and the people of a number of other nations . . . " (279). He and his superiors assumed they had the "right to determine who should and should not inhabit the world . . . " (279). Implicit here is a telling characteristic of genocide. As practiced by the Nazis, the crime involved acting outside of the framework of humanity, that is, being beyond the "earth" and deciding who should and should not inhabit it.[2] In other words, the "crime against humanity" implies taking a standpoint *outside* of humanity. Given that all moral justification draws its sense from the human framework—the framework that includes its ethical, social, and religious ideals—to stand outside of this is to exceed such sense. It is to enter into a realm of senselessness that incapacitates moral judgment.[3] Here, the "hurt" suffered by humanity does not just involve its impoverishment through the elimination of one of its possibilities of being and behaving—the possibility that had been realized by the eliminated population. It includes the enforced suspension of the framework that allows people to recognize and react against this impoverishment.

The ethical imperative that follows from this analysis is that of preserving the context that permits moral judgment. For the person acting, the demand is that of integrating one's standpoint within a framework where it can achieve moral sense. The practical import of this imperative extends far beyond events like the Holocaust. It appears, for example, in a number of contemporary ethical issues. Many of these center around genetics and bioengineering, where recent advances push us beyond the contexts that once guided our thinking. Thus, we are now in the process of overcoming the biological limits of human existence. The technology of implanting frozen embryos in surrogate mothers does not just make the time and place of birth an open issue; it also raises the question of the discarding of the unused embryos. Are the latter alive or not? Do we have any responsibilities to them? How far do they have to develop before they elicit a moral as opposed to a strictly utilitarian response? Parallel questions occur when we consider the end of life. According to one leading theory of aging, we die because the cellular repair process in our organism ceases after a definite, genetically determined time. Making this process continue by inhibiting the timing mechanism that shuts it off, thus, involves the theoretical possibility of living indefinitely. Should we attempt to realize this? What would a life be like that had no end?

How would this affect our relations to the old? Given that the whole of human experience is that of biological finitude—i.e., of living with the inevitable approach of death—we have no ready answers.[4] Our progress in the technologies of genetic manipulation confront us with similar aporia. These technologies now allow us to make life-forms with specific qualities. In the not too distant future, it is conceivable that completely new organisms could be created. As the biologist Wolf Singer noted: "[T]he complete synthesis of the elements that can develop into an organism has become conceivable" (Singer 1996, 19). The question that these prospects raise is what, if any, limits should be put on applying this new knowledge. How far, for example, should we apply the technologies of genetic manipulation to ourselves?

Discussions on this point invariably recall the Nazis' attempts at selective breeding. This common practice of animal husbandry was applied to humans. Singer observes, "It was only when the racist ideologies adopted these, in some sense, natural experiences of genetic manipulation that we were shocked . . . " (19). The Nazis did not just decide that certain "inferior races" should not share the earth, they also thought that a certain genetic type (blond, northern European) should prevail. Is what is shocking here the fact that their decisions were arbitrary and based solely on power? Or are we shocked by the fact that such decisions were made at all, i.e., that the Nazis assumed a standpoint that allowed them to take them? If it is for the latter reason, then contemporary developments are equally disturbing. Thus, the advances in bioengineering force us to consider the ethics of taking up a standpoint that decides, not on possibilities *within* humanity, but rather on the possibilities of humanity itself. This standpoint necessarily stands outside of humanity, even though the people who occupy it are members of some human group. Recent developments in brain research and the replacement of human with artificial intelligence raise similar considerations about the standpoint that would use the powers they afford us. So does modern warfare. Our present capabilities of mass destruction are still such that those who would exercise them could decide, not just the fate of various human groups, but that of humanity itself.

The sense that something is wrong with the standpoint assumed by those who would make such decisions can be expressed in terms of the contradiction it implies. Formally, the contradiction concerns the concepts of ground and grounded. It involves decision makers, situated within the human framework and, hence, *grounded* in humanity and its relations, assuming the position of a ground of humanity. Any group that decides what humanity should be—i.e., decides not just its future, but on the "nature" of the humanity that is to have a future—makes a decision whose justification cannot be drawn from the existing human framework. The formal contradiction, then, is between being grounded by such framework and assuming a position whose justification necessarily stands outside of it. Ethically speaking, the contradiction involves the fact that moral justification draws its sense from the human framework. To leave this framework is, essentially, to leave ethics behind. It is to enter a moral vacuum where the call to justify one's actions is undermined by the absence of justification implicit in occupying a standpoint beyond humanity.[5]

The Abstract Subject

To examine how we arrived at this position is the objective of the first chapter. In outline, however, the account can be reduced to two factors. The first is the enormous increase in our technical powers since Galileo and Descartes initiated modern science. Our technologies have given us abilities with regard to nature, warfare, and political manipulation that exceed the human scale. Coincident with this has been the development of the notion of the individual subject as an essentially autonomous agent. This second factor is deeply entwined in the first: the modern idea of autonomy is correlated with the demands of modern science. Thus, Descartes in his *Meditations* marks the beginning of the modern conception of selfhood with his reduction of the subject to the "I" of the "I think." This subject, whose understanding focuses on the numerable aspects of the world, can, according to Descartes, be considered apart from its body. When we do this, we abstract the subject from all the particular conditions—such as sex, age, and social position—that might affect its observations. The scientific motives for regarding the subject as a disembodied, independent observer are readily apparent. Every such observer, when properly trained, is equivalent to every other. Each can perform the same scientific experiments without fear of being influenced by external factors, since each limits himself or herself to the selfhood that, ideally, is only a "pure" autonomous observer of the abstract and measurable aspects of reality. However valuable this limitation may be for scientific progress, it obviously represents an abstraction from the general framework of humanity. Carried to the extreme, it cuts off the self from the resources required to make ethical decisions. Here, of course, we must distinguish the paradigm of the subjectivity that accomplishes scientific work from the self that is the object of this work, e.g., the self as studied in sociology, psychology, brain research, and so forth. It is the former that takes up the stance of the autonomous observer. The result is not merely the accumulation of enormous, almost superhuman technological powers; it is the association of these with the subjectivity that uncovers them, a subjectivity that proceeds by abstraction from the human framework.

Descartes's point in engaging in this abstraction is to escape the particularities of our embodiment. His attempt is to proceed beyond what is relative to such particularities to what is objectively true, that is, to what is true in itself—for example, those universal laws of nature that hold always and everywhere. His insight is that to the point that each observer is substitutable for every other, such laws come into focus. A similar thrust towards universalization informs the moral thinking of modernity. Its most radical expression occurs in Kant's account of freedom. Beginning with the commonplace observation that people are morally responsible only for their voluntary actions, Kant defines such actions as autonomous. These are actions where the will determines itself by itself. In his words, the autonomous will has the "property . . . of being a law unto itself (independently of every property belonging to the objects of volition)" (Kant 1964, 108; 1955a, 440).[6] Thus, the free individual does not just determine how he will react to the circumstances confronting him. His self-determination requires him to abstract from these circumstances. The best way to describe this radical position is in terms of the distinction Kant draws between autonomy and heteronomy. The will is heteronomous when its choices are determined by something other than itself. What then controls it is the desire to achieve a given result—for example, the desire to gain a specific object. In such a situation the will, according to Kant, is *not* free. The actual agent is not the self, but rather the world. The world acts through the person by means of the inclinations its objects cause in him. The world is thus what controls his will. The upshot is that to be autonomous, i.e., self-directed, one must "set aside altogether the influence of inclination and, along with inclination, every object of the will" (Kant 1964, 68; 1955a, 400). This includes even the results one wishes to achieve.[7] Such an abstraction is necessarily also an abstraction of the willing subject from its situating context. Insofar as this subject abstracts its motives from the particularizing influence of the world, it is, like Descartes's pure observer, no different from any other agent. How could it distinguish itself, given that to reach the autonomous agent, we must "abstract from the personal differences between rational beings, and also from all the content of their private ends" (1964, 101; 1955a, 433)?

As in Descartes, the gain expected from this abstraction is an access to what holds independently of the particularities of our situation. When we abstract from the particularities of our nature and situation, what

remains are the universal moral laws that exist as the Kantian parallel to
the universal laws of nature. Kant's move is, thus, from autonomy to
universality. In his words: "Since I have robbed the will of every induce-
ment that might arise for it as a consequence of obeying any particular
law, nothing is left but the conformity of actions to universal law as
such, and this alone must serve the will as its principle. That is to say, I
ought never to act except in such a way that I can also will that my
maxim should become a universal law" (Kant 1964, 70; 1955a, 402). This
last is the formula of the categorical imperative. To apply it is to see if
your maxim could "become through your will a universal law of nature"
(1964, 89; 1955a, 421). We do so when we universalize our maxim—i.e.,
attempt to see what would happen if everyone always adopted it.
Suppose, for example, your maxim is that a person can make false
promises to get out of a difficulty. Imagining this to be a universal law,
you see at once that such promises would never be believed. The maxim
cannot be universalized without making impossible the purpose of
promising (1964, 90; 1955a, 422). Now, to universalize a maxim is to
abstract the person following it from any particular situation. He cannot
plead any particular circumstances to justify his conduct. What must
motivate him is simply the maxim itself—or, rather, the objective, universal law it exemplifies. Robbed of any motive that might spring from
the consequences of obeying this law, nothing can make him follow it
but himself. He alone must bind himself to follow it. As autonomous or
free, nothing else will serve.[8] Given this, two conclusions follow. On the
one hand, we have to say with Kant that "the principle of autonomy is
the sole principle of ethics." On the other, it is clear that the "categorical
imperative . . . commands nothing more nor less than precisely this
autonomy" (1964, 108; 1995a, 440). It does so whenever it commands us
to universalize our maxims. As conceived by Kant, this universalization
both abstracts us from the world and commands us to act
autonomously, i.e., independently of it.

    If we take modernity in terms of its twin ideals of individual
autonomy and universality, then these two parallel abstractions, the
Cartesian and the Kantian, can be said to define it. The Cartesian
abstraction is epistemological. Through strict rules of method, it
abstracts the knowing subject from the particularities of its situation.
The Kantian abstraction is moral. It separates the willing subject from all
motivations springing from its particular circumstances. In both cases
the advantage promised is the ability to stand outside of and
autonomously judge one's situation. Thus, a Cartesian would explain the
special qualities of our bodily sensations by taking up the standpoint of
the universal, mathematically describable aspects of reality. She would,

for example, account for how we see a certain color by considering the electromagnetic waves striking our retina and the causal chains this initiates in the physical structures of our eyes and brain. Her explanation would be in terms of the universal laws governing such causal chains. Her evaluation of our subjective experience would proceed from this basis. In the Kantian parallel, the basis is the universal moral law. The abstraction required when we universalize our maxim separates us from the particularities of our situation. It thereby gives us the distance required to evaluate our response to it. What allows us to judge rather than just conform to the situation we find ourselves in is, in other words, the perspective of the universal law.

The difficulties with these abstractions parallel their advantages. In neither case is it clear that in taking up an external perspective we can really grasp what we are supposed to judge. How far, for example, is seeing color reducible to its universal physical description? Locke, writing a generation after Descartes, had his doubts. He writes: "We are so far from knowing what figure, size or motion of parts produce a yellow color, a sweet taste, or a sharp sound, that we can by no means conceive how any size, figure, or motion of any particles, can possibly produce in us the idea of any color, taste, or sound whatsoever: there is no conceivable connection between the one and the other" (Locke 1995, 445; Bk. IV, ch. 3, sec. 13). The same reflections caused Leibniz to affirm: "Perceptions . . . are inexplicable by mechanical causes, that is to say, by figures and motions."[9] The point of these philosophers (as well as their modern counterparts) is that the abstraction that was supposed to help us explain our felt qualitative experience actually made it unintelligible.[10] The same point may be made with regard to Kant's abstraction. Is the situation where we might need to make a false promise adequately accounted for by universalizing our maxim? Kant's ethics forbids us from taking account of the consequences: neither the harm we hope to avoid nor the good we expect can be considered in evaluating it. Here, the very radicality of Kant's procedure apparently eases the process of evaluation. In his descriptions, the method of universalization appears to be simplicity itself. Yet the resulting abstraction from the circumstances of an action has its price. It deprives us of the information required to evaluate it. As in the Cartesian account of our perceptual experience, essential elements are lacking. The result is that Kant's abstraction makes unintelligible the ethical act as it is *actually enacted*. The advantage promised by his procedure is clear. Kant promises us the ability to act and judge independently of the circumstances that frame us. The difficulty is that the separation from circumstances required for such autonomy deprives us of the context that is essential to its sense.

The Task

To avoid this separation is to return to the ethical imperative of
preserving the context that permits moral judgment. It is to accede to the
demand of integrating one's standpoint within the framework where it
can have its human sense. This is the framework that includes the judge
within the judged. In the chapters that follow, I will lay the groundwork
for an ethics shaped by this demand. At its basis will be a model of the
self that recognizes its essential situatedness within the human framework. The result will be an ethics that refuses to stand outside of humanity. Its norms will promote those decisions that work to integrate the
self within the whole that is humanity. Thus, the decisions informed by
this ethics would constantly reaffirm the possibility of taking an ethical
action by situating the self within the context that gives its action the
sense that allows it to be ethically evaluated.

In all this there is an overriding assumption. This is that the
resources required for ethical judgment can be found within the context
of the human community. This implies that in our interactions with
others we gain the possibility of evaluating rather than simply conforming to our situation. In other words, the assumption is that in the very
process of being framed (or situated) by others, we gain the possibility
of judging this framing. If this is true, then neither a Cartesian nor a
Kantian abstraction is required for ethical action. Rather, the independence or autonomy needed for such action is given by the frame itself.
To establish this is to show that our being within the human context is
the very thing that gives us the capacity to judge this context. The task
here is to show how our being with others both situates us in and
abstracts us from this situation, how it both provides the self with the
particulars required for judging and yields the distance necessary to
make a judgment. With regard to those who did resist the Nazis, it is to
see how their escaping their situation sprang from their facing it, how
their resistance was rooted in avoiding the enforced suspension of the
human situation.

A further element in the task ahead is implicit in the title of this
book. To call it *Ethics and Selfhood* emphasizes the point that a coherent
theory of ethics requires an account of selfhood. This is because ethical
theories, being about human actions and purposes, are also about our
selfhood. Even when they do not make it an explicit theme, a conception
of the selfhood of the agent still lies at their basis. When this is inade-
quate—that is, when this conception fails to capture the complexity of
the human reality required for ethical action—the ethics they propose is
undermined. The best way to counter this is to face the issue directly.

Ethics must take up the task of advancing a theory of selfhood that is adequate to its conception of our moral responsibilities.

To accomplish this, I shall take ethics as a kind of "transcendental clue" to the nature of selfhood. Assuming that moral actions are, in fact, possible, I will ask: What must be the nature of the self that engages in them? This question is not meant to advance a hypothetical conception of our selfhood—a conception whose only basis is an assumed set of ethical norms. My purpose is not merely to deduce the subjective conditions of the possibility of ethics. Beyond being deductive, my approach will also be phenomenological. Thus, the conditions uncovered will be taken as "clues"—that is, as pointing to where one should look for the evidence of this selfhood. The goal is to establish the nature of our ethical selfhood phenomenologically. On one level, this means regarding the direct evidence we have of its being and behaving, its successes and failures to live up to its ethical ideals. It is this spirit that the research material from the Yad Vashem Archives on those who rescued Jews will be introduced. On another level, the task involves an account of the constitution of this selfhood. Here the effort will be to exhibit the arising of those elements of our selfhood that make moral action possible. The work that follows, thus, has a dual focus. It is as much about selfhood as it is about ethics. Often, in the same chapter, it will move back and forth between these two themes, sometimes combining them as it attempts to gain both a conception of ethics adequate to our selfhood and one of selfhood adequate to our ethical sensibilities.

The Alterity of Selfhood

What, then, is the notion of selfhood that is called for? Put in the broadest possible terms, it is one that involves an inherent alterity. Traditionally, this has been understood in terms of the opposition of the individual and the collective aspects of our selfhood. This alterity has had various expressions. Both Plato and Kant, for example, see it in terms of the opposition of appetite and reason. My reason, regarding the sensuous promptings of my appetites, tells me whether I should follow them. It is what provides me with the ability to distance myself from myself and ethically evaluate my sensuous appetites. It is, in fact, because our selfhood embodies both—in Kant's words, because "we consider ourselves as belonging to the world of sense and yet at the same time to the intelligible world"—that we experience the tension between what we desire and what we know is right. This tension may be considered to be the experiential basis for our sense of the "ought" (Kant 1955a, 453-54;

my translation throughout). With Aristotle and Mill, our appetites are opposed not so much by reason as by the settled habits acquired through our socialization. In giving us a fixed character, our habits allow us to overcome the momentary impulses of our appetites. Darwin gives this opposition a biological interpretation, one that bases ethics on our inherited instincts. He sees our selfhood as split between our self-regarding instincts—those which find expression in appetitive impulses—and our social instincts. The former, while often violent in their passion, are not long lasting. The latter, in binding us to the members of our tribe, have a steady force. Here, the sense of the "ought" is taken as arising from the tension between the two instincts. Regarding the spent force of a momentary impulse from the more steady perspective of the social instinct, we feel a certain remorse, one springing from the thwarted social instinct. This prompts us to feel that we should not have given way to our momentary fears and desires—e.g., that we ought not to have abandoned our friends in a moment of danger, that we ought to have shared our food with them rather than keeping it for ourselves, and so on. Freud, to take a final example, psychologizes this division in our selfhood. It appears as the opposition of the id and the superego. The id is the place of our instinctual appetites. It is where they first make their organic presence felt. The superego, by contrast, exhibits the influence of others in their socializing us. Thus, it continues the influence of our parents in their action of imposing on us their moral strictures. It also includes, in Freud's words, the influence of "the family, racial and national traditions handed on through them, as well as the demands of the immediate social milieu which they represent" (Freud 1989, 3). For Freud, our sense of conscience originates in the superego's critical regard of the id's impulses.

The history of ethics, which I relate in chapter 3, is described in these terms. It is a history of the attempts to bring these opposing factors together, that is, to form from them a coherent picture of our selfhood. The difficulty faced by all such attempts is that of integrating the transcendence that results from our self-alterity. Thus, for Plato and Kant, the division between reason and appetite is so radical that it splits our selfhood between the intelligible and sensible worlds. Our "true" or "real" self belongs to the former. Our sensible, embodied self is relegated to the latter. The transcendence of the "true" self vis-à-vis its sensuous bodily presence yields the distance that assures it of the autonomy of its judgments. But the price paid is too high. Not only is there a loss of context for our ethical judgments, there is also a question of how they can have a practical effect. How do the freedom and reason that pertain to one world become manifest in the other? Those writers who attempt to overcome this by naturalizing this division—i.e., making it part of one and the same appearing world—do not face this problem, but they also lose the advantage that Plato and Kant promise. They leave us with the task of balancing the claims of one part of the self against the other without sufficiently opening up the distance necessary to adjudicate their claims. Symptomatic of this are the questions they leave us with. There are no ready answers when we ask: Which set of instincts should we follow, the social or the private, self-regarding ones? Should I always heed the voice of the superego against the promptings of the id, or should I realize (as Freud urges) that its commands are also flawed? Similarly, how do I know when the training that has socialized me is correct? Can I trust the character that society, through its laws and education, has imposed upon me?

How, then, is our self-alterity to be understood? How can we grasp it such that we can integrate the transcendence it affords us into the world in which we live and act? The tradition gives us a kind of transcendental clue. It reveals that what opposes appetite is actually the internalized presence of our others. Understood psychologically, this presence is that of the superego. It internalizes the authority of our others. For Freud, it is "only when the authority is internalized through the establishment of a superego . . . that we should speak of conscience or a sense of guilt" (Freud 1962, 72). When we give the same presence a biological interpretation, it appears as Darwin's social instinct. For Aristotle and Mill, the internal presence of others is that of the habits and character resulting from our socialization. As for Plato and Kant, others manifest themselves within us in the guise of reason. Thus, as Plato has Socrates admonish Callicles in the *Gorgias*, Callicles, in limiting himself to his appetites, cannot acknowledge others. In fact, "he is incapable of social life" (Plato 1971, 117; *Gorgias*, 507e). Here, reason pulls us into the intersubjective sphere. It does so by giving us a perspective beyond that of the privacy of bodily pleasure. For Kant, this perspective is that of the moral laws that reason proposes to itself. Others are present as the implied referent of their universality. They make this presence felt when the self asks what would happen if everyone followed a particular line of conduct. This constantly reoccurring reference to others points to a basic reality of our human condition, one that all these authors have had to confront: We are embodied beings who live with others. As a consequence, we are present to ourselves both organically and socially. Both sorts of presence have their demands: We have to satisfy our bodily needs and appetites. We must also "get along" and "go along" with one another. A major task of any practical ethics is to assist us in balancing the two—i.e., help us sort out our obligations both to ourselves and to our others. In terms of providing a coherent theory of the selfhood that engages in ethical action, the task is to integrate the transcendence necessary for judgment with the embodiment required for practical action. The self must be able to distance itself from itself, but not to the point that it uncouples the world in which it acts from that in which it knows. There must be no unbridgeable divide between the two.

Empathy and Self-Alterity

What is the paradigm of selfhood that meets these requirements? It is, first of all, one that recognizes that each of us is an embodied individual. As such, we are subject to a range of appetites directed, in the first instance, to our bodily well-being. Embodiment signifies singleness of perspective. In an immediate sense, we see only out of our own eyes, we feel only what our flesh reports to us. No person can perform the bodily functions of another person. Thus, no one can eat for you, sleep for you, and so on. Both your organic birth and death are unalterably your own. Our body, then, manifests our selfhood in its irreplaceable uniqueness. This uniqueness, however, is always being resituated by others. This cannot be otherwise, given the essential plurality of our condition. From conception onwards we are in relation to others. We are dependent on them and almost immediately after birth begin our efforts to bind our caregivers to ourselves. Because we rely on others, we must be able to gauge their actions and intentions. Thus, as we mature, our essential plurality manifests itself in our capacity for empathy. It shows itself in our ability to take up—on a number of different levels: emotional, imaginative, and intellectual—the standpoints of our others. When we do so, our self-presence undergoes a double shaping. On one level, each of us remains his or her organically unique self. On another, each takes up the selfhood of the other.

One way to see what happens to us when we do adopt the standpoint of the other is to see the effect on ourselves, while reading a novel, of our imaginatively entering into the world of one of its characters. Doing so is letting her world become our own. It is to feel her clothes on our skin, experience her rush of emotions, and so on. If we ask where this character "is", we cannot say that she is in the letters, words, or pages of the novel. Neither can we say, since in many cases the author is deceased, that she necessarily is in the author's mind. Is she, then, in the mind of the reader? Not in any natural scientific sense. The character is not "in" us—i.e., in our brain—like an object in a box. Rather, she is present insofar as we are "in" her, that is, insofar as we imaginatively take up her character, letting ourselves be shaped by her environment.

The type of understanding functioning here involves embodiment. The self, in this action, takes on, embodies, the features of what it understands. The paradigm is one where, instead of saying "I observe heat," I affirm that "I *am* hot." This "am" signifies that the selfhood that engages in this sort of understanding is itself a function of the embodiment it imaginatively takes on. Empathy—understood in its etymological sense of a "feeling in" another person—is characterized by this kind of understanding.[11] In allowing me to feel in and through another, empathy doubles my sense of myself. Thus, the understanding that allows me to read a novel inherently involves self-alterity. Overlaid on my sense of myself as defined by my environment, I have a sense of myself as another, i.e., as defined by the *different environment* that situates the other. This other is "in" me as "other" than me. As such, he abstracts me from my situation. To the point that this gives me the distance, the autonomy, that is required for its ethical appraisal, literature, in allowing me to live through the other, has an inherent ethical function.

Since from birth onwards we are always with others, this paradigm of empathetic understanding implies that selfhood is inherently dual, that it always manifests a split in our self-presence. I experience this split most dramatically when I confront the other who is in need. My empathetic apprehension of his need interrupts my enjoyment. Adopting his standpoint, I feel the hunger of the other overlaid on my satiety. I feel it as the bread snatched from my mouth. Separated from myself by taking up the standpoint of the other, I regard my own satiety from his need. Doing so, I am put into question. Confronting myself, I have a conscience. Hearing its "voice," I ask myself, in and through this other, why he is in need and I am not. On a more general level, the duality of my self-presence raises the question of the relation of the true for me and the true for my others. It presents me with the task of arriving at positions I can share with others. This task is both inter- and intrasubjective. It is both, because such others are both outside and within me. They externally confront me and are an inherent part of my selfhood insofar it is for-itself, i.e., able to stand back and regard itself.

The following chapters will explore this paradigm of selfhood in some depth. When they do so, it will be in terms of the claim that the presence of the other *in* us as *other* gives our self-presence a certain tension. Its self-regard is stretched between its desires and those of its others, between its own perspectives and truths and theirs. My claim will be that we experience this tension as the "ought" of ethics. Regarding ourselves from the perspectives of our others, we evaluate our conduct. As a result, we say that we ought not to give way to certain inclinations or, correspondingly, we ought to oblige others in certain ways. Such self-separation is our freedom insofar as it liberates us from being defined by our immediate environments. It is also our framing, since it places us in the human context that provides us with our ethical criteria. It is, in other words, not by standing outside of this context that we gain the autonomy needed for judgment. The displacement required is, rather, provided by our being resituated by our others. Such resituation, insofar as it places us in their contexts, opens us up to possibilities of the human condition. In doing so, it gives us the data required for ethical evaluation.

Life and the Excess of Self-Alterity

Can this paradigm account for the rescuers of the Jews? The documentary evidence is that they acted largely on their own. Rather than expressing the sentiments of their largely anti-Semitic contexts, their actions opposed these. How, then, can it be said that their others gave them the autonomy they needed for ethical action? More broadly, the question is: How does an encounter with another person induce the self-separation that allows you not just to transcend yourself, i.e., exceed your particular perspective, but also transcend the rules of your society? How, in fact, does the other's calling you into question result in your being able to call society itself into question? The answer comes from the peculiar nature of the relation of rescue. The relation has a unique one-to-one, unconditioned quality. As such, it abstracts you from society. Thus, as the accounts stored at Yad Vashem indicate, the circumstance that initiated the act of rescue was generally that of a face-to-face encounter with the victim. The rescuer experienced this as a unique, nontransferable responsibility imposed on him by the other. If the rescuer did not act to save the other, his life would be forfeit. The rescuer's experience of the appeal of the other as unavoidable and unconditioned stemmed from the recognition of what was at stake. This was the other's life itself in its irreplaceable, unconditioned quality. The intuition here is that without life nothing else is possible. Without it, we cannot act, we cannot value, we cannot judge. In fact, given that without life, there are no human possibilities, we have to say that life itself *exceeds* these in being the unconditioned ground of everything else. As such, there are no grounds I can appeal to in order to avoid its appeal. Its exceeding quality, thus, causes me to exceed myself. In its absolute demand, it places an obligation on me, an "ought" that is beyond the rules of my society. To put this in terms of empathy is to observe that when I take up the standpoint of the endangered person, I let myself be shaped by the thought of my own annihilation. Facing death through the other, I experience the contingency of my own life. Asking myself why I have shaped it in this way rather than in another manner, I place it in the frame of a series of possibilities that collectively exceed those that I have realized. This exceeding, which comes from the exceeding quality of life, thus causes me to exceed myself. It is my self-separation, my ability to transcend and, hence, judge my situation.

Why, then, did most people ignore this demand coming from the life of the victim? Why did they not have the intuition just described? Stereotyping, I will argue, prevented them from recognizing what was at stake. Such stereotyping, which typically positioned the victim as an exploiter of society, as a "virus" or a form of "vermin," reduced the life at risk to a limited and distasteful set of possibilities. As such, it masked its exceeding quality.

Ethics and Politics

As we shall see, this exceeding quality is correlated to the possibility of self-concealment. To the degree that I am open to the possibilities of my others, i.e., "understand" them in the empathetic sense, I also understand that I am capable of more than I can possibly manifest. By virtue of this, I have an inherent hiddenness. In deciding to actualize one set of possibilities rather than another, I choose what to reveal and what to conceal from my others. Here my very freedom as both self-exceeding and as exercising choice can be seen to be socially constituted. Others, in their informing me of life's possibilities, inform me of the choices that make freedom real. Insofar as they reposition me, they cause me to exceed myself. They, thus, stock my autonomy with a set of possible ways of being and behaving that exceed those given by my immediate environment. By virtue of this, they turn the self-transcendence they occasion into the self-exceeding of freedom. They give my acting the possibility of the new, the unforeseen.

The upshot of this argument, which chapter 6 makes in some detail, is that our ethical selfhood is not something inherent, not a natural quality given at birth. It is, rather, given in and through the human framework. As such, it can be undermined and even, at the extreme, eliminated as this framework is progressively impoverished. The ethics that grows out of this is informed by the demand of keeping open the possibilities for ethical judgment and action. Concretely, this means maintaining the possibilities that underlie our self-transcendence and self-exceeding.

Translated into politics, we have the call to preserve the diversity of our human condition. This can be put in terms of what this ethics implies with regard to society's having a conscience. As I noted, an individual's conscience is based on his self-alterity, i.e., on the other's being "in" him as part of his self-presence. To the degree that a person allows himself to be called into question by this other, he has a conscience. For a society to have a conscience in this way, its collective self-presence must express a similar alterity. For this to occur, different forms of its self-presence have to embody different aspects of our human condition. Each must be essential to this condition as presently constituted. Each, however, as just one among many such forms, only partially expresses this condition and, hence, depends on other such expressions. Incapable of reducing the others to its own perspective, each, then, can be called into question by the other expressions of what it means to be human. Providing a society with the means to have a conscience means giving institutional expression to these different forms. It requires that each be given the power to call the others into account for their actions. As examples of the forms of the human condition, I will make use of Hannah Arendt's trinity of labor, making, and socio-political action. Other forms could be added to these, without impairing the argument. What is essential is the goal, which is that of giving society the means to call itself into question. Negatively, this involves the structuring of our social and political life so as to prevent its collapsing into a single expression of the human condition. Positively, the demand is that we settle our conflicts through negotiation. By this I mean a process that keeps open the alternatives whose claims it mediates. Such negotiation is our responsibility to the essential plurality of our human condition. It responds to and keeps open the alterity that defines and enriches it.

1

Selfhood and Certainty

The Axiomatic Subject

It has long been a commonplace that while modern philosophers have excelled in the more abstract branches of their discipline, they still fail to come up to the standards of the Greeks when it comes to formulating a coherent theory of ethics. The difficulty does not involve their skills at argument or the subtlety of their ethical insights. In the latter, they are probably superior to the ancients. The problem revolves around the modern concept of the self. Attempting to position it as normative, that is, as providing standards for both knowing and acting, they ended by abstracting it from the world. As a result, they eliminated the context required to make sense of the self. The history of how this happened is instructive. On the one hand, it leads to the insight that if this abstraction does rob the self or subject of its intelligible sense, then this sense must come from the world. On the other, it points to the way we should conceive the self if we are to put forward a coherent theory of its capability for moral action.

The intellectual climate of today, with its multiple timidities born of the collapse of the philosophical paradigms of modernity, stands in sharp contrast to the optimism of the period when these paradigms were first fashioned. This is particularly true of the modern conception of the self. It arose in the great expansion of outlook that followed the discoveries of the fifteenth and sixteenth centuries. On the one hand, it seemed as if everything was possible. On the other, this very wealth of possibilities threatened to overwhelm all inherited certainties. Different peoples were discovered with different customs. Not only were the Europeans confronted with ancient, self-sufficient civilizations with different religious and civil traditions, they also faced a bewildering variety of primitive tribes and customs. Such experience prompted Montaigne to write in his essay, "Of Cannibals," that "we have no other criterion of truth and reason than the example and pattern of the opinions and customs of the country wherein we live" (Montaigne 1949, 77–78). Montaigne's skepticism with regard to our criteria for truth achieved a radical literary expression in Cervantes's *Don Quixote*. In this international best-seller of the seventeenth century, dreams have the force of reality for the don. He explains any evidence to the contrary as the result of the "enchanters [who] have persecuted, are persecuting, and will continue to persecute me" (Cervantes 1949, 722). Evil and all-powerful, they make it impossible to decide on what precisely is real, what is a dream and what is not. At issue in this novel is not just Montaigne's genial cultural relativism. At stake is the relation of reality and illusion. The success of the don's arguments threatens the certainties by which we distinguish the two.

It is precisely these certainties that are the object of Descartes's method of doubt. Its point is to overcome our skepticism by radicalizing it. Thus, Descartes begins his *Meditations* by noting that from his "earliest years," he has "accepted many false opinions as true." Realizing that everything "concluded from such badly assured premises could not but be highly doubtful and uncertain," his aim is to set them all aside "and start again from the very beginning" (Descartes 1990, 17). To do this he imagines the equivalent of the enchanters that persecute the Don. They reappear as a "*mauvais génie*." Descartes supposes "that . . . an evil spirit, not less clever and deceitful than powerful, has bent all his efforts at deceiving me" (22). How, then, can he tell whether he is dreaming or awake? It seems, in fact, "that there are no conclusive indications by which waking life can be distinguished from sleep" (19). If this is true, then Descartes at once achieves his goal, which is "to destroy generally all my former opinions." They all rest on the belief in the reality of what his senses report to him. This, however, is precisely what the supposition of the *mauvais génie* undermines. To be faithful to this supposition is to engage in a radical resolution: Descartes will "abstain from the belief in things which are not entirely certain and indubitable no less carefully than from belief in those which appear to [him] to be manifestly false" (17). In other words, whatever is not absolutely certain will be set aside. Everything that counts simply as opinion will be eliminated as no more certain than the fiction of a dream.

This devaluation of opinion can be seen as a deframing—one that dislocates the self and its usual processes of inquiry. Normally, I situate myself through a whole series of unexamined assumptions. I assume that a certain pair of people are my parents, that those I interact with in society are actually who they say they are, that behind the pictures on the television and the voices on the radio real events are transpiring—that the whole is not an illusion. As part of this assumption, I take for granted that within the whole itself are the means for correcting whatever discrepancies I may find. If a certain element I thought was true turns out to be incorrect—if, for example, someone lies to me—the presumption is that inconsistencies will arise. They will lead me to closer examination of the situation and a discovery of the truth. The assumption here is that the criteria for certainty are within the whole itself. Each element is framed by the whole such that each implies the others—this, in such a way that we can go from what we know to what we do not know.[1] Such a procedure does not, of course, imply absolute certainty. Certainty is relative to the context. As Aristotle noted, "precision cannot be expected in the treatment of all subjects alike." The proper goal is "clarity within the limits of the subject matter" (Aristotle 1962, 5; *Nic. Eth.* 1094b 13–14). In a totality of mutually implicit elements, what is ultimately certain is simply the whole itself. The whole is the ultimate, situating frame. As such, it is the object of Descartes's doubt. If I cannot trust my perceptions, all the evidence the totality offers to me is devalued. I cannot use any of its relative certainties to inquire into the doubtful. One can also say that in demanding a certainty *within* the whole that only the *whole itself* can have, Descartes deframes the normal process of inquiry. He robs it of the use of everything that is "not entirely certain and indubitable," thereby eliminating the normal context of inquiry.

What replaces this context is a deductive system of premise and conclusion. To inquire becomes to deduce what we seek from a premise that cannot be doubted. The uncovering of such a premise is, of course, the point of Descartes's assuming "that everything I see is false." His goal is to uncover what resists this assumption. He compares it to the fulcrum that Archimedes claimed could be used to "move the earth from its orbit" if only it were "fixed and immovable" (Descartes 1990, 23). The model here is obviously mathematics. The Archimedean fulcrum he is seeking is an axiom. It is both a "truth which is certain and indubitable" and a principle from which other truths can be derived. Two features characterize axiomatic systems. The first is the distinction between the axioms and the propositions derived from them. The truth of the propositions following from the axioms depends on the truth of the axioms, but the reverse relation does not hold. In fact, one cannot prove an axiom. If an axiom could be proved it would not be an axiom, but rather a member of the propositional set derived from axioms.

Axioms are grounds rather than members of these propositional sets. As such, they are *outside of the framework* they set up. The second feature is that only those propositions validly derived from the axioms are a part of this framework. In other words, what cannot be so derived cannot be part of the system of truths the axioms define. Certainty, then, is not a matter of mutual implications within a system. Still less is it something resting on the whole itself. It rather comes from the axioms that stand outside of the propositions they ground. If they are certain, then so is everything validly derived from them. These derived propositions can be used to validly prove further propositions. Everything else, however, is groundless. As not being derived from the axioms, it must be excluded from the deductive process. We can thus see how Descartes's effort to find an Archimedean fulcrum and the wholesale destruction of his previous opinions imply each other. As he writes in the *Discourse on the Method*, the goal is to accept only those items that "conform to the uniformity of a rational scheme" (Descartes 1955a, 89).

Philosophically speaking, the modern conception of selfhood begins when Descartes positions the self as his Archimedean fulcrum. Given that what is to be deduced is nothing less than the world itself—that is, the world that we experience and claim as "real"—this move immediately transforms what counts as a "self." Such a self cannot be part of this world; its content cannot be derived from it. This becomes apparent once we consider what remains when we reduce the self to an *ens certissimum*—"an absolutely certain being." The self that is completely indubitable is not a person having parents, social relations, and so on. It is not an individual with a "face, hands, arms, and all this mechanism composed of bone and flesh and members" (Descartes 1990, 25). All these could be the illusions of a dream. In Descartes's words, it could well be "that I have no senses; . . . that body, shape, extension, motion and location are merely inventions of my mind" (23). What cannot be doubted is only the self that might be subject to such illusions. To be subject to them is still to exist. Thus, even if a *mauvais génie* bends all his efforts to deceive me, "there can," Descartes writes, "be no slightest doubt that I exist, since he deceives me" (24). Of course, given that bodily extension is one of the deceptions he might be imposing on me, my self-certainty has to exclude the fact of embodiment. In other words, in terms of self-certainty, I have to say "that I am entirely and truly distinct from my body." Since the certain cannot depend upon the doubtful, it also follows that I "can be or exist without [this body]" (74).

The "I" that Descartes is referring to is the self that is being positioned as an Archimedean fulcrum. Such a self stands outside the world of "body, shape, extension, motion," and so on. In itself, it is only a *non*extended "thinking thing." "Thought," Descartes asserts, "is an attribute that belongs to me; it alone is inseparable from my nature" (Descartes 1990, 26; see also 74). Thought, here, is a generic term. It includes such things as doubting, understanding, affirming, denying, willing, imagining, and sensing—in short, all the elements we designate by consciousness (27). What it does not include are the *correlates* to these actions. The correlates can be doubted; they could be fictions provided by the *mauvais génie*. What cannot be doubted is simply our attending to them in these different activities. Strictly speaking, the self that does attend to them is not any one of these activities. It does not change with the change of conscious contents. Rather, as Descartes asserts, "it is one and the same mind which as a complete unit wills, perceives, and understands. . . ." Since I cannot say I am a different mind when I will or understand or sense, as I often perform these activities simultaneously, these activities do not point to different "parts" of myself. "I am," rather, "a thing which is absolutely unitary" (81). What I am, as later thinkers have pointed out, is only a unity of attending that persists through these different activities.

Such remarks result in a radical deframing of the self. They position the self as outside of the totality for which it is supposed to serve as an Archimedean fulcrum. Since this totality is nothing less than the world, selfhood thus becomes emptied of all worldly content. In Descartes's words, what I cannot doubt is "that indescribable part of myself which cannot be pictured by the imagination" (Descartes 1990, 28). It cannot, since as completely nonextended it is not part of the experienced, physical world. Its status as a thoroughgoing unity also moves us to distinguish it from the descriptions of consciousness—e.g., those of willing, sensing, and so on—taken as distinct activities. What we are left with is the notion of a self as an essentially contentless unity. Distinguished from all its possible objects, it becomes objectively anonymous. It cannot be named or described in terms of any of the objects it attends to. As a unity of attending, it also separates itself from the content of the changing acts of consciousness.[2] Thus, to the degree that we attempt to make it indubitable—i.e., serve as our Archimedean fulcrum—it escapes our grasp. Descartes's foundational, axiomatic method thus leaves us in the curious position of attempting to base objective knowledge on what can, itself, never be objectively known.

To fill this out, we have to turn to the underlying problem the *Meditations* tries to resolve. This is the problem posed for knowledge by embodiment. Behind the specter of the *mauvais génie* is the thought that nature itself—specifically Descartes's nature as a mixture of mind and body—might be deceptive. Thus, in the First Meditation, the *mauvais génie* is taken as an evil, all-powerful god who has created Descartes such that he always errs. To those who doubt the necessity of supposing such a god, Descartes replies, "[T]o whatever degree less powerful they consider the author to whom they attribute my origin, in that degree it will be more probable that I am so imperfect that I am always mistaken" (Descartes 1990, 21). As he puts the same point in the last Meditation, the origin of the doubt raised by this specter was that "pretending not to know the author of my being, I saw nothing to make it impossible that I was so constructed by nature that I should be mistaken even in the things which seem to me most true" (73). Thus, it seems most true "that in an object which is hot there is some quality similar to my idea of heat; that in a white, or black, or green object there is the same whiteness, or blackness, or greenness which I perceive; that in a bitter or sweet object there is the same taste or the same flavor, and so on for the other senses" (77). None of this, however, is true. These apparent qualities have their origin, not in the objects apprehended, but in the peculiar structure of Descartes's senses. The purpose of these senses, however, is not objective truth, but rather survival. In Descartes's words, my bodily senses are there "only to indicate to my mind which objects are useful or harmful" to my embodied state (79). As such, the information they provide is strictly relative to it. The question, then, is: How can we get beyond this relativity to apprehend what pertains to the objects themselves?

It is at this juncture that the self plays its role as an Archimedean fulcrum for Descartes's system. In doubting everything else, I cannot doubt the self that is doubting. In this very inability to be doubted, the self functions as an epistemological axiom. We can derive from its indubitability the two essential standards for knowing. The first of these is clarity: we are absolutely clear on the fact that we exist, any doubts to the contrary being overwhelmed by the sheer fact of our self-presence. The second is distinctness: we cannot confuse our own being with any other's. The existence that we affirm is distinctly our own. This holds, in particular, when we attempt to deny our existence. The selfhood that we cannot deny clearly distinguishes itself from all that can be doubted as pertaining to ourselves. Descartes thus writes of the affirmation of his existence, "[I]n this first conclusion there is nothing else which assures me of its truth, but the clear and distinct perception of what I affirm" (Descartes 1990, 34). He turns this into an epistemological axiom when he adds, "Therefore it seems to me that I can already establish as a general principle that everything which we conceive very clearly and very distinctly is wholly true" (34). In other words, to the degree that our perceptions and thoughts of corporal objects approach the clarity and distinctness of our grasp of ourselves, we can be equally certain of the reality of their objects.

How do objects exhibit this exemplary clarity and distinctness? In what way are we to conceive them so that they become clear and distinct? For Descartes, there is a ready answer to these questions—one that points to the numerable aspects of reality. Numbers are both clear and distinct. Between any two of them, no matter how close in the number series they are, there is a clear difference that prevents us from confusing one with another. Given that clarity and distinctness are standards of truth, Descartes can therefore assert, "[E]verything which I conceive clearly and distinctly as occurring in [corporal objects]—that is to say, everything, generally speaking, which is discussed in pure mathematics or geometry—does in truth occur in them" (Descartes 1990, 76). Descartes's focus is on these objects' "size or extension," their shapes (considered as a "limitation" of extension), the relative positions and the change of these positions, as well as their "duration" and "number." All these factors can be measured; hence, all can be conceived "clearly and distinctly" (41). What is excluded from this list of numerable aspects are the immediate givens of our five senses: the colors, odors, tastes, sounds, and tactile qualities (the smoothness, roughness, softness, hardness, etc.) of the bodies we encounter. Not only do these shifting sensuous qualities lack clarity and distinctness, but what they present points more to ourselves than to the objects we grasp. Specifically, they point to the particularities of our perceptual organs. As Descartes's analyses of bodily illnesses such as jaundice and dropsy indicate, changes in our bodily state result in the change of the sensuously appearing object. To require that our bodily senses grasp the object as it is in itself is, thus, to embrace a contradiction. In demanding that what our senses present *not* be relative to our bodily state, we require that our bodily organs be somehow independent of our body.

The move towards the numerable aspects of the object is intended to overcome the relativity of embodiment. This overcoming is through an abstraction. To apply number to bodies, we have to count. Counting, however, requires that we abstract from what we count everything that does not pertain to the unit we employ. For example, in counting apples, the unit I employ abstracts from all individual differences between the apples. The same holds when I count fruit. Here the unit—understood as that by which each of the things I count is one—abstracts from the differences of different types of fruit. In counting very different objects, I must, in fact, abstract from all their given features and consider each of them only in its quality of being one. Now, it is not just in their numerability that the lengths, positions, and motions of bodies require abstraction. Even before we apply numbers to them, the grasp of these features already presupposes increasing levels of abstraction. Thus, we must abstract from color to consider length as such. Similarly, the grasp of position requires that we attend only to the relative location of a body, while to apprehend motion as motion, we must abstract again to focus on the change of position. For a grasp of velocity or *quantity* of motion, this change of position must itself be quantified and considered in relation to a quantity of duration. Each such abstraction is a move away from the peculiarities of our embodiment. A body's perceived color depends on the structure of our eyes. Its length, expressed as a number of units, does not. The same holds for its position, as expressed by its x and y coordinates on a Cartesian grid. What apprehends the object in such terms is, to use Descartes's phrase, "solely an inspection by the mind."[3] In such an inspection, what the bodily senses present is abstracted from, since it pertains more to us than to the object itself.

To get to the object in itself requires, of course, more than simply abstraction. This abstraction must be directed towards what Descartes calls the "corresponding variations" in the actual as opposed to the sensuously present objects. The sensuous qualities of the objects point to myself—i.e., to the structure of my bodily senses. The changes of these qualities, however, point beyond this to corresponding changes in the actual objects. As Descartes reasons, nothing can come from nothing. Every perceptual event must ultimately have some objective cause. Thus, "from the fact that I perceive different kinds of colors, odors, tastes, sounds, heat, hardness, and so on, I very readily conclude that in the objects from which these various sense perceptions proceed there are some corresponding variations" (Descartes 1990, 77). These variations are to be taken as changes in the numerable aspects of the body. A Cartesian would assert, for example, that to a change in sound there corresponds a change in the numerical frequency of the sound wave. Of course, the change in the sound wave is actually quite different from the change in heard sound, which is experienced as a change in pitch. As Descartes admits, "these variations are not really similar to the perceptions" (77). This, however, is to be expected. It is a function of our proceeding beyond what is specific to ourselves to what pertains to the object in itself. The lack of similarity between the heard pitch and the frequency at which the pressure ridges in the air strike the ear is based on a double abstraction. Objectively, we abstract from the sound all its felt qualities. Its nature becomes reduced to a mathematically describable account of the motion of groups of particles striking the eardrum. Subjectively, we abstract from the self that investigates the nature of the sound all the special features of its embodiment. Insofar as we apprehend the sound only through "an inspection by the mind," we actually enact Descartes's distinction of mind and body. As pure, disembodied observers, not only do we overcome the problem for knowledge posed by our embodiment; each of us also becomes the ideal scientific witness whose observations are repeatable by every other properly trained observer.

The difficulties with this solution are not with its practice, which has actually worked quite well in the centuries that have seen the development of modern science. They concern rather the attempt to make sense of this practice. How do we understand the scientist that engages in it? Can she be grasped in terms of the science that she accomplishes? In other words, can her activity be understood in terms of its results? Such questions recall the fact that an axiom is outside of the system it grounds. If Descartes's ideal, disembodied observer does function as an axiom, this observer must also stand outside of the system it determines. This system, however, is modern science itself. This implies that the scientist's functioning to determine science cannot, itself, be understood in scientific terms. That this is the case follows from the self's disembodied status. This status is essential for the self's indubitability. It is thus required for it to serve as an axiom for the clarity and distinctness that mathematics exhibits. The nonextended self, however, can have none of the features that mathematics fastens on in pursuit of Cartesian science. Bodies have figure, size, motion, and numerable parts. A completely nonextended self does not. If the world explored by science consists of such qualities, the nonextended self of the scientist is absent from this world. Not only can we not grasp its functioning in terms of this world, it is impossible to see how it can be in contact with it. At what physical point does the nonextended touch the extended? Bodies touch by coming into contact at their extremities, but the nonextended self has no extremities. The problem here is not just that of trying to imagine how this self would receive any information (any "data") from the extended world. It is how it would communicate at all with it. In *The Passions of the Soul*, Descartes proposes that the soul communicates to "the machine of the body" by means of a "little gland," the pineal. Moving the gland, the soul moves the body (Descartes 1955b, 347; art. 34). Yet, given that between the extended and the nonextended there can be no point of physical contact, this obviously will not work. The difficulty here, as Locke pointed out, is that we lack even an idea of the connection between the two. The nonextended self must first perceive the world in its sensuous features to perform the abstractions that present the world as it is in itself—the world of primary (numerable) qualities such as sizes, shapes, and motions. Yet we cannot explain such sensuous perceptions in terms of such qualities. As we earlier cited Locke, "[W]e can by no means conceive how any size, figure, or motion of any particles, can possibly produce in us the idea of any colour, taste, or sound whatsoever: there is no conceivable connection between the one and other" (Locke 1995, 445; bk. 4, chap. 3, sec. 13).

What we confront here is an instance of the basic aporia that bedevil modernity's twin ideals of individual autonomy and universality. These ideals come together in the attempt—characteristic of modernity—to make the subject normative. By this we mean the attempt to draw from it universal standards. In Descartes, this takes the form of transforming the self into an *ens certissimum*, a being whose certainty is such that it can stand as a standard for all other claims to knowledge. Thus, the method of doubt is intended to position the subject as an autonomous source of certainty. Its goal is the self as an axiom from which universal standards of clarity and distinctness can be drawn. The result, however, is the transformation of the self into the opposite of this: the self becomes the most obscure element in the Cartesian "system." What makes it obscure is the abstraction required to position the self as an ultimate standard. This abstraction is a deframing—a pulling the self out of the world in which it normally functions and has its sense as an embodied individual. What this transformation points to, then, is the inability of the self to sustain this abstraction. It indicates its essential dependence on the frame that both situates and particularizes it.

The Subject as Synthesizer

Kant repeats Descartes's attempt to make the self normative and attains roughly the same result. Once again the endeavor is motivated by the search for certainty. As before, it is prompted by the specter of skepticism—this time raised by the empiricism of Hume. Limiting himself to the "ideas" that can trace their origin to impressions, Hume declares that "there is nothing in any object, consider'd in itself, which can afford us a reason for drawing a conclusion beyond it" (Hume 1973, 139; bk. 1, pt. 3, sec. 12). All the conclusions we draw come not from objects, but from the habits we gain through our experience of them. Similar sequences of experience, when repeated, breed a habit (or "custom") of expectation. We come to expect that the experiential patterns connecting objects will repeat themselves. Such expectation is our only basis for inference. We may, for example, imagine that some necessary connection exists between two objects—the one being thought as the cause of the other—

but, in fact, as Hume writes, "Objects have no discoverable connection together; nor is it from any other principle but custom operating upon the imagination, that we can draw any inference from the appearance of one to the existence of another" (103; bk. 1, pt. 3, sec. 8). In this view, all inference is actually a species of association. It is limited to moving between the experiences we associate because of their resemblance, contiguity, and frequent conjunction. This limitation implies that we cannot infer from experience the existence of something underlying experience. We are limited to the immediate givens of experience. This means, according to Hume, that "we have . . . no idea of substance distinct from that of a collection of particular qualities [given as contents of our perceptions]" (16; bk. I, pt. I, sec. 6). When, for example, the self trains its view on itself, it finds nothing substantial, but only a "bundle or collection of different perceptions" (252; bk. I, pt. 4, sec. 6).

Kant's response to this is contained in his famous "Copernican turn." Accepting Hume's argument that the knowledge of necessary "apriori" connections cannot be drawn from objects, he seeks it in the subject. In his words: "Previously it was assumed that all our knowledge must conform to objects. But all attempts to establish something apriori about them through concepts which would increase our knowledge have failed under this assumption. We should try then to see if we would not make more progress in the tasks of metaphysics by assuming that objects must conform to our knowledge" (Kant 1955c, 11–12; B xvi). To see objects as conforming to our knowledge is, Kant adds, to see the experience through which they can be known as *conforming to our concepts*. It is based on the suppositions that "experience itself is a type of knowledge requiring understanding; and understanding has rules which I must presuppose as being in me prior to objects' being given to me. These rules find expression in apriori concepts with which all experiential objects must conform and agree" (11–12; B xvi). Such rules of the understanding are rules of synthesis, the very synthesis that results in objects' being given. The rules are "apriori" in the sense of being prior to such givenness. Their necessity is simply that of subjective conditions for the possibility of experience. Whatever violates them cannot be experienced, since all objective experience occurs through the operation of these rules of synthesis.

Kant's reply to Hume is, thus, to trace the necessity of inference, not to objects, but to the subject that experiences these objects. When I assert, for example, that every event has its cause, the concept of "cause" expresses a category of the understanding to which objects must conform. This is because the assertion expresses a rule of my understanding, one I constantly use to make sense of my world. Were something to suddenly appear without any possible cause, I would probably assume that I was dreaming or hallucinating. In any event, I would not take the object as actually given—i.e., as part of the real world. I simply don't put together what I see so that things just pop in or out of existence without any reason.[4] Now, this "putting together" is *my* act of synthesis or combination. What synthesizes is the subject itself. In Kant's words, combination, "being an act of the self-activity (*Selbsttätigkeit*) of the subject, can only be performed by the subject itself" (Kant 1955c, 107; B 131). It is the subject (rather than any object) that combines what it sees to make sense of its world. In Kant's words, "combination . . . is an act of the spontaneity of its ability to represent (*Vorstellungskraft*)" an objective world (67). The upshot is that the synthesizing subject becomes what Kant calls "the transcendental ground of the necessary lawfulness of appearances composing an experience" (Kant 1955b, 93; A 127, my translation throughout). Behind the lawfulness of appearances is the lawfulness of the subject putting together these appearances. It is the subject's following given rules in its understanding of its world. Following them, it makes sense of its experience—that is, it interprets this experience as proceeding from objects that are actually "out there." The experience that does not conform to these rules never gets this interpretation. Thus, the subject never experiences objects "out there" violating this lawfulness.

The result of this Copernican turn can be expressed in three mutually implicit characterizations of the self. First and most obvious is the positioning of the self as normative. Kant calls the self the "ground of the necessary lawfulness of appearances" because the rules of its understanding determine the universal structures of appearance. These rules can be called norms insofar as objective experience must meet their standards if it is to be possible. The essential concept here is that of synthesis, the rules of the understanding being those of synthesis. It is, then, by virtue of its action of synthesis that the self that understands has its normative position. Such synthesis or combination "can only be performed *by the subject itself*." This means that "we cannot represent to ourselves anything as combined in the object without ourselves first having combined it . . . " (Kant 1955c, 107; B 130). With this we come to the subject's second characterization, which is its absolute unity. The fact that all combination requires a combiner implies that the combining subject must itself be uncombined. Otherwise it would be the *result* rather than the ground of combination. It, however, is this ground, since it alone can combine. One can also say that since combination can only be performed by the subject, if the subject were itself combined, there would have to be another subject behind it acting as *its* combiner. If this last were combined, the same reasoning would obtain. To avoid this regress, we thus have to assert that "nothing multiple is given" in the combining subject (110; B 135). Like Descartes's mind or self, it must be conceived as a "thoroughgoing identity" (87; A 116).

The fact that the subject is an uncombined unity immediately positions it beyond the categories of the understanding. This follows because the rules of the understanding are rules for combination. They express the "universal and necessary connection of the given perceptions" required if we are to grasp an objective world (Kant 1995d, 298 §19, my translation; see also 1995d, 304; §21a). Thus, the categories of our understanding, such as substance, causality, unity, and so on, apply to the appearing world because the rules embodying these categories determine the perceptual connections through which objects appear. Given, however, the fact that the combining subject must itself be uncombined, none of these categories can apply to it. Thus, the third characterization of the subject is negative. The synthesizing subject cannot be described in terms of the categories. Even the category of unity, insofar as it contains the thought of the unity of the multitude of perceptions composing an experience, does not apply to it. The unity of the subject, "which precedes apriori all concepts of combination," Kant asserts, "is not the category of unity" (Kant 1955c, 108; B131). The unity that "first makes possible the concept of combination" is not the same as the unity that is a category of the understanding. The same holds for all the other concepts by which the understanding makes sense of its experience. They do not apply to the subject in its "thoroughgoing identity." We cannot, for example, say that this subject is causally determined. To do so would link its appearances in a necessary chain. But the subject in its thoroughgoing identity is prior to these appearances. As prior, it may be characterized as inherently free. Such freedom, however, signifies simply our inability to apply the category of causality to it. Its status as an uncombined combiner is such that it is completely undetermined by the experience it makes possible. None of its categories apply to it. In its action of combination, it thus enjoys a complete autonomy. It determines itself in the "spontaneity of its ability to represent" the world.

The difficulties of this position are similar to those we found in Descartes's account of the self. Both Kant and Descartes, in positioning the subject as normative, abstract it from the context in which it has its sense. Thus, as just noted, none of the categories, taken as rules of combination, apply to it. Kant, for example, may speak of a "transcendent affection" as providing the sensuous material required for subjective syntheses. The attempt, however, to explain how an object can "affect" our sensibility immediately runs into difficulties once we realize that we cannot speak here of "causality" in Kant's terms. The category cannot apply to the subject "in itself," i.e., the subject actually engaged in synthesis. How, then, does the world affect the subject? As a noted Kant scholar says, "'[A]ffection' cannot be causation in Kant's sense. But then, what else can it be?" (Robinson 1989, 279). Once again, we face the question of how the self or subject can interact with the world. For Descartes, the problem involved the nonextended nature of the normative subject. The difficulty, as Locke noted, is that the categories applicable to the extended world—those of "size, figure, or motion"—do not apply to this subject: We cannot conceive how an account employing such categories can explain subjective experience. The difficulty for Kant is even greater. It involves the inapplicability of *all* our categories. Such categories express the way we make sense of our world. They compose the framework of our understanding in its most general terms. The *actual* subject—the subject that acts—stands outside of this frame.

In Kant's account, the subject does not just escape the framework of appearing sense; it is also outside of appearance as such. To see this, we must note with Kant that all appearing requires connected perceptions. It is, for example, through the perspectivally connected series of perceptions that spatial-temporal objects appear. Limited to a single unconnected intuition of an object, we would have only a momentary apprehension of one of its sides. This is insufficient to even distinguish it from its background. For this, we have to connect (and, thereby, "combine") the appearances that pertain to it. By virtue of this action, these appearances become presentations (*Vorstellungen*) of one and the same object. This object, which is the referent of all the momentary apprehensions, gathers in itself their time determinations. It persists through them. The same process applies to the subject's own appearance. As an acting combiner, it connects its momentary self-intuitions. The acting self is prior to such action. Its appearance to itself, however, is determined by the result of this action. As temporally extended, it appears in and through the multiplicity (or "manifold") of perceptions it connects. Thus, for Kant, while I do have an immediate (if fleeting) consciousness of myself as the combiner, if I want to intuitively grasp myself or my extended activity of combining or connecting, I must do so in terms of the manifold I have combined. The subject that appears through this is temporally extended; it persists through all the momentary perceptions that form the manifold. The uncombined subject that engages in this combination is, however, not temporally extended. It cannot be if it is the ground rather than the result of this action of combination. In fact, since all appearing requires combination of the manifold, as uncombined, the acting subject cannot appear. Combination is its function; yet, as a combiner, it falls outside of the appearing made possible by combination.

According to Descartes, the I that thinks is that "indescribable part of myself which cannot be pictured by the imagination" (Descartes 1990, 28). I know that I exist as a thinking being, but what I know cannot be described in terms of the appearing world. My self-presence is thus both certain and indescribable. The same points hold in Kant's account of the self. According to him, "I exist as an intelligence which is conscious solely of its power of combination" (Kant 1955c, 124; B 158). Yet such consciousness, insofar as it is directed to what is uncombined, never becomes descriptive. In Kant's words, the subject's "consciousness of itself is very far from being a knowledge of the self . . . " (123; B 158). In fact, he adds, "I have no knowledge of myself as I am but merely as I appear to myself" (123; B 158). Such appearance is in terms of the results of combination: I can intuit myself as existing in time, as persisting through it. Given this, I have to say with Kant that my "power of combination . . . can be made intuitable only according to the relations of time." Since, however, this power is nontemporal, it "can know itself only as it appears to itself . . . " (124; B 158–59). This cannot be otherwise, given that the inner sense by which we grasp ourselves "presents even ourselves to consciousness only as we appear to ourselves, not as we are in ourselves" (120; B 152–53). What then is the status of Kant's account of combination? Is it a description of the appearing or actual self? As Edmund Husserl remarked, Kant's procedure seems to leave us with "a mode of the subjective which we, in principle, cannot make intuitive to ourselves either by factual examples or by genuine analogy" (Husserl 1962, 116). To make it intuitive is to remain with the appearing subject. The actual subject, however, is positioned on the other side of the categories of appearance. It is their ground, but precisely as such it escapes being categorized by them. This cannot be otherwise, since the categories of the understanding, which we employ to make sense of appearance, cannot apply to the acting subject.

The positioning of the subject "in itself" as noumenal or nonappearing does not just exclude it from the framework of intelligibility set up by the categories. As just noted, it renders deeply problematic Kant's account of subjective synthesis. The account is intended to position the subject as normative—that is, as an autonomous source of certainty. Kant's "Copernican turn" sees it as the answer to Hume's skepticism. The result, however, is a transformation similar to that which we encountered in Descartes's account. The subject, positioned as normative, becomes the most obscure item in Kant's system. We cannot know anything of its nature "in itself." Even the descriptions of

its action of synthesis—the very actions that position it as normative—
are deeply problematic. We can use none of the categories this action
establishes to render Kant's account of it intelligible. Thus, as in
Descartes's account, the very attempt to position the subject as normative eliminates the context required to make sense of the subject. Its
normativity depends upon its being as a synthesizer, but such being
(which is that of an uncombined combiner) abstracts it from the appearing world. Thus, once again we face an abstraction that is a deframing in
the sense that it pulls the subject out of the framework of world. Once
again the resultant obscurities indicate the inability of the self to sustain
this abstraction. Ontologically, they point to its inability to be independently of the frame.

These difficulties indicate the necessity of reversing our view of the
self. If the subject or self that is abstracted from the world loses its intelligible sense, this sense must come from the world. This implies that the
self, rather than being autonomous, is essentially dependent on its situating framework. Rather than being unaffected by the world, it must be
open to it. Such openness is not just epistemological, not just a matter of
the self's knowing being dependent on the givenness of the world. It is
also ontological. Aristotle's original expression of this ontological openness remains instructive. Speaking of the self simply as mind or intelligence, he writes, "[B]efore mind thinks," that is, before it grasps an object,
"it has no actual existence" (Aristotle 1964, 164; *De Anima* 429a. 24). It is
"potentially identical with the objects of its thought"—indeed, this potentiality is its openness. But, as he adds, it "is actually nothing until it
thinks" (168; 429b. 31). We can express this openness in more modern
terms by speaking of temporalization. According to Kant, all "our representations . . . are subject to time, the formal condition of inner sense.
Time is that in which they must be ordered, connected and brought into
relation" (Kant 1955b, 77; A 99). On the level of "inner sense," the sense
by which we grasp our conscious processes, we are, formally regarded,
simply a series of temporal relations. From this point of view, our openness to the world is the openness of time. This explains why, in temporal
terms, the mind is nothing before it thinks. The nothingness of Aristotle's
potential (or "passive") mind points to time's lack of inherent content.
This lack is time's openness. Since it lacks any content of its own, time per
se is capable of exhibiting every sort of content. One could say that this
capability rests on its moments being empty containers—or rather, place-
holders—of possible contents. This, however, has to be qualified insofar as
it is this very lack of any inherent, distinguishing content that undercuts
the notion of time's having discrete moments. Since what distinguishes the

moments is the content that fills them, time's lack of inherent content is a correlative of the continuity of time.

If subjectivity is a field of temporal relations, the openness of time implies that its content must come from its objects. Its being as such a field *is,* in other words, *its openness* to what is not itself. Given the variety of situations the subject can find itself in, this openness implies a number of possible forms of subjective existence. As a field of temporal relations, the subject is capable of as many forms as time has. We can, for example, speak of subjectivity as sheer nowness, subjectivity as temporal flowing, subjectivity as the forms of objective synthesis, subjectivity as our being-there in and through other persons (our being timed by them), and even of subjectivity as the unidirectional flow of objective causality (the flow that allows us to suppose that our own inner relations are subject to causal laws). Each corresponds to a different situation of the subject—or, what is the same, an openness to a different type of object. When I grasp a mathematical relation (when at the moment of insight I am no longer conditioned by the before and after of time), then I exhibit the first form of subjectivity. I exhibit a very different form playing with others as a member of an ensemble. All of this, of course, assumes that the subject actually is the field of temporal relations grasped by inner sense. For Kant, however, the field is the subject only as it appears, not as it is in itself. With his focus on normativity, Kant takes the appearing subject as the result of the nonappearing synthesizing subject. Not to take this step is to stay with the sense of subjectivity as temporality. To think through this sense, however, is to engage in the reversal that returns us to the Aristotelian conception of the subject as an openness. Rather than being taken as the result of the subject's synthetic action, temporality, in this view, becomes the subject's ontological condition. Time, in other words, is understood as the openness of subjectivity. Thus, rather than being regarded as the author of time, the subject is seen as temporalized by the world, its different forms resulting from different temporalizations.

To pursue the epistemological and ontological implications of this reversal would lead us too far afield. They have, in fact, already been discussed elsewhere.[5] The ethical implications are, however, of concern to us. My goal in the following chapters will be to draw them out. Here I will only note the challenge they pose for any attempt to base an ethics on the sense of selfhood they define. Kant's account, for all its difficulties, has a great advantage. Its positioning the subject beyond the world gives it the autonomy to judge the world. It is not limited to expressing its particular situation; its actions are not just a response to it. As autonomous, the subject can ethically appraise its response. It can set its own criteria for judging its actions. Behind this autonomy is Kant's positioning of the subject as the combiner of its experiences. Such combination generates, not just the apparent object, but also the time through which this persists. As such, it is responsible for all the temporal relations, *including those of causality*, that characterize the appearing world. Its freedom is a function of this. As a ground of time, the subject "in itself" is prior to time. As prior, it has the ontological autonomy that it expresses in the voluntary actions that are subject to ethical standards. The task faced by an ethics that sees the self as temporalized by the world is to establish the self's autonomy *in these terms*. It is to see it as a function of the self's being so temporalized. If, for Kant, the self's freedom is grounded in its being before time, the challenge here is to see this "before time" through time. It is to see the escape from time occurring through the self's being temporalized by the factors that situate it. As we shall see, these factors include the other persons it encounters. The experience of other selves does not just situate the self, giving it a place in the intersubjective world. Being temporalized by such experience also desituates or decenters it. It pulls the subject or self out of the world that is centered on itself. As such, it gives the self-centered subject a certain "inner distance" from itself. When properly understood, this inner distance will be seen to form the core of its autonomy.

The task of seeing the "before time" through time can be put in terms of the dichotomy that Kant and Descartes leave us with. The appearing world for both Cartesian science and Kantian ethics is a place of necessity. Nothing within it occurs without a prior cause, the linking of cause and effect continuing without apparent beginning or end. The self, however, escapes this determination. Whether we take it as nonextended or as prior to time, it becomes the place of a nonappearing freedom. The necessity for taking it as such is obvious for both ethics and science. Only a free self can be called to account for its actions. It is morally responsible only for its voluntary actions. Similarly, only a free self is free to scientifically investigate the world. Given that the laws of knowing (e.g., the laws of mathematical and logical inference) are distinct from those of causality, the knowing self must have a sufficient independence of the laws of causality to follow those of knowing. The dichotomy, then, is between framing and freedom. It is between a situating, necessarily determining world and a self that escapes its determination. The way to escape this dichotomy is to redefine both self and world. It is to engage in a reversal that sees the escape from the frame as inherent in the frame itself.

A theoretical account of how our being timed by others both situates us and supports our autonomy will have to wait till chapter 6. A concrete example of this, however, is readily available: literary works continually offer us instances of framing and escape from the frame. The characters whose lives we imaginatively enter into as we read literature show how our actual others both frame and deframe us. Rather then presenting us with a sterile dichotomy between necessity and autonomy, literature avoids this altogether. It points to a way of relating the self to the world that is quite different from the accounts provided by Descartes and Kant. In the next chapter, I will examine how it does this in the context of the difference between the sciences and the humanities.

2

Empathy and Self-Presence

The Sciences and the Humanities

The division between the sciences and the humanities that begins with Descartes is actually one of two different types of understanding. To an extent far beyond what its founders could conceive, the understanding fostered by the sciences is global. Scientists all over the world share their results, collaborate, and make progress together. The universal understanding that science expresses ignores racial and political boundaries. Crossing borders without difficulty, its collective enterprise declares itself to be open to anyone independently of his or her cultural background. The reasons for this character have already been noted. They stem in large part from the modern, scientific project of mathematizing nature. The project originally arose from skepticism regarding our senses. It was discovered that our sense perceptions are *not* given to us to provide accurate information about the inherent qualities of objects. Their purpose is our bodily preservation rather than truth. They are given, Descartes writes, "only to indicate to my mind which objects are useful or harmful" (Descartes 1990, 79). To move beyond this pragmatic concern, we have to attend to the numerable aspects of what we perceive. Grasping these, we apprehend what pertains to the objects in themselves. This grasp is, of course, an abstraction. Abstracting from the so-called secondary qualities of bodies—that is, their tastes, smells, colors, and so on—we abstract from those things given to us by nature for our preservation. This is also an abstraction from our embodiment, that is, from our physical selfhood as a sensing subject. Only the "I" of

37

the "I think"—the "I" that grasps the primary, numerable qualities of bodies—is taken into account. This is the "I," Descartes assures us, that can be considered apart from the body (74). The gain here is in the universality of our understanding. Since selfhood is reduced to the status of a disembodied, pure observer, each observer is substitutable for any other. Each can perform the same crucial experiments and observe the same results, since each limits himself to the selfhood that is a correlate of these abstract and measurable aspects of reality. There is, then, a double abstraction that makes possible the universality of science. We abstract from the embodiment of both the scientist and nature. The nature that is the same for everyone is the nature that is graspable in terms of universal, mathematically formulatable laws; this is the nature that has been stripped of its sensuously embodied presence. The same holds for the scientist whose observations can be universally confirmed. All the cultural and physical particularities that set this individual apart have been discounted.

When we turn to the humanities, we find a very different view of the understanding. The focus of the humanities is on the qualia of nature, its sensed existence. Colors, tastes, sights, and sounds are all crucially important. A person's appearance can affect his role in history. A historian can legitimately ask, for example, about Joan of Arc: How charismatic was she? Did she have a penetrating voice and manner? How was she able, through her visions, to sway the French peasants and nobles? As these questions indicate, the focus here is on Joan's embodiment, both physical and cultural. It is on her embodied presence as it reflects a specific cultural environment. We cannot turn to the "hard" sciences to answer these questions. Their universal understanding is based on an abstraction from specific national cultures. What they focus on is *not* culture, but rather what *transcends* its boundaries. No such abstraction, however, is possible in the humanities. If they abstract from culture and more generally from embodied selfhood, they lose their objects entirely. They must focus on such items. Given this, a different paradigm of understanding is required in their case. It must involve a different sense of universalization.

Understanding as Embodiment

A good example of understanding in the humanities is provided by reading a foreign novel. Reading Kawabata's *The Sound of a Mountain*, for example, a North American becomes immersed in the world of its chief character Shingo (Kawabata 1970). The skill and intensity of Kawabata's description is such that the reader becomes Shingo, an older man living in a Tokyo suburb in the 1950s. The reader sees the world through his eyes, tastes what he tastes, feels the kimono he wears on his skin. All of this gives the peculiarity of humanistic understanding. At its most immediate and direct, it is a living *as* another by a living *in* the other. It is a sharing of the other's embodiment. It is "empathy" in the sense of *feeling* or experiencing *in* the other's body. To ask how humanistic understanding is possible is to ask how such empathy is possible. What is its basis? Are there, as some suggest, "universal" features of mankind, features that allow us to cross cultural borders? Instructed by the Cartesian paradigm, the temptation is to seek such features by abstracting from the peculiarities of embodiment. Yet the selfhood grasped by disregarding such particulars would, at the limit, be the abstract, disembodied one presupposed by the sciences. That the selfhood in question is not such is shown by the peculiar universality of cultural artifacts. These artifacts, like Kawabata's novel, work through their particularity. The more particular the understanding they manifest, the greater, often enough, is their appeal. It is not his sharing in universal features that makes Shingo appeal to us. It is rather his uniqueness, his rootedness in a particular culture and time.

What, then, is the basis for our understanding Shingo's particularity? If an appeal to universal or common features washes out the uniqueness that is the special object of our understanding, to what should we appeal? How can our understanding work if it is denied its abstract, universal objects? The dilemma can only be resolved by broadening the notion of understanding. What is required is a shift in our paradigms. We must move from the scientific model of *understanding through observing and abstracting* to one of *understanding through embodying and particularizing.* A corresponding shift is required in the notion of the self that understands. The observing self distinguishes itself from its object, which it regards at a distance. In Descartes's paradigm, this self is autonomous and disembodied. It grasps its objects, not through the senses, but through the understanding that abstracts, counts, and measures. The embodying self, by contrast, understands through overcoming the distance between itself and its object. Its understanding is through its own states. As noted in the introduction, its paradigmatic mode of expression is not "I observe," as in "I observe heat," but rather "I am," as in "I am hot." The universals grasped by this form of understanding are the shared features of the self's states. They express what is common to its sensuously embodied environment. The paradigm here is understanding through flesh. Universalization, rather than abstracting from the fact of having an embodied standpoint, takes flesh as its prior basis.

In a general sense, the condition for the possibility of this second, humanistic understanding is the "transparency" of selfhood. Rather than having any given features, the self is transparent to such features. It lets them appear through itself. The previous chapter put this in terms of the openness of time: precisely because it lacks any content of its own, time, per se, is capable of exhibiting every sort of content. In any given individual, this openness—which, in a formal sense, is subjectivity—is limited by the senses. Each sense, when active, fills time with a specific type of content. In allowing this content to appear, each sense becomes the place of its actualization as a sensuous content. This may be expressed in terms of Aristotle's observation that "the actuality of the sensible object *qua* sensible is in the sensing subject" (Aristotle 1964, 149; *De Anima* 426a. 10). Our five senses provide examples of what he means: the actual taste is in the tongue, the actual odor is in the nose, and so on. By "*actual*" is meant the *acting* taste, odor, and so on. Aristotle's corresponding term is *energeia*, signifying not just actuality, but also being-in-act, being-at-work. Thus, to say that the actuality of the odor is in the nose is to say that it is at work there. The nose manifests the odor's presence. It lets it appear through itself. The same holds for each of our senses. It also holds for our selfhood insofar as it is a sensing self. Such a self is the place of sensuous presence. As such a place, it takes on its features from its environment. The contents it manifests spring from the nature of the objects it perceives. Insofar as we judge and understand on the basis of what we perceive, the self that understands is also shaped by its environment. It becomes the place where its intelligible relations can be present—in Aristotle's words, the "place of the forms" that specify *this* environment (ibid., 165; 429a. 27). These forms can be "universal" or common features; but, as just noted, they are this by being features of particular, sensuously embodied environments. Their basis is not abstraction, but rather embodiment.

As noted in the preceding chapter, the dichotomy that modernity leaves us with is that between framing and freedom. The positioning of the self as the place where environments come to presence avoids both alternatives. This is because it evades their basic presupposition, which is that of seeing the self's relation to the world in axiomatic terms. The axiom stands as a ground; it explains why the grounded is as it is. When Kant takes the subject as free, he sees the subject as the ground of the causal lawfulness of the appearing material world. Those who understand the subject as determined reverse this relationship. They explain the subject's actions by the causality of the material world. For Kant, the material world is reduced to its representation in the conscious subject. For the materialist, by contrast, the subject is reduced to the world. It is grounded (explained) by its material, mathematically describable "axiomatic" processes and laws. Thus, the first alternative sees the material world's claim to be the world "in itself" as an illusion, while the second takes consciousness itself as an illusion. In the latter view, as Dennett expresses it, "we are all zombies. Nobody is conscious" (Dennett 1991, 406). In both cases, the categories of the ground absorb those of the grounded. Since, however, the ground, as an axiom, is necessarily distinct from the grounded, this absorption is also an elimination. It is the replacement of one category by another—either the material world by subjectivity or subjectivity by the material world. To avoid this, we have to think of the relation of self and world in different terms. In fact, the embodiment that characterizes the self's grasp of the world positions it as neither a ground of nor as grounded by the world. Rather than functioning as a determining ground, the self is simply the "place" of presence. The world's coming into presence both *requires and determines* this place. Thus, without the self, its environing world cannot appear. This world's coming into presence, however, is what situates the self as a particular place of presence. It gives the self a definite content, making it a "this." Such determination does not reduce the self's consciousness to an illusion. Similarly, the self's role in providing a place of presence for the world does not reduce the world to a mere content of consciousness.

Both alternatives are excluded by the notion that being is where it is "at work," i.e., *is* where it functions by embodying itself. To say, in these terms, that color is in the eye is to assert that color is color by being at work in the eye, that is, by functioning in and through a particular bodily environment. The "ground," here, if we could use this term, is not outside of the grounded. Rather it manifests itself through it. It only functions as a ground *through* the grounded. Thus, color only exists in the eye. It can as little be reduced to the electromagnetic waves of the environment as such waves can be reduced to the conscious content of color. The waves that "ground" color only function as its basis in the environment of the eye. Their presence as color is through their operating in this bodily environment. The point here is that we cannot search beyond the actual presence of a color—or, indeed, of any entity—for the ground of such presence. This ground "is"—i.e., is "at work" acting as a ground—in the embodied functioning that manifests an entity. If we grant this, we cannot reduce the material world to its presence in the self nor such presence to the nonconscious processes of the material world. The concrete phenomenon of coming to presence

requires both. Because it does, we cannot axiomatize either the self or
the world to make it serve as an external Archimedean fulcrum. The paradigm of understanding as embodiment may thus be distinguished by its
refusal to situate the functioning ground outside of the grounded. In this
refusal, it both avoids the deframing discussed in the preceding chapter
and gives us a way of seeing how our understanding can include itself
among the items it understands.

Empathy and Embodiment

There are a number of practical, but not insurmountable, limitations in the paradigm of understanding through embodying. On the
most basic level they involve the fact that our first, most immediately
shaping environment is the body. We experience the world in and
through our bodies. Our bodily senses are the place of the world's sensuous presence. The nature of this presence shapes the self that experiences through embodying. Given this, the different bodies men and
women have shape different selfhoods. This difference affects their self-
understanding. Men and women can, of course, understand each other
by abstracting from these bodily differences, which, in any case, are
hardly total. But when they do so, they fail to grasp each other in their
specificity. Men are not grasped as men, nor women as women. The
same holds for the other bodily differences, such as those having to do
with age or capacity. The understanding that functions through a child's
body is distinct from that of an adult, which, again, is distinct from that
of an elderly individual. Each age group has a distinct set of abilities—a
distinct "I can"—that affects the way its environment presents itself to it.
For example, what is out of reach of the child is not "there" for him in
the same way as it is for an adult. A person lacking the capacity to see
presents an even stronger contrast. Distances in his environment must be
gauged by sound or touch. In the blind person's world, departure is present through decreasing sound, while length is sensed by bodily contact.[1]
To actually grasp each group as such is, of course, more complicated
than crossing the biological, bodily divides of sex, age, or impaired
capacities. Cultural considerations also come in. Different cultures have
different interpretations of the body. They have different body images.
These often affect the body as a place of presence, affecting the self-
understanding that is based on this presence.

In spite of these limitations, a good novel does allow us to cross
biological and cultural barriers. In particular, it shows how the empathy
that crosses these divides is possible. To define such empathy, one can

say that the possibility a good novel realizes is that of oneself as another. It symbolically presents through its prose the tastes, smells, textures, sounds, and sights of a different environment. When I use my imagination to fulfill or make vivid the intentions given in its text, not just an environment is represented. As I imaginatively enter into the life of a character in the novel, my own subjectivity undergoes a doubling. In this, the novel represents the subject to itself as another by providing him with an alternate environment. In other words, the subject's transparency is such *that it can undergo a double shaping*. It is both itself, defined by its given environment, and it is another insofar as it makes vivid this second environment. The identification that allows me to see myself as another is not based on an empty universalization. I do not abstract from the distinguishing features of the two selves to regard what is the same. Its basis is rather a self-transformation. It is a representing oneself as another by imaginatively placing oneself in the other's defining world. The same thing can happen when another person is actually present. Genuine empathy, in taking up the other's standpoint, enters into the other's environment. As such, it disrupts self-presence. It makes it dual by including the other.

The notion of this disruption is impossible in the Cartesian paradigm that takes the self as an objective observer. Such a self never encounters another. As Merleau-Ponty remarks, "The existence of other people is a difficulty and an outrage for objective thought" (Merleau-Ponty 1967, 349). For such thought, other people stand as objects. They appear over and against the observer, who distinguishes himself from them as a subject who, for all intents and purposes, is a disembodied self. There is, then, in Merleau-Ponty's words, "a contradictory operation" required for objective thought to grasp another. Confronting another person, " . . . I ought to both distinguish him from myself, and therefore place him in the world of objects, *and* think of him as a consciousness, that is, the sort of being that has no outside and no parts . . . " (349, italics added). In other words, I have to conceive him both as an object and as a nonextended conscious subject. Such a disembodied consciousness, which is simply a sheer attending, has "no outside" and hence cannot be made objective. A solution to this impasse is possible only by redefining what counts as a self. Selfhood must be taken as embodied. For Merleau-Ponty, the self's embodiment places it within the perceptual world, making it graspable by another self. As he asks, "If my consciousness has a body, why should not other bodies not 'have' consciousness?" (351). Of course, for the presence of the embodied other to be that of a self, we have to take the self as defined by its embodiment. By virtue of its being embodied, the self must gain its sense as a specific place of presence, one where the world that surrounds it can appear in all its sensory richness. So regarded, selfhood should not be thought of as inhabiting a body as if it were something placed in a box. On the level of what Aristotle called the "passive intellect," selfhood is particularized through its bodily senses. Each, as I noted, provides it with a specific set of contents. When it acts, its agency becomes personal by being situated.[2] Thus, its bodily action always starts off from a specific place. The bodily abilities that form its "I can" are related to a given surrounding world. This does not mean that the self's unity is given by its body, taken as a physical entity. If one self is to have the possibility of genuinely encountering another self, its agency cannot flow from any *pregiven* unity. This entails that it cannot be conceived as either a Cartesian thinking substance or as a Kantian "transcendental unity of apperception." Still less can it be thought of as an objective physical structure, taken as a unity prior to and independent of its surrounding world. For intersubjective contact, the self's unity, rather than being pregiven, must be given by its situating environment. This is what allows one person to encounter another by attuning himself in empathy to the other's situation. The encounter is, in other words, also a kind of self-transformation.

Selfhood, in this encounter, is a function of the embodiment I imaginatively share in taking up the other's standpoint. The sense a "self" has here can be expressed by answering the question: Where is Shingo? This character is not "in" the letters or the pages of the novel. We cannot say that Shingo is in the deceased author's mind. He is not even in the reader's mind, if this is taken in a Cartesian, Kantian, or natural scientific fashion. Shingo, rather, is where I am as I read the novel. Reading it, I take up his character, imaginatively becoming it. Shingo is in the selfhood I assume in placing myself in his environment. This does not mean that in doing so, I leave my own selfhood behind. It remains, since it continues to be defined by my bodily situation. My selfhood does, however, undergo a certain doubling. In my becoming Shingo, it is not as if the distance between myself and this imaginative other is closed by a fusing of two distinct unities. One is rather overlaid on the other. This doubling of selfhood is implicit in all empathy, in all humanistic understanding. Ontologically, it follows from the notion that being is where it is at work. My being, for example, involves being the place where my body is at work as living flesh. My body is both my first situating environment and that through which my surrounding world works on me. This being bodily situated defines my agency—making it "mine." Beyond this, however, the others I encounter are *also at work* in me. The result is the social functioning in which my agency is "mine" only as part of a context that includes the agency of others—the agency of my others acting in and through me.

Insofar as I am both myself and my others, my self-presence includes both. The result gives my self-presence its characteristic ambiguity. My self-presence is in part a function of my organic being. I am present to myself in my pleasures and pains. My agency is shaped by the appetites and fears that flow from my embodied state. Yet, because I do not live alone, I am always being resituated in terms of others. Such others are also part of the way I view myself. They are "in" me as other than me; that is, they present me to myself as an other, an other that is overlaid on myself. Functioning as both an organic and social being, I thus regard the world from both my own and my others' standpoints. I take into account what is "true for me" and what is "true for others." Concretely regarded, such truths point to a task: that of arriving at agreements I can share with others. This happens whenever I attempt to mediate between my own self-knowledge and what others say about me. This mediation is actually a "negotiation" of my self-presence. In the back-and-forth that this term implies, I attempt to find an acceptable solution to often competing claims. Such negotiation should not be thought to involve self and others as pregiven units. The ambiguity of self-presence is also that of the functioning self. I act through myself; but others also act through me. The self that includes both must maintain its unity through negotiation. Its unity as an acting self is the *result rather than the cause* of the negotiation. Thus, the failure of the negotiation signifies the self's inability to function as a whole both organically and socially. Given this, the primary task of the self is that of managing the dualities of self-presence involved in its being with others. It maintains itself as a functioning self through negotiating the differences involved. Its unity, rather than being taken for granted, is continually at issue in its functioning.

Ethics and Embodiment

Discussions concerning the nature of the self may seem to some to be a side issue in ethics. They are, however, essential to the contention of this book. Its guiding premise, as noted in the introduction, is that the difficulties of modern ethics can be traced to the failure of its conception of the self. Autonomy is central to this conception. Such autonomy, in alienating the self from the context it judges, makes the self lose the framework required for judgment. Kant's conception of ethics is exemplary in this regard. It is based on a universalization that separates us from our situation. To arrive at the universal law, we must abstract not just from flesh but from all the differences based on this—in Kant's words, we must abstract from all "personal differences between rational beings, and also from all the content of their private ends" (Kant 1964, 101; 1995a, 433). For Kant, this abstraction is required to uncover the self's autonomy, the autonomy that pertains to it as it is "in itself," i.e., as it is in its inherent nonappearing (noumenal) being. Such being is, by definition, distinct from the appearing world that situates the self. Now, if we want to avoid the difficulties entailed by this position, we need a different sense of the self—one that includes the judging subject within the judged. Such self-reference demands that we place the self in the world; and this, as we have seen, requires that the self be taken as embodied. Thus, the understanding that functions in ethics must assume embodiment: it has to take selfhood as defined by its situations. This includes, in particular, those situations in which the self encounters its others. Thus, in contrast to the Kantian conception, such understanding never leaves the basis of flesh. It cannot, if selfhood implies embodiment. To leave flesh behind would amount to leaving selfhood behind; and this would strip the ethical law of the very subjects it is supposed to apply to. The universalization that avoids this cannot, then, abstract from embodiment. It must, instead, base itself on its common features. More precisely, its basis should be what is common to the standpoints a person assumes in empathy—i.e., what remains in the self-transformations involved in the doubling of selfhood.

To state the obvious, what does remain is flesh. The flesh implied by having an embodied standpoint is both prior to all universalization and assumed by all ethical understanding. The doubling of our selfhood in the self-transformations occasioned by empathy also remains. Both must be the starting point of ethical reflection. In its broad outlines, the ethics that results can already be sketched out. The duality of our self-presence points to a certain inner distance in ourselves, a distance from which we can gain a perspective on ourselves. The ethics that is based on this is an ethics of judging one standpoint by another. Insofar as we do not leave flesh behind, it is also an ethics of being called to respond in the flesh to this judgment. The response, in other words, is not simply theoretical. Insofar as its basis is the embodiment assumed by empathy, the response must manifest this. Being called into question by my other has to involve my embodied being. The hunger of the other, for example, does not just call forth a theoretical response. It snatches the bread from my mouth when I take up the other's standpoint. To take it up is to experience the demand that I relieve his or her wants.

At issue in all such responses is not just the sorting out of obligations I have to myself and others; it is the presence underlying these obligations. I must come to terms with the duality of my self-presence that is occasioned by empathy. I have to negotiate the competing claims this makes on me. The ethical system I adopt is, in fact, a set of rules for negotiating these claims. Here, the answer to the question "Why be ethical?" concerns the selfhood that is the result of such negotiation. Being ethical is its preservation. The ultimate sanction of morality is that ethical failure involves its progressive loss. It results in the self's increasing inability to function both organically and socially.

The attempt to base ethics on the duality of selfhood has much to recommend it. The Kantian and the other systems of ethics that might be ranged against it also have their advantages. How can we know which is closer to the truth? One way of deciding is to note that a fact that is truly fundamental should be encountered by every acute observer. Thus, the more fundamental a fact is, the more likely it is to be implicit in different approaches to ethics—this, at least, insofar as they are based on genuine observation. At issue here, however, is nothing less than the selfhood implied by ethics. Thus, if this selfhood is, in fact, dual, the major writers on ethics, *Kant included*, must have come to terms with it. Seeing how this is, in fact, the case requires what may be called a "phenomenological" or descriptive history of ethics. Its task will be to uncover the ways in which the various forms of ethical theorizing arise from the fundamental fact of the division of our self-presence. Insofar as this division rests on our embodiment, the following chapter, in outlining this history, will also indicate the ways in which embodiment has shaped ethics. The goal here is not just to present a descriptive history, but also to relate our position to this tradition. This will clarify the issues facing us if this position is to be secured.

3

The Divided Self:
A Phenomenological History of Ethics

Plato and Kant

Plato's Rhetoric

For Plato the duality of our selfhood is one of appetite and reason. The self that is determined by appetite takes pleasure as the good. The self determined by reason chooses pleasure only insofar as it leads to the good (Plato 1971, 105; *Gorgias* 500a). For this rationally directed self, to know the good is to do it. In the dialectic that is, concretely, the working out of Plato's ethics, reason constantly tries to persuade the appetite that it is mistaken about the good. In Plato's writings, their conversations take the dramatic form of dialogues between Socrates and various interlocutors. The back-and-forth of the dialogues manifests the ongoing attempt to negotiate the difference between the two selves. In the *Gorgias*, Plato's most extended treatment of ethics, Socrates plays the role of reason. The self that is defined by its appetites appears in the form of three increasingly strident respondents: Gorgias, Polus, and Callicles. All three are proponents of oratory or rhetoric.

The question that the *Gorgias* continually returns to is the place of oratory in the state. Gorgias defines oratory as "the ability to convince by means of speech a jury . . . and any other gathering of citizens whatever it may be" (Plato 1971, 28; *Gorgias* 452e). This conviction, he admits, is "the kind that engenders belief without knowledge" (32; 454e).

It is, for example, not the conviction produced by arithmetic (25; 450e). It does not persuade by teaching, but rather by appealing to what its audience wants to hear. Its target is pleasure rather than knowledge. Socrates sums up this description with a pair of proportions. The first proportion is: "[C]ookery is to medicine as beauty culture is to physical training" (47; 465b). The proportion concerns the arts having to do with the body. According to Plato, there are two genuine arts, physical training and medicine, and two counterfeits of them, beauty culture (or cosmetics) and cookery. The genuine arts aim at the actual health of the body. While training keeps the body fit, medicine cures it of its disorders. The counterfeits simulate their results. Thus, the healthy glow that physical training brings to our appearance is counterfeited by cosmetics; similarly, the sense of well-being that health and medicine bring is simulated by the pleasure provided by a well-cooked meal. In both cases, the counterfeit provides the semblance, but not the reality of what the genuine art aims at. The same point holds for the proportion having to do with the arts of the soul. For Plato, popular lecturing (or sophistry) is to genuine legislation and the debates that inform it as oratory is to the justice that is the object of a trial. Legislation, with its rules, is here understood as "training" the citizen's soul, while justice is taken as "curing" it of its disorders. Popular lecturing, which lobbies for particular laws on behalf of special interests, is the counterfeit of legislation; while oratory, which persuades through special pleading without imparting knowledge, provides a false semblance of justice. Plato combines both proportions by asserting that "popular lecturing is to legislation as beauty-culture [is] to training, and oratory [is] to justice as cookery [is] to medicine" (47; 465c). The first of each pair "makes pleasure its aim instead of good." It is not really an art since "it has no rational account to give" of its practices (46; 465a). It simply takes note of what provides pleasure and adds it to its repertoire. Knowledge, however, is required to practice medicine, craft legislation, or provide justice. The mere accumulation of examples is not sufficient. One has to know something of the nature of the body to practice medicine. The legislative art requires a knowledge of political and constitutional processes. Similarly, the mere ability to persuade does not assure the justice of the jury's verdict.

Does this mean that we should banish cooks, beauticians, lobbyists, and lawyers from the state? That Plato's position is more nuanced than this appears in Socrates' own use of rhetoric at the end of the dialogue. When the reason he appeals to fails to convince Callicles, Socrates tells of the punishments and rewards of the next world: a tale obviously fashioned to work on Callicles' fears and desires. Plato also has Gorgias relate how his brother, a doctor, had to rely on Gorgias to persuade his patient to undergo medical treatment. What moved the patient was not the brother's medical knowledge; it was Gorgias's rhetorical skills. Were Callicles and the patient guided by reason, such interventions would be unnecessary. In fact, had we complete knowledge and were we totally guided by reason, there would be no place for oratory in our state. All persuasion would be like that provided by arithmetic: reason alone would compel us. Similarly, if knowledge were absent and we were totally guided by appetite, oratory or rhetoric would be all-powerful. Nothing would contradict the rhetorical appeal to our desires and fears. Neither, however, is the case. Our condition is between these extremes; and this means that we cannot do without rhetoric's ability to persuade. At best, we can only control it, using it, as Gorgias did, for some benefit.

Divisions in the Self

Our middle state between knowledge and ignorance, reason and appetite, points to a corresponding division in our selfhood: we are both reason and appetite. Plato expresses this division in a number of ways. There is, for example, the divide between convention and nature. The two, Callicles asserts, "are inconsistent" (Plato 1971, 77; *Gorgias* 4822e). In a passionate speech, which Socrates helps clarify, he outlines their differences. By nature, Callicles asserts, "the better man should prevail over the worse and the stronger over the weaker" (78; 483d). By convention, Socrates adds, "equality, not inequality, is right" (86; 489a). Nature declares that "right consists in the stronger seizing the property of the weaker and the better ruling the worse and the more gifted having an advantage over the less" (85; 488b). Convention, however, asserts that "ambition is base and wrong, and that wrong-doing consists in trying to gain an advantage over others" (78; 483c). Nature is the state of the strong overpowering the weak. Convention, Callicles declares, consists of those rules by which the weak constrain the strong (78; 483 b-c). The focus of nature is on individuals, on "those who are stronger and capable of getting the upper hand" (78; 483c). Conventions, however, refer to collectives. Their rules are based on the agreements that men make; and they are enforced by their collective strength (85–6; 488d–489b).

To sum up, a state based entirely on "nature," as Callicles defines it, would be a winner-take-all state. At the limit, it would be a tyranny with all power and wealth concentrated in one person. At the opposite extreme, the state that embodied convention's strictures against ambition and seeking an advantage would enforce a total equality. All the differences springing from nature would be suppressed.[1] Given that neither alternative is really viable, a functioning state must somehow come to terms with both extremes. Politics, in fact, exists between the two. Taken as the art of public negotiation, its ongoing task is the reconciliation of nature with convention. Its goal is to give space to both natural winners and collective values. The functioning state is the result of this negotiation. Its unity, rather than being pregiven, depends on its success in this negotiation. The same point, incidentally, can be made with regard to marriage. What is natural in marriage is the sexual bond. Considered as a "contract," marriage is a convention. The marriage itself exists in the ongoing balance between sex (nature) and contract (convention). It falls into difficulties when it is reduced to one or the other.

For Plato, the nature-convention distinction mirrors the inner division that exists within the self. Nature, with its focus on what is inborn, speaks to our bodily being—i.e., to its inborn talents and capacities for pleasure and pain. Convention, which requires agreement and, hence, communication with others, shifts the focus to "speech" and "reason"— both words being translations for the Greek term *logos*. Another expression of the difference between our bodily and our rational aspects is the distinction Plato draws between bodily pleasures and the good that is apprehended by reason.[2] Having gotten Callicles to admit that there are "better and worse pleasures," the question arises of a standard to judge between them (Plato 1971, 104; *Gorgias* 499c–e). Given that there are "good and bad pleasures," the standard cannot, itself, be pleasure (105; 499e–500a). It must, in fact, be some good we wish to obtain, be this health, a particular career, or some other goal. Thus, to take a contemporary example, it is not the pleasure it affords us, but the long-term consequences for our health that make us decide that smoking is a "bad" pleasure. This decision is a product of our reason, which, in this instance, opposes our bodily desires. Such desires are immediate. Reason, however, looks at the consequences. It regards alternatives in terms of what they will lead to. Thus, it projects the present forward in terms of the consequences of alternative actions. What informs its evaluation of these consequences is some standard of the good—in this case, health.

There is, according to Plato, a teleological relation between this standard and the pleasures we are evaluating. The good that is the standard is the goal, while the pleasures have their worth only as means for achieving this good. This means, Plato writes, "we should embrace pleasure among other things as a means to good, and not good as a means to pleasure" (105; *Gorgias* 500a). His advice regarding means and ends presupposes that we can reason out the consequences of our actions. It also assumes a certain self-separation. There must be a kind of temporal distention of the self, one that stretches between the immediacy of pleasure and the future as laid bare by reason. Regarding my pleasures, I am both in the present and ahead of myself. I evaluate a present pleasure from the standpoint of the self that I want to be. Suppose, for example, I want to be a marathon runner and I realize that I ought to quit smoking. This "ought" assumes both the self I am as I smoke and the self that stands as my goal. The "ought" has its sense in terms of my regarding myself in the light of my goal. In the model that sees pleasure and the good as a relation of means and ends, self-control thus implies self-separation. The self that is controlled is the present self, the self that is controlling is the future self—the self that stands as my end or goal. When I abandon myself to pleasure—when, in Plato's words, I allow my "appetites to go unchecked" and "attempt to satisfy their endless importunity"—my self-separation collapses. This self-separation is implicit in "the appropriate kind of order" that Plato sees as characterizing the healthy soul (116; 506e). The order in question keeps open the inner distance that allows self-control. My freedom demands this, since when the distance collapses, I fall into slavery. Reduced to the immediacy of pleasure, I lose all ability to oppose my desires. Needless to say, both sides of the divide are required for this inner distance. My experience of the "ought" and the freedom it implies is framed both by pleasure with its rootedness in the present and by reason with its analysis of the consequences of pleasure.

Another expression of the division between appetite and reason appears in the distinction between the solitary and the social self. Pleasure—particularly bodily pleasure—is private. There is no objectively true or false with regard to assertions of pleasure. Since we cannot dispute what another person claims he feels, the realm of pleasure is, epistemologically speaking, that of the "true-for-me." It is the realm of private appearance as opposed to public reality. This is why Socrates tells Callicles that the person who allows his "appetites to go unchecked" cannot acknowledge others. In fact, "he is incapable of social life" (Plato 1971, 117; *Gorgias* 507e). To live with others, we require *logos*—i.e., speech and reason. Both are public. Thus, the conventions that language assumes with regard to usage presuppose others. So do the agreements and social conventions that language makes possible. The same presupposition holds for reason insofar as it involves publicly acknowledged standards of evidence and proof. Its realm, in contrast to that of pleasure, is the domain of the "true-for-everyone." Its object is public reality as opposed to private appearance. The division in myself between reason and appetite is, thus, also a division between my social and my private self. If I wish to maintain my unity, I have to add the "true-for-everyone" to the "true-for-me"; what appears to me (the realm of appearance as appearance) must be conjoined to the real. As already noted, this involves balancing my own self-knowledge and what others say about me in order to arrive at truths I can share with others. To pursue this goal, neither side can be abandoned. I have to endure the tension between the solipsis- tic truth of pleasure and the objective truth of the world I share with my others. The tension, one can say, is that between myself and the others who are "in" me as part of my unity. Such others call my truths into question and, in doing so, call on me to respond. The self that exists in this tension is called forth as a respondent. Its others are "in" it as an ontological basis for its being as a respondent.

All of these divisions are capable of collapse. The breakdown of the self is the collapse of the tensions involving appetite and reason, plea- sure and the good, present immediacy and future goals. It is the undoing of such distinctions as nature versus convention, the private versus the social self, the true-for-me versus the true-for-everyone. In Plato's terms, this breakdown is the self's "dis-cordance." It is the loss of the "order" that is appropriate to the soul. This is why Socrates asserts that what is at issue in the debate is Callicles' selfhood. Failure to engage in it means that Callicles "will remain at variance with himself his whole life long" (Plato 1971, 76; *Gorgias* 482b). The point that can be taken from this admonition is that the debate between appetite and reason is essen- tial to selfhood. More generally, it is that ethics may be defined as the ability to engage in the debate, i.e., the ability to negotiate between the different sides of our selfhood. Such negotiation is required if we are to live the tensions that inform human existence.

Sovereignty and Rule

If the above were the complete story of Plato's ethics, this book would be much shorter. A large part of it would consist in commenting on the passages where Plato develops his ideas. Plato, however, both makes *and undermines* his point about the duality of our selfhood. The undermining comes through his position that reason should rule in the soul. As his *Republic* makes clear, the relation of reason to pleasure (of ruler to ruled) is not democratic.[3] Its model is one of command and obe- dience. Behind this view, as Hannah Arendt points out, is a fateful equa- tion of freedom with sovereignty. The analyses of the *Gorgias* imply that freedom exists in the self-separation occasioned by the division between appetite and reason. Both are required for its exercise. The equation of freedom with sovereignty or rule, however, assumes that the freedom of one element is equivalent to the other element's lack of freedom. Reason's "rule," then, can be understood as a coercion and repression of desire. As repression, it exercises a "tyranny"—a rule from without in the Greek sense.[4] Discussing "that identification of freedom with sovereignty which has always been taken for granted by political as well as philosophic thought," Arendt notes its fallacy: if freedom required sovereignty, none could be free. In her words, "If it were true that sovereignty and freedom are the same, then indeed no man could be free, because sovereignty, the ideal of uncompromising self-sufficiency and mastership, is contradictory to the very condition of plurality." The point here is not that we are dependent and, hence, require others. Freedom is impossible "not, as the tradition since Plato holds, because of man's limited strength, which makes him depend upon the help of others." If this were the case, then "the recommendations the tradition has to offer to overcome the condition of non-sovereignty and win an untouchable integrity of the human person" might be of some avail. "Yet," as she notes, "if these recommendations were followed, the result would not be so much sovereign domination of one's self as arbitrary domination of all others or, as in Stoicism, the exchange of the real world for an imaginary one where these others would simply not exist" (Arendt 1958, 234). Where the tradition goes wrong is in assuming that the difficulty is practical. This is to misunderstand the human condition, which is one of "plurality." In our terms, it is one where the self both implies and is founded on its others. The elimination of others is the self's elimination. Given this, a person's freedom is not enhanced by overcoming others and their freedoms. The exercise of freedom demands the latter as the context in which it can operate. In the public realm, this exercise manifests itself as political action. It shows itself in the contention and negotiation that inform the life of a democratic state. Within the soul, freedom shows itself in the persuasion rather than the tyranny of reason. This is because the self's situated quality within the body politic is also reason's within the soul. Neither can be "free" outside of the context in which it operates.

That such a view is ultimately *not* embraced by Plato appears in his description of the trial of the souls that enter the underworld. Callicles had earlier reproached Socrates for being incapable of defending himself in the state. If someone were to arrest him, Socrates, he asserted, "would be in a daze and gape and have nothing to say." If Socrates were dragged into court, however poor the prosecutor, Socrates "would be condemned to death, if [the prosecutor] chose to ask for the death penalty" (Plato 1971, 82; *Gorgias* 486b). Socrates' "counter challenge" is that Callicles would be equally incapable of defending himself in the trial before the judge of the underworld (148; 526e–527a). In the description that ends the dialogue, the dead are "tried naked." To "ensure complete justice," Socrates adds, "the judge too must be naked and dead himself, viewing with bare soul the bare soul of every man as soon as he is dead . . . " (143; 523e). This procedure has two results. On the one hand, the dead lose their worldly identities. The judge "summons them before him and inspects each man's soul, without knowing to whom it belongs" (144–45; 524e). On the other hand, the dead are completely exposed. As Socrates says of the naked soul, "once it is stripped of the body, all its qualities may be seen, not only its natural endowments but also the modification effected in it by the various habits which its owner has formed" (144; 524d). The underworld, then, is the place of unrestricted presence, of total unconcealment, of "truth" (*a-letheia*) in the sense of complete unhiddenness. By virtue of such exposure the self loses its defining situatedness. In fact, this complete exposure is the end of its being in the world.

This becomes apparent once we realize that everything *in* the world has parts that are seen and parts that are hidden. The sides that we see of a cube, for example, hide the parts that we do not see. The seen are in the foreground, the unseen in the background. As Merleau-Ponty has pointed out, to posit the cube in itself, i.e., the cube with all six of its sides equally present, is to abstract the cube from our consciousness of it. Given our embodied status, we always grasp things in terms of their horizon—i.e., in terms of foreground and background. The world of appearances for us is always that of partial presence. The full presence of the object is thus the absence of appearance. It is, in fact, the absence of consciousness, which by virtue of its embodied status is always perspectival, always an apprehension from one perspective, from one point of view among many.[5] The same holds for our moral apprehension. Our being in the world means that we only see one aspect of a person at a time. The person himself, by virtue of his situatedness, can only partially reveal himself. Like any other being in the world, he has his necessary foreground-background structure. Those features that do not pertain to his present circumstances are concealed (i.e., shoved into the background) by those that do pertain.

If to be in the world is to be in horizon, can we eliminate this foreground-background structure and still talk of apprehending a person? Plato, with his talk of stripping the body from the soul, assumes that we can. To eliminate embodiment is to eliminate the perspectival character of consciousness. It is to deprive it of that which places it "in" the world, situating it at one place rather than another. What remains, according to Plato, is reason or mind. The disembodied reason exercised by the judges grasps the souls of the dead from every side all at once. The paradigm here seems to be the mind's grasp of the "ideas"—the (εἴδει)—that Plato positions as the truth of reality. To grasp the idea is to apprehend what is essential to a multitude of individual instances. The latter may show themselves with varying characters, but the ideas themselves are always "the same with themselves," everlasting in their self-identity.[6] Their presence is complete and nonperspectival. Basing ourselves on the etymology of the word for idea (εἶδος),which comes from the Greek word signifying "to look at," we can call the ideas "the invisible looks" of reality.[7] They are "invisible" because to see them one must look beyond the world of individual realities. They are "looks" because they are the presence of such realities as they are in themselves. Ἅιδης (Hades), the Greek term Plato uses for the underworld, has a spelling practically identical to the term signifying invisibility in Greek—ἀιδής. This indicates that the realm of Hades, insofar as it dispenses with bodies, is also an invisible kingdom. It thus invites us to see the realm of Hades as a metaphor for the world of the ideas, the "invisible looks" of reality. The judgments carried out in Hades correspond to those in the realm of the ideas. In both cases, the judgment that is passed abandons our being in the world. This may be put in terms of Plato's position that what can be predicated of the ideas cannot be predicated of the things for which they are ideas. The idea of smallness, Plato reminds us, is not a "small" idea; the idea of largeness is not itself "large" (*Parmenides* 131d). We cannot, for example, say that the idea of a triangle is itself "triangular." All of these attributes apply to bodies. They do not apply to the ideas in their invisible, disembodied presence.[8] The ideas, then, are supposed to both ground our knowledge of the world and express a standpoint that stands outside of the world. The same holds for the judgments that obtain in the underworld. Abstracting from our being in the world, they are supposed to have the last word on it.

The difficulties involved in judging the world from a standpoint beyond it have already been considered. The task they leave us with is a dual one: we have to break the connection between freedom and sovereignty. Freedom must be thought of independently of the sovereignty that isolates it. Equally, we have to redefine reason or mind such that its moral apprehensions correspond to the situated character of the self. In both cases, the task is really the same: that of including the person and his standpoint within the framework of his judgments and actions. To draw from this a transcendental clue to the nature of our selfhood is to return to Plato's intuition that the divide between reason and appetite is that between the social and the solitary aspects of the self. As we are both appetite and reason, it points to the others within us situating us. The freedom that is distinct from sovereignty will, in a subsequent chapter, be seen to be occasioned by these others.

Kantian Obligation as Self-Separation

Socrates' final advice to Callicles in the *Gorgias* is to aim at "the reality rather than the appearance of goodness" (Plato 1971, 148; *Gorgias* 527b). This may also be taken as Kant's admonition. For Plato, the distinction between the real and the apparent is ultimately one between the intelligible ideas and sensible things, the predicates of the ideas *not* being those of the things. Kant's parallel division is between the intelligible and the sensible worlds. As he continually stresses, the categories of the latter are *not* those of the former. The result of this division between the intelligible and the sensible worlds is thus a task parallel to the one Plato imposes on us. For Kant it is to combine these two worlds to provide a unified stage for moral action. The challenge is to integrate the reality of the "true" self with the framework of its appearing.

When, with Kant, we distinguish between these two worlds, we also differentiate the selves that pertain to them. Correlated to the sensible world is the appetitive self. Its law is that of inclination. All of its imperatives are "hypothetical," that is, they follow the "if . . . then" form of the hypothetical syllogism. Their form is: *if* you want to achieve some advantage, i.e., satisfy some inclination, *then* you must take some particular action. The selfhood that follows inclination is embodied. It is both situated and driven by need. Insofar as its actions are determined by objects, its agency is ultimately not its own. This means, in Kant's words, that its "will does not give itself the law [of its actions], but the object does so in virtue of its relation to the will" (Kant 1964, 108; 1955a, 441). The world in which this self is situated is here the ultimate agent. It acts through the willing self. It does so to such an extent that, as Kant admits, "it is absolutely impossible for experience to establish with complete certainty a single case in which the maxim of an action, in other respects right, has rested solely on moral grounds" as opposed to inclination (1964, 74; 1955a, 407). The impossibility rests on the character of the appearing world (of which the appearing self is simply a part). As already noted, this world is structured by the category of causality. Its very objectivity as there for everyone demands that nothing occur within it without a prior cause, the cause being something worldly. Thus, the actions of the selves within the appearing world can always be traced to things in the world. These things move us through the desires they arouse.

If the sensible world were the whole story, there would be no moral action in the Kantian sense. Such action demands the addition of the intelligible world. The self that is correlated to this world is ruled by reason. It is motivated, not by inclination, but by rational self-consistency. Its question is not: "How do I get what I want?" It is: "What would happen if everyone acted as I did?" Could I, for example, will that everyone lie to get out of a difficulty? Since if everyone lied, no lie would be believed, there is an obvious inconsistency here. It is one that we embrace whenever we lie. Lying, we desire that others not lie. In fact, a lie is most effective in a world where everyone has complete confidence in the truth of what people say. In willing our lie to succeed, we thus both affirm and deny that people should lie. In Kant's words, there is "a contradiction in our own will" when we will the success of our lie. We both will "that a certain principle [of truth telling] should be objectively necessary as a universal law and yet subjectively should not hold universally but should admit of exceptions"—that is, we will that the principle should not apply to ourselves (Kant 1964, 92; 1955a, 424). In such remarks, we find a ready test for whether we are contradicting ourselves. The test of our self-consistency is whether or not our maxims can be universalized. As Kant notes, "some actions are so constituted that their maxims cannot even be *conceived* as a universal law of nature without contradiction." In the case of others, even though there is not "this inner impossibility, . . . it is still impossible to *will* that their maxim should be raised to the universality of a law . . . , because such a will would contradict itself" (91; 1955a, 424).

The same universalization is also a self-separation. When I ask what would happen if everyone engaged in some action, I separate this action from every particular situation in which it might occur. I thus leave out of account the particular inclinations called forth by such situations. The self that poses this question thus considers itself apart from the sensible world and its determinations. It distinguishes the rationally motivated self (the self that seeks to preserve its self-consistency) from the appearing self. The latter is the self whose embodiment situates it and fills it with needs. Its determination follows the various hypothetical imperatives required to satisfy these needs. The self that determines itself according to the standard of rational self-consistency has, by contrast, only a single, categorical imperative. This is to see if its maxim could "become through [its] will a universal law of nature" (Kant 1964, 89; 1955a, 421). Doing so, it understands itself as autonomous. It takes itself as determined by the single imperative that *it sets for itself*.

According to Kant, were I exclusively in either the intelligible or sensible worlds, I would have but a single determinant for my will. In his words, "If I were solely a member of the intelligible world, then all my actions would perfectly conform to the principle of the autonomy of a pure will; if I were solely a part of the world of sense, my actions would have to be taken as in complete conformity with the natural law of desires and inclinations . . . " (Kant 1964, 121; 1955a, 453). In the first case, I would follow only my reason. In the second, appetite would be all-determining. In fact, however, I belong to both worlds. Their separation is also my self-separation. I am both a rational and a sensing, desiring self.[9] My sense of ethical obligation begins with this. To cite Kant again: "[W]hen we think of ourselves as under obligation, we look upon ourselves as belonging to the sensible world and yet to the intelligible world at the same time" (1964, 121; 1955a, 453). The words "at the same time" point to the fact that one aspect of ourselves is overlaid on the other. Both form part of our self-presence. The sense of obligation arises when we regard the promptings of desire from the standpoint of reason. We ask, regarding some particular action that inclination urges, "What would happen if everyone acted so?" The contradiction that appears makes us realize that we "ought" to act differently.

This "ought" is not a statement that either a will ruled entirely by inclination or a "pure will" determined by reason alone would recognize. The imperative stating the ought does so for a will undergoing both determinations. This, Kant writes, is "a will that does not perform an action straight-away because the action is good." Knowing the good, the person still might act contrary to it (Kant 1964, 82; 1955a, 414). The "ought," thus, has its sense in a context where the decision is open. The duality of self-presence that keeps it open is, in fact, a basis for *both* our morality and immorality—i.e., for both our following and not following what we ought to do. When we violate the categorical imperative—when, for example, we lie to gain an advantage—we do not thereby abandon the standpoint of the intelligible world. Lying, we still presuppose it. In willing the success of our lie, we will that the world in which we lie be one where no one (else) lies. This universal standpoint, which we adopt to assure our credibility, overlays the particular standpoint in which we seek some special advantage. To be immoral, we need both standpoints. We have to be capable of both reason and inclination. When we act immorally, we generally resolve the contradiction between the two by changing the universal law into a general law. We transform it into a law that, holding for the most part, does admit exceptions (92; 1955a, 424). Nevertheless, we insist that it hold for the others we deal with—e.g., the person we lie to when we enter into some agreement. He, categorically, should tell the truth!

The duality of standpoints required for being either moral or immoral excludes both the animals and God from the human sense of either. Animals cannot be blamed or praised, since they necessarily follow the law of nature. As for the "perfectly good will" of God, it is necessarily "determined only by the concept of the good." This means that "for the divine will . . . , there are no imperatives: 'I ought' is here out of place, because 'I will' is already of itself necessarily in harmony with the law" (Kant 1964, 81; 1955a, 414). These remarks imply that what prevents us from automatically acting according to the necessity of our nature is our being in both worlds: we are not automatons, because we have both reason and sense. The freedom that encompasses ethical choice requires both as its frame. It requires, first, that I be present to myself as a member of an intelligible "kingdom of ends," a kingdom whose members form "a systematic union of different rational beings under common laws" (1964, 100; 1955a, 433). My "union" with the others occurs because each of us wills according to universal maxims. Each thus wills what all others could will. In the second place, ethical freedom requires that I be present to myself as sensuously embodied, i.e., as expressing a particular standpoint and having particular inclinations. This dual requirement signifies that I experience the freedom implicit in my "ought" by living in the tension of both worlds. Working out the "ought" in a concrete situation, I have to combine both. I have to negotiate between my self-presence as sensuously embodied and as a member of this "kingdom of ends." The implication here is that my ethical selfhood—the selfhood that experiences the "ought"—arises in this process.

Kant, of course, does *not* draw this implication. From a Kantian perspective, any negotiation that does occur is extremely one-sided. To have a moral life, my inclination must submit to my reason. My freedom demands that reason must rule, i.e., exercise a sovereign dominion over desire. Thus, once again, we find the fateful equation of freedom with sovereignty that we saw in Plato. As with Plato, its ultimate foundation is ontological. It is based on taking the distinction between the real and the apparent as a distinction in being. Thus, for Kant, the two forms of selfhood are not on the same footing as regards their being. My real, actual self is the self that is determined by reason. It is the self as it is "in itself," i.e., the self quite apart from the way things appear. By contrast, the self that experiences inclinations is not the actual, acting self, but only its appearance. The same distinction can be made about the worlds that these selves pertain to. Thus, the intelligible world that my real self belongs to is the actual world, i.e., the world as it is "in itself." As for the sensuous world that situates the desiring self, this is not the world "in itself," but only its appearance. To make this distinction into an ontological relation, we have to say that the apparent depends on the real such that it cannot *be* without the real. Ontologically, then, the intelligible world is taken as the basis of the sensible. As Kant formulates their relation, "the intelligible world contains the ground of the sensible world and therefore also of its laws." This means that "in respect of my will, for which (as belonging entirely to the intelligible world) it gives laws immediately, it must also be conceived as containing such a ground" (Kant 1964, 121; 1955a, 453).

With this division into the real and the apparent, all the previously mentioned difficulties reappear. They revolve around the fact that to follow the laws given by the intelligible world is to follow the categorical imperative. This, however, is to deprive selfhood of its specifying (and, hence, defining) situation. The selfhood that results is, of course, autonomous. It enjoys a complete freedom vis-à-vis its environment. As free, it is a member of Kant's "kingdom of ends." The price it pays for such membership is, however, high. It is nothing less than the loss of all particularity with regard to its will. This is because we can only conceive this kingdom "if we abstract from the personal differences between rational beings, and also from all the content of their private ends" (Kant 1964, 101; 1955a, 433). As free, then, the autonomous self is like every other self. Only the pure form of its willing—that of the universality of its maxims—remains once it enters this kingdom. There is, needless to say, a certain paradox here. It comes to the fore when we ask: Who is actually willing according to these universal maxims? Whose autonomy is Kant actually referring to?

The paradox underlying these questions embraces the self in terms of its action, its appearance, and its causality. The paradox of action is that of the ownership of freedom. On the one hand, I have to say with Kant that my freedom is my very selfhood. It is because I am autonomous that I am "price-less." I am without price because nothing has a purchase on my will. As independent of my situation, I cannot be bought (Kant 1964, 102; 1955a, 435). This very autonomy, however, comes at the price of my individuality. The freedom that the abstraction from my environment affords me is not "mine" in the sense of pertaining to a specific actor. Such freedom, in fact, has no finitely human owner. This may be put in terms of Kant's position that a rational being is both a subject and a head of the kingdom of ends. He is a subject "when, although he makes its universal laws, he is also himself subject to these laws. He belongs to it as a *head* when as the maker of laws he is himself subject to the will of no other." As the head, in other words, he subjects himself to the laws he makes. This self-subjugation is necessary, since as the head he enjoys complete autonomy. Is this autonomy his as an individual, human actor? Kant's answer is contained in the remark he adds about the rational being that assumes the position of headship: "The position of the [head] he can maintain, not in virtue of the maxim of his will alone, but only if he is a completely independent being, without needs and with an unlimited power adequate to his will" (1964, 101; 1955a, 433–34). The position of the "head" of the kingdom is, then, ultimately God's. Thus, although my freedom is my selfhood, its exercise in making and acting on universal laws does not just make me like everyone else, it also seems to collapse me into God. My will, in its identity with all other wills that follow the categorical imperative, is identical to the divine or holy will.

To put this in terms of the paradox of appearance is to observe that I have my individuality only as an appearing self. This is the self that is situated and individualized by its surrounding sensible world. It is the self that has its identity as a "this-here-now," that is, as a definite position in space and time from which the surrounding world is viewed. Its identity, we can say, is that of a center, a point *from which* spatial and temporal distances are marked—for example, so many yards from my "here," so many minutes from my "now." To abstract myself from this world is to lose this centering. Losing this, however, I lose my individual selfhood. The result is a kind of seesaw of relations. I am an individual in the world of sense, but not, Kant assures me, an independent actor. I lose this individuality in the world of reason (the intelligible world), but, then, according to Kant, I gain independence. Once again the paradox of ownership opens up: I have to ask whose independence this is.

The same paradox may be put in terms of causality by recalling that the self is independent only to the point that it follows reason. The laws of reason are, however, not those of the causality that structures the appearing world. The premises of a syllogism, for example, do not "cause" its conclusion in the same way that one gravitating body causes another to move towards it. The logical, static relation of premise to conclusion is not that of the causally determined *temporal* sequence of appearances that structures the sensible world. Logical relations belong to the intelligible, as opposed to the sensible, world. The world that does appear thus cannot reveal whether the subjects within it are following reason or simply acting out of appetite. To the point that they actually have an independent rational agency—i.e., actually follow moral as opposed to causal laws—such subjects do not appear. To the degree that they do appear, one can always doubt their freedom. Since, however, freedom is the essence of selfhood, this doubt touches not just their appearing but also their being. The specter it raises is that of solipsism. The appearing world, to the point that it excludes freedom, can offer us no evidence of genuine others. A subject, limited to it, could well believe that it was a solitary self. Following Kant, this self could, of course, appeal to the intelligible world, i.e., to the others with whom it supposedly shares the kingdom of ends. Such an appeal, however,

simply translates the difficulty, since, as already indicated, in this kingdom of ends individuals tend to collapse into each other. The paradox of
causality is, thus, that of the appearing of the individual agent. A person,
to the degree that he is free, exercises an agency that cannot appear in the
causality that structures the sensible world. To be recognized as free he
must, paradoxically, give himself as not being able to be given in this
world. His appearance must indicate his inability to appear.

The task that Kant's thought leaves us with is that of thinking freedom "in" the world. As already noted, this is the task of combining
framing with the escape from the frame that is freedom. Insofar as we are
framed by the appearing world, this involves showing how this world
"gives" what cannot be given in its strictly sensuous terms. Chapter 6, in
describing the constitution of our selfhood, will undertake to explain
how this comes about. It will also show how our freedom arises as part
of the same constitution. The solution it offers will, however, only be
comprehensible in terms of the alternatives offered by the tradition.
How do they conceive of freedom in terms of the world?

Darwin and Freud

Ethics and Instinct

Freedom involves self-separation. When I do not separate myself
from myself, when, for example, I live simply in the immediacy of some
pleasure, I lack the distance to judge or resist the pleasure. To conceive
of freedom as "in" the world is, accordingly, to understand this inner
distance or self-separation in terms of the world. This involves seeing the
world as affording us the resources by which we can escape the immediacy of our situation. It is to see the world as not just centering us, but
also as pulling us out of our self-centeredness.

For Darwin, who conceives the world in biological terms, both
actions are biologically based. Our self-alterity is, for him, a function of
our instinctive life; our self-separation is actually a separation of
instincts. This means that, on the one side, we have our self-regarding
instincts. These are directed to the "search after pleasure or happiness"
(Darwin 1967a, 490). On the other side are found our "social instincts."
In Darwin's words, they "have been developed for the general good . . .
of the species," this being defined as "the rearing of the greatest number
of individuals in full vigor and health, with all their faculties perfect"
(490). The distinction between the two types of instinct appears in the
example of a person rushing into a burning building to rescue someone.

At the time, "he can hardly feel pleasure" in his action, which he performs unreflectively, "without a moment's hesitation." Yet, Darwin adds, "should he afterwards reflect over his own conduct, he would feel that there lies within him an impulsive power widely different from a search after pleasure or happiness; and this seems to be the deeply planted social instinct" (490). In this example, the social instinct overrides the self-regarding instinct for self-preservation. For the person who immediately draws back from the attempt, the reverse is the case. The drive to preserve himself overcomes the impulse to save another person. Normally, neither instinct predominates to the exclusion of the other. Each can serve as a standpoint for regarding the impulses of the other. Thus, the person who hesitates may judge the impulse to rescue to be foolhardy. Yet he may also see his hesitation as the sign of cowardice. These two attitudes, which can be simultaneous, indicate our self-alterity. Their basis is the duality of our instinctive life. It is both directed towards our self-preservation and the preservation of others.

The evolutionary origin of this duality is not hard to find. Our survival in primitive times depended on our success *both* as individuals and as tribes. The competition between individuals fostered their self-regarding instincts. Those who could best preserve themselves and compete for mates passed on the characteristics that favored their success. Their self-regarding instincts are those inborn drives and corresponding patterns of behavior that favor success in the competitive struggles within a tribe. Those characteristics that favored the survival of the tribe itself would equally tend to become inherited instincts. In Darwin's words: "A tribe including many members who, from possessing in a high degree the spirit of patriotism, fidelity, obedience, courage, and sympathy, were always ready to aid one another, and to sacrifice themselves for the common good, would be victorious over most other tribes; and this would be natural selection" (Darwin 1967a, 500). Its members, in other words, would pass on these psychological characteristics and, hence, the instincts underlying them. The success of their tribe would "select" for them by allowing its members to survive and breed at the expense of the members of the competing tribes. The extermination of the latter would, of course, be the elimination of the biological basis for their social instincts. They could not pass them on.

Were there no conflict between the characteristics that tend to preserve the individual and those that tend to preserve the tribe, there would be no conflicts in our instinctual life. The biological basis for our self-alterity would vanish and, with this, according to Darwin, our sense of conscience. Conflict, however, is built into this division. The individual members of the tribe cannot both preserve themselves and "sacrifice themselves for the common good." They cannot be simultaneously self-centered and altruistic. As a result, there is often "a struggle in man between his social instincts, with their derived virtues and his lower, though momentarily stronger impulses or desires" (Darwin 1967a, 494). Since an individual is always a member of his tribe, his social instinct is continuous in its action. At the moment of danger, however, the instinct to preserve himself may outweigh this. If, at the expense of his tribe, he yields to it (or to some other self-regarding instinct) he will feel the sting of conscience. The remorse he experiences is, Darwin writes, "analogous to the feelings caused by other powerful instincts or desires, when left unsatisfied or balked" (494). It is "the sense of dissatisfaction" caused by the balking of the social instinct. Of course, to feel such remorse, one has to have the ability to compare past and present impressions. This, how-ever, happens incessantly. Thus, a person naturally "will be driven to make a comparison between the impressions of past hunger, vengeance satisfied, or danger shunned at other men's cost, with the almost ever-present instinct of sympathy . . . " (484). The thwarting of the latter, leads to "remorse, repentance, regret, or shame." The person, Darwin concludes, "will consequently resolve more or less firmly to act differ-ently for the future; and this is conscience; for conscience looks back-wards, and serves as a guide for the future" (484).

The Darwinian parallel to the Kantian working out of the ought is apparent from the above. Instead of the conflict between appetite and reason—that is, between our membership in both the sensuous and the intellectual worlds—we have the struggle between two opposing sets of instincts. For such a struggle to be a moral one there must, of course, be a certain amount of intellectual development. The "mental facilities" of our species must be sufficiently developed so that the "images of all past actions and motives would be incessantly passing through the brain of each individual" (Darwin 1967a, 472). In other words, each individual must become self-conscious in the sense of being aware of his past actions and his intentions for the future. Such self-awareness, however, is not yet morality. The individual must also have a sense of approving or disapproving his past and his intended future actions. In Darwin's words, " . . . [W]e rank all actions of a certain class as moral, if per-formed by our moral being. A moral being is one who is capable of com-paring his past and future actions or motives, and of approving or disapproving them" (482–83). The moral being, in other words, is the person who says to himself: "I should not have done that, I will not do that in the future." For this, he requires more than the powers of memory and anticipation; he needs some standard to judge what he remembers or anticipates doing. This is what the social instinct provides.

When the individual disapproves of what he did, it is because he sees that "the enduring and always present social instinct had yielded to some other instinct, at the time stronger, but neither enduring in its nature, nor leaving behind it a very vivid impression." The impression of the social instinct is "always present," while the impressions of the self-regarding "instinctive desires, such as hunger, are in their nature of short duration; and after being satisfied, are not readily or vividly recalled" (472). The superior force of the impression created by the thwarted social instinct thus overwhelms the vanishing sense of satisfaction of the act that disregarded it. With this we have "that feeling of dissatisfaction or even misery, which invariably results . . . from any unsatisfied instinct . . . " (472). We have, in other words, the sting of conscience.

Were we guided solely by the social instinct, i.e., had we no self-regarding instincts, this sting of conscience would not occur. We would automatically follow its impulses. The same holds were we limited to the self-regarding instincts, such as hunger, sex, individual preservation, and so on. In neither case would we perform an act that we would later regret. We experience the "ought" precisely because we are subject to both types of instinct. Experiencing both, we experience the "struggle as to which impulse should be followed" (Darwin 1967a, 473). The "ought" occurs as we regard the consequences of following one set of instincts in the light of what happened when we followed the other set. In Darwin's words, " . . . [S]atisfactions, dissatisfaction, or even misery would be felt, as past impressions were compared during their incessant passage through the mind. In this case an inward monitor would tell the animal that it would have been better to have been followed the one impulse rather than the other. The one course *ought* to have been followed, and the other *ought* not; the one would have been right, the other wrong" (473, italics added). Needless to say, were we completely moral and only yielded to the demands of our social instincts, we would not avoid the sense of dissatisfaction that comes from thwarting instinctive impulse. Our self-regarding instincts, such as hunger, while of "short duration," must also be satisfied if they are not to overwhelm us with their periodic demands. Realistically, then, the only solution to our being subject to both types of instinct is an ongoing negotiation between the two. We must, somehow, learn to balance their demands.

Judgment and Instinct

To see conscience as arising from the "struggle as to which impulse should be followed" does not yet tell us how we decide between our impulses. Given that some sort of negotiation is required, the question of its basis naturally arises. We have to ask: Where, in Darwin's scheme, is that part of the self that, seeing both sides, adjudicates their demands? This part cannot itself be a social or self-regarding instinct. Not only would this prejudice its action, but the very notion of instinct disqualifies it from reasoning out the merits of the competing claims. "The very essence of an instinct," Darwin writes, "is that it is followed independently of reason" (Darwin 1967a, 491). It does not reflect, but works automatically. What does decide must, then, be a faculty separate from instinct.

It is tempting to see this faculty as "reason" in its traditional sense of *logos*—the term signifying not just reason but also speech. So understood, reason is taken as the specific difference of humans. To define man as a "rational animal" is to say that he alone is capable of action "in accordance with logos."[10] We know this because he can speak, i.e., give reasons for his actions. Animals cannot do this. It may be, as Darwin claims, that the Paraguayan monkey "when excited utters at least six different sounds, which excite in other monkeys similar emotions." It is certainly the case that the domesticated dog's vocabulary includes "the bark of eagerness . . . of anger . . . the yelp or howl of despair . . . the baying at night, the bark of joy . . . " and so forth (Darwin 1967a, 491). Yet such actions, by which the animal reveals its emotional states, do not qualify as *logos*. In no case do animals explain their actions.

This line of thought, which makes reason a specific difference, is deeply problematic for Darwin. To prove man's descent from a "lower form" of life, Darwin points to the features humans have in common with the other animals. Common features indicate a common ancestry and, hence, show a common descent from an original stock. If, however, as Darwin's critics urge, there are some features that are unique to man, features that point to the uniqueness of his origin, this argument cannot be made. Chief among these features, they claim, are his reasoning ability and the moral sense that is based on this.[11] Thus, to secure his theory of evolution, Darwin must interpret both so that the difference between men and animals is one of degree rather than kind.

This is why Darwin breaks the tie between reason and speech. Even though animals cannot speak, i.e., cannot explain their behavior, their actions show that they can associate. Reason, Darwin claims, is "intimately connected" with "the association of ideas." As such, it admits of various degrees. A pike, he relates, dashed its head against a glass partition whenever it attempted to catch the fish on the other side. After three months, however, even its "feeble mind" was capable of associating these attempts with the violent shock it received. As a result, it did not attack the fish when the partition was later removed. "Now with monkeys . . . ," he adds, "a pain or merely a disagreeable impression, from an action once performed, is sometimes sufficient to prevent the animal from repeating it." Drawing the inference, Darwin asks: "If we attribute this difference between the monkey and the pike solely to the association of ideas being so much stronger and more persistent in the one than in the other, though the pike often received much the more severe injury, can we maintain in the case of man that a similar difference implies the possession of a fundamentally different mind?" (Darwin 1967a, 454). If we cannot, then the difference between the savage and one of the higher animals is only one of degree: "The savage . . . would take notice of much slighter circumstances and conditions and would observe any connection between them after much less experience" (455). The savage is, thus, much quicker in drawing associations than the higher animal. "But," he adds, "the higher animals differ in exactly the same way in this power of association from those low in the scale, such as the pike, as well as in that of drawing inferences and of observation" (455). As the context makes clear, the sense of reason at work in this argument is that of drawing inferences from observations. This, however, is treated as association. The pike, for example, in its ability to associate one event with another, is understood as gradually drawing the inference: if I do this (attack the fish), then this happens (I get a shock). The same pattern of association, Darwin claims, is behind the fact that both the dog and the savage search for water in the same way. Both "have often found water at a low level." This coincidence has, thus, "become associated in their minds. . . . and, in both, [searching for water by proceeding to lower levels] seems to be equally an act of reason, whether or not any general proposition on the subject is consciously placed before the mind" (455).

To grasp the novelty of this view of reason, we have to contrast it with its pre-Darwinian sense, which includes both logic and speech. An anecdote from a textbook in elementary logic gives the essence of what was traditionally taken as the ability to reason:

While talking of his early experiences as a priest, an elderly abbé responded to the comment that the secrets of the confessional must often be of a kind disturbing to a young man, by admitting that it had indeed been so in his case, as the first confession he ever heard was a confession of a murder. Shortly after the abbé's departure his visit was mentioned to a later caller, a local proprietor and notability, who remarked that the abbé and he were very old acquaintances. "Indeed," he added, "I was the abbé's first penitent." (Sinclair 1950, 45)

Hearing this tale, we conclude that the later caller was a murderer. We come to this conclusion by identifying the murderer with the abbé's first penitent and this penitent with the later caller. Formally, we see that if $a = b = c$, then $a = c$. Reason, in its traditional sense, is the ability to do this. Such ability involves both speech and logic. We can draw the logical inference because we can use words to hold our concepts stable. Stable, self-identical concepts allow us to formalize our inferences. We can, for example, say that if all a's are b's and all b's are c's, then all a's are c's. The conclusion here is independent of the particular content of the a's, b's or c's. To assert that humans are rational—i.e., language-using—animals is to say that they can draw such conclusions. Hearing a series of assertions, they can abstract from their contents and use the symbolism of words to regard their forms. Using these to infer, they can draw a conclusion that was not present in any of the individual premises they started with. Animals cannot do this because they cannot talk. They can, of course, associate. Association, however, is the opposite of the abstraction needed for language and logical inference. Association works from the pairing of specific contents. Seeing Peter, for example, reminds me of Paul, since I have often seen them together. Inferring, however, proceeds by abstraction from the contents that must be attended to if they are to serve as a basis for association.

The abstraction at work in reason is also a liberation. Using reason to work out our goals, we can create the distance that frees us from our already experienced environment. Thus, for Plato, reason, in working out the future, grounds our self-alterity. It gives us the perspective to stand back and judge that aspect of ourselves that is defined by the immediacy of desire. A parallel point is made by Kant. Taking up the standpoint of reason, I stand outside of myself as I exist in the sensuous world. This standing-outside is my freedom. It is what allows me to judge myself and my actions. It permits me, for example, to adjudicate between the competing impulses of my social and self-regarding instincts. When, however, I reduce reason to association, this becomes impossible. Association cannot provide the escape from immediacy that counts as freedom, since, by definition, it is fixed by the environment, i.e., by the particular circumstances that call up association. Darwin, in reducing reason to association, thus naturalizes both reason and the morality it founds. Reason, for Darwin, cannot stand outside of our natural life so as to morally judge its course. As association, reason is simply a facet of this life.

Ethics and Extermination

The limitations of this view become apparent once we draw out the consequences of Darwin's position. In a telling aside, Darwin calls "the moral sense of consciousness . . . one of the highest physical faculties of man" (Darwin 1967a, 471). The point of calling our moral sense a physical faculty is to rank it among the other inheritable characteristics of our nature. Thus, just as a person's physical qualities, such as hair or skin color, can be traced back to his ancestors, so can his moral qualities. Insofar as they are based on his physical makeup, they are equally inheritable. This means that "if bad qualities are transmitted, it is probable that good ones are likewise transmitted." It is "known," Darwin adds, "that the state of the body, by affecting the brain, has great influence on the moral tendencies" (492). This holds not just for individuals, but for their races. Their physical differences are accompanied by differences in their moral traits. Both, Darwin concludes, must be heritable. In fact, he asserts, "except through the principle of the transmission of moral tendencies, we cannot understand the differences believed to exist in this respect between the various races of mankind" (493). Darwin's insistence on this point is not accidental. The view that different races have different moral characteristics and that such characteristics, rather than being culturally based, are biologically transmitted is essential to his position. It is what allows him to explain the evolutionary development of our moral sense. The features that make up this sense have been selected for on the basis of the advantages they offer in the struggle for existence. They are, in this sense, no different than physical characteristics.

The implications for ethics of this view may be seen by noting the two elements required for natural selection. The first is the pressure of competition for scarce resources. This is the result of there always being more individuals born than the environment can adequately support. The second is the variability of the features of these individuals.[12] Because of the first, only a portion of the newborn will survive and breed offspring. The second element—random variability—distributes their chances. Those individuals who survive do so, generally, because of some variation giving them a competitive advantage. This holds both for their instincts and for their more readily observable physical characteristics—skin color, length of limbs, and so on. In both cases the logic of evolution implies extermination. In animals that are social the extermination includes that of competing social groups. Thus, the moral qualities that make a tribe "victorious over most other tribes" are chosen by "natural selection" precisely because they result in the extermination of these competing tribes (Darwin 1967a, 500). Since closely allied forms compete for the same resources, the competition between them is generally the most severe. The races of man, however, are only incipient species. The competition of such closely allied forms thus naturally results in extermination. In Darwin's view, this holds even in our present day. He observes, for example, that "the civilized races have extended, and are now everywhere extending their range, so as to take the place of the lower races" (502). This leads him to the prediction: "At some future period, not very distant as measured by centuries, the civilized races of man will almost certainly exterminate, and replace, the savage races throughout the world" (521). In fact, the problem of the extinction of one of these "lower" races is, from the perspective of evolution, no different than "that presented by the extinction of one of the higher animals." "The New Zealander," he observes, "seems conscious of this parallelism, for he compares his future with that of the native rat now almost exterminated by the European rat" (550).

These remarks raise the question of how a morality based on evolution would judge the racism and genocide that marked the last century. If different races have different moral tendencies and these are heritable, there is, in fact, a basis in nature for racial stereotyping. One can speak of "the careless, squalid, unaspiring Irishman," contrasting him with "the frugal, foreseeing, self-respecting, ambitious Scot" (Darwin 1967a, 505). One can acclaim "the great stream of Anglo-Saxon emigration to the west" as that which "gives purpose to all other series of events," including those of Greece and Rome (508). Indeed, one can see "much truth in the belief that the wonderful progress of the United States, as well as the character of the people, are the results of natural selection"— the same selection that gives an advantage to the English over the French Canadians (508). The success of one people at the expense of another is, in this context, both natural and moral. It is natural because biological evolution is a matter of struggle for existence, a struggle that results in "the survival of the fittest." The traits that evolve are those that give success in this struggle. Thus, the morality that develops is one that allows a tribe to succeed over its competitors, a success that usually involves the competitor's extermination. Given this, we cannot say that the success that involves extermination is immoral. Natural selection involves extermination. Morality itself, however, is a product of natural selection. Its standards rise through tribe supplanting tribe. In Darwin's optimistic phrasing, "At all times throughout the world tribes have supplanted other tribes; and as morality is one important element in their success, the standard of morality and the number of well-endowed men will thus everywhere tend to rise and increase" (500). In such a context, to say that this supplanting is immoral is to condemn the very process that gives us morality. We cannot do it without involving ourselves in a kind of performative contradiction. Our very act of condemning this extermination presupposes the moral sense that is derived from its process.

The same point holds with regard to helping the unfortunate members of our society. Insofar as this action works against the natural selection that gives rise to morality, we cannot really say that it is moral. In fact, from an evolutionary perspective, it is actually harmful. It reverses the progress of evolution. As Darwin puts this:

> With the savages, the weak in body or mind are soon elimi-
> nated; and those that survive commonly exhibit a vigorous
> state of health. We civilized men, on the other hand, do our
> utmost to check the process of elimination; we build asylums
> for the imbecile, the maimed, and the sick; we institute poor-
> laws; and our medical men exert their utmost skill to save the
> life of every one to the last moment. . . . Thus the weak mem-
> bers of civilized societies propagate their kind. No one who has
> attended to the breeding of domestic animals will doubt that
> this must be highly injurious to the race of man. (Darwin
> 1967a, 501)

This means that if checks are not found for preventing "the reckless, the vicious and otherwise inferior members of society from increasing . . . , the nation will retrograde" (507).

Darwin's attempt to conceive of the self-separation that grounds ethics in natural, biological terms thus ends in paradox. Actions that we commonly take as moral—for example, helping the sick and infirm—become immoral. Actions that we regard as immoral—most notably, genocide—appear to lie at the basis of morality. Obviously, something is missing in this attempt. Rather than providing us with any way to stand against and judge the framework that determines us—here conceived in terms of natural selection—morality becomes one of its expressions. The escape from the situation provided by Darwin's division of our instincts is, therefore, more apparent than real. The "others" that for Plato and Kant were represented by the universality of reason are not really cap-tured by Darwin's social instinct. The virtues springing from the social instinct, Darwin notes, "are practiced almost exclusively in relation to the men of the same tribe" (Darwin 1967a, 487). This cannot be otherwise, since they were selected because of the advantages they offered the tribe. To get beyond this limitation we need to speak of the inner presence of others in terms that exceed those of the development of our instincts. As Freud saw, we have to cross the divide separating biology from culture.

Structures of the Self

For both Plato and Kant, our primary access to others is through reason. In Plato, this occurs in the back-and-forth of the arguments that make up the *Dialogues*. Reason, for Socrates, is an intersubjective phenomenon. This means that others are present to me in the dialogues they provoke. As other than me and yet "in" me, they exist in my calling myself into question and in my calling myself forward to respond to this. They thus exist in the examined life that Socrates constantly urges on his hearers. For Kant, such others are the implicit referent of the universalization demanded by the categorical imperative. To universalize my maxim is to ask what would happen if every one followed it. Others here are not so much partners in dialogue as the totality of possible rational agents. To the point that they can universalize their maxims, they are members of the kingdom of ends. Their presence in me as other than me is that of the nonappearing in the appearing. They represent the intelligible as opposed to the sensible world. Darwin's biologization of our self-separation interprets it as a separation of instincts. Others are "in" me as other than me insofar as their presence is manifested in those social instincts that draw me out of myself. The others within me are those unthinking drives that impel me to act on behalf of other persons. My self-presence on the instinctual level thus contains more than I (as a self-regarding individual) can contain. There is a blind alterity within this presence that constantly disquiets it with the demands of others. With Freud, a new formulation of self-alterity occurs: others become part of the self as a set of internalized parental and cultural demands. They are in me as forming one of the functioning components of the system that is a self.

As the later Freud schematized it, three structures make up the system of the self: the id, the ego, and the superego. The superego is a designation for the "special agency" that "prolongs" the influence of our parents in their action of imposing moral strictures on us. According to Freud, it "includes in its operation not only the personalities of the actual parents but also the family, racial and national traditions handed on through them, as well as the demands of the immediate social milieu which they represent" (Freud 1989, 15–16). Opposing this agency is the action of the id. The id "contains every thing that is inherited, that is present at birth." Above all, it contains "the instincts, which originate from the somatic organization and which find a first psychical expression here [in the id] . . . " (14). The instincts, in other words, "represent the somatic demands on the mind" (17). The id is that place where they first come to presence, i.e., achieve some form of psychic expression.

According to Freud, there are "only two basic instincts, Eros and the destructive instinct." The aim of Eros or the "love instinct" is "to establish ever greater unities and to preserve them thus—in short, to bind together." The goal of the destructive or "death instinct" is "to undo connections and so destroy things" (Freud 1989, 18). Darwin's social and self-regarding instincts, with their focus on "the preservation of the species" and "self-preservation," are in part akin to Eros. When, however, they are aggressively directed against other individuals or tribes, they also manifest the death instinct. Freud's division, thus, cuts across Darwin's. In Freud's eyes, it is more fundamental, since it explains the apparent multiplicity of our instinctual life. This, he writes, is due to the fact that "in biological functions the two basic instincts [love and death] operate against each other or combine with each other." To use Freud's examples, "the act of eating is a destruction of the object with the final aim of incorporating it, and the sexual act is an act of aggression with the purpose of the most intimate union" (18). As such examples make clear, the id may be regarded as analogous to the appetitive part of the soul. The inclusion within it of the death instinct points to the fact that the consumption that satisfies appetite is also a destruction.[13] Now, for Freud, the check on appetite is not so much reason as the others implied by reason. Internalized and made concrete as the presence of our parents and society, these others form our superego. Their inner voice gives us a standpoint outside of ourselves that is also within us. Viewing and judging the demands of the id from within, the superego makes its demands felt as the voice of conscience.[14]

While the id represents "the influence of heredity" and the superego that of others, "the ego," Freud writes, "is principally determined by the individual's own experience, that is, by accidental and contemporary events" (Freud 1989, 16). It is the place where the "real external world" is acknowledged and dealt with (14). The opening up of the self to this world involves the repression of the id. Parental prohibitions first cause the child to reflect on its instinctive impulses. It learns to cope with these "by deciding whether they are to be allowed satisfaction, by postponing that satisfaction to times and circumstances favorable in the external world or by suppressing their excitations entirely" (15). To guide it, the child must attend to reality—i.e., to the intersubjective world that includes its parents. Its motives for doing so stem from its helplessness. Since its survival depends on its parents, the child must have their approval. It must take thought vis-à-vis the instinctive demands that press upon it. Separating itself from their immediacy, the child has to consider their possible effects on those on whom it depends. When its instinctual demands are inappropriate, i.e., lead to parental disapproval, the child must repress them. Its selfhood, which previously yielded at once to the pressure of desire, thus acquires through these actions the inner distance that is both a *self-separation* and an *openness* to the real, intersubjective world. With the internalization of the action of its parents and their successors, i.e., with the appearance of the superego, the maintenance of this openness becomes part of the functioning of the self. The "ego" names its result. Phenomenologically regarded, it is the self's openness to reality.

The position of the ego as such openness does not mean that it cannot be described as acting. When, however, it is so described, we have to understand the self as the actor. The "ego" in such descriptions stands as its representative. It stands for the self understood as an actor within the real world. It *is* the self's interface with the actual world. This is the way we should read Freud's assertion, "An action by the ego is as it should be if it satisfies simultaneously the demands of the id, of the super-ego and of reality—that is to say, if it is able to reconcile their demands with one another" (Freud 1989, 15). At stake in this reconciliation are both the self and the ego, taken as one of its structures. The failure of the reconciliation undoes the self's relationship to the real world. This, however, makes it impossible for the self to act in relationship to it.

This may be put in terms of the fact that the ego, as our openness to reality, is contested ground. The demands of the superego and the id are opposed both to each other and to reality. In an adult, the superego's focus is largely determined by the past strictures of a vanished childhood. As for the id, its focus is entirely internal. The drives that comprise it are indifferent to the dangers they pose to the self in the real world. The self, however, cannot simply dismiss their demands. Its very openness as ego is, as just noted, a result of their action. It arises through the repression of the id by the internalized intersubjective voice that is the superego. Thus, the self requires their opposition. It also requires that neither encroach too far on the other. The complete success of the id would destroy its relation to reality. So would the victory of the superego. To avoid this, the self must constantly negotiate between their sets of conflicting demands. It has to balance its bodily (instinctive) self-presence with its self-presence as shaped by others. Since the self is both organic and social, its unity depends on the success of this action. This action is an action of both the self and of the ego, taken as its representative. The "ego" is the opening to reality created by the opposition between the superego and the id. The opening is kept open by the delicate and continuous process of negotiating their conflicting demands. Since this negotiation can only succeed by regarding also the real and its demands, it requires the ego. The ego, then, both acts for the self and is the result of the success of its action.

Illness and Recovery

The failure of the negotiation is the collapse of the self's openness. Overwhelmed by the demands of the id and superego, the ego "tries to cling to reality in order to maintain its normal state." When it fails, these demands (which ignore the real world) "succeed in loosening and altering the ego's organization, so that its proper relation to reality is disturbed or even brought to an end" (Freud 1989, 50). At the extreme, the result is "psychosis"—i.e., the collapse of the system that is the self. Freud's description of the "neurotic ego" is an account of this system in peril. The still functioning but "weakened" ego, he writes;

> is no longer able to fulfill the task set it by the external world (including human society). Not all of its experiences are at its disposal, a large proportion of its store of memories have escaped it. Its activity is inhibited by strict prohibitions from the super-ego, its energy is consumed in vain attempts at fending off the demands of the id. Beyond this, as a result of continuous irruptions by the id, its organization is impaired, it is no longer capable of any proper synthesis, it is torn by mutually opposed urges, by unsettled conflicts and by unsolved doubts. (60)

The loss of memory Freud refers to is the result of repression. What an individual cannot "synthesize"—i.e., interpret and integrate into his experience—he rejects and represses. Particularly in early childhood, emotionally charged events that do not fit in with the child's normal experiences are rejected and confined to the "unconscious." The same happens to those events whose subsequently divined sense threatens the self's integration (36). In the weakened ego this repressed material shows its presence not directly, but through symptoms. A symptom is a pattern of behavior, deeply disturbing to the patient, that cannot be explained in terms of his actual situation or his consciousness of it. It is a sign that "the real external world" no longer completely guides his conduct. What moves him are the elements of his unconscious that do not (as they do in psychosis) directly appear, but rather take on the forms of symbolic substitutes. Such substitutes are actions that satisfy on a symbolic level a person's repressed wishes or, alternatively, place him in a situation where these wishes cannot, in fact, be realized.[15]

Curing the patient involves ridding him of symptoms. This, however, requires that the repressed material causing these disturbances be made conscious. As Freud puts this: "Symptoms are not produced by conscious processes; as soon as the unconscious processes involved are made conscious, the symptoms must vanish. . . . Our therapy does its work by transforming something unconscious into something conscious, and only succeeds in its work insofar it is able to effect this transformation" (Freud 1965, 290–91). Two presuppositions are at work in this assertion. The first is that curing the self involves "an extending of its self-knowledge—i.e., extending the area of its conscious possessions" (Freud 1989, 56). The second is that consciousness is the realm of the self's freedom, such freedom being a condition of the possibility of its being cured. The singularity of the psychoanalytic cure may be brought out by contrasting it with the cure of bodily illness. Knowledge of the cause of an illness such as AIDS does not by itself yield the power to intervene in its process. For this, we require additional technical powers. In a psychic process, however, knowledge and recovery go hand in hand. Of course, for the patient to gain such knowledge he must be helped to overcome his resistance to reexperiencing emotionally disturbing material. The instinctive urges that forgotten events imposed upon him have to be faced. Yet once such resistances are overcome and the materials in question become conscious, the assumption is that the ego can freely dispose of them. In terms of the validity of the cure, it is, then, "a matter of indifference" whether the overcoming of resistances "results in the ego accepting, after a fresh examination, an instinctual demand which it has hitherto rejected, or whether it dismisses it once more, this time for good and all" (58). The important thing is that the ego be given this choice. This requires that the unconscious demand (as well as the actual circumstances that originally incited it) be made conscious. Making both conscious makes them part of the real world. In bringing, say, a traumatic event to consciousness, the patient acknowledges that it actually occurred, that it was real. The ego, however, is the self's openness to reality. Thus, whether the ego accepts or rejects the demand, "the compass of the ego has been extended" (58).[16]

This extension goes hand in hand with the unmasking of the patient's symptoms. They are shown to be the result of unconscious materials. As Freud describes the analytic process, "we restore order in the ego by detecting the material and urges which have forced their way in from the unconscious, and expose them to criticism by tracing them back to their origin" (Freud 1989, 60). As a result, the patient knows the original of which the symptom is only a symbolic expression. This knowledge gives him the ability to critically appraise and transform his behavior. He can, for example, choose not to repeat the behavior that helped him cope in childhood with an instinctive demand. He can realize that it is no longer appropriate. The effect of analysis is, then, not just to transform a patient's "unconscious and repressed" material into conscious contents "and thus return it once more to the possession of his ego" (61). In making him acknowledge the hidden determinants of his actions, it transforms the latter into items he can choose or refuse to realize. The extension of the patient's self-knowledge is, thus, simultaneously an extension of the patient's ego, an increase in his sense of reality, and a widening of his freedom.

Ethics and Analysis

Given that we have to be free to make moral choices, Freud's account of psycho-analysis seems to position it as a necessary propaedeutic to ethics. In extending the "compass of the ego," analysis appears, at very least, to establish the conditions for the possibility of ethics. Such conditions include the information and skills necessary to negotiate between the demands of the id and the superego. With the analyst's help, the patient is able to overcome the strict prohibitions of the superego, thereby weakening the self's resistances to the demands of the id. This lessening of their opposition allows previously unconscious material to be made conscious and thus be subject to moral choice. The unmasking of symptoms that accompanies this process does not just extend our sense of reality; it increases that inner distance that is the ego taken as the self's openness to the real world. This inner distance, understood as separating the self from the immediacy of desire, is the condition that makes possible a moral life. Implicit here is, thus, a double ideal. Analysis, by extending the self's openness to previously unconscious material, aims at the *maximum increase of consciousness*. It also, thereby, aims at a *maximum of freedom*. In the ideal condition, the patient has a complete choice regarding the contents of his selfhood. Correspondingly, his symptoms disappear, since the unconscious material that occasioned them has been made conscious. Freed of his symptoms, the patient is free to take moral responsibility for his life.

Tempting as it is, this ideal is only an illusion. Its realization would, in fact, be the dissolution of the self. Thus, the ideal of making unconscious material conscious can proceed only so far. The resistance of the self to this process is not without cause. Its sanity depends upon the success of its efforts to keep most of it down. This means that the process of analysis mimics, as it were, the process of the breakdown of the self in psychosis. In Freud's words,

> [W]hat comes about in the analytic treatment as a result of our efforts can also occur spontaneously: a material which is ordinarily unconscious can transform itself into preconscious material and then become conscious—a thing that happens to a large extent in psychotic states. From this we infer that the maintenance of certain internal resistances is a *sine qua non* of normality" (Freud 1989, 62).

This does not mean that we are free to increase such resistances. Too much repression is as destructive to the self as too little. It can lead to a downward spiral in which the energy of the repressed instincts gets channeled to the superego. Using this energy to increase its repression, the superego, acting as our "conscience," draws additional energy from this further repression, which it uses to become even more severe. As Freud describes this downward process: "Every renunciation of instinct now becomes a dynamic source of conscience and every fresh renunciation increases the latter's severity and intolerance" (Freud 1962, 75). Aggression plays a central role in this increase of severity and intolerance. Initially, as Freud writes, the child's aggression is directed "against the [parental] authority which prevents him from his first, but nonetheless his most important, satisfactions" of his instincts (76). The child, however, cannot revenge himself on the parent. His only way of escaping from his helplessness is to identify himself with his parent's authority. He internalizes this authority in the form of the superego. In Freud's words: "The authority now turns into his super-ego and enters into possession of all the aggressiveness which the child would have liked to exercise against it" (76). Thus, "the original severity of the super-ego does not represent" the severity of the parent's authority; "it represents rather one's own aggressiveness towards it"—i.e., toward the authority of the parent who demanded the renunciation of the child's instinctual satisfactions. Each further renunciation increases this aggression, which the superego redirects against the instinctive impulses. The result is a cycle of renunciation and aggression in which the superego grows increasingly severe. Since this process takes no note of the actual world—which, in any event, is *not* the superego's concern—the self is once again threatened with a loss of its sense of reality.

The freedom that psychoanalysis offers us is, thus, limited by the system that is the self. Too little or too much repression unbalances the self. Since the amount of unconscious material that can become conscious is strictly limited, so is the ideal of complete control of our actions. Ethically regarded, our responsibility is bounded by what we can be conscious of. What psychoanalysis teaches is that this can never be complete. It is not just that we are never fully aware of the springs of our actions—i.e., know whether their motives lie in duty or appetite. We also cannot be certain of the extent to which our actions are responses to the "real, external world" or simply symptoms—i.e., are responses to "unconscious" materials. The "voice of conscience" is no help in this quandary: the superego that incorporates it is just one member of the system that is ourselves. Like Darwin's social instinct, it lacks the necessary transcendence to judge the system of which it is simply an aspect.

Thus, as Freud's descriptions make clear, the superego has its own liabilities. Although it is, according to Freud, the origin of conscience, its judgments need not be ethical. This is particularly the case when, in a cycle of renunciation and aggression, the superego's strictures become increasingly intolerant.

This, of course, is where analysis is supposed to help us out. The work of the therapist is to increase our self-knowledge. She should instruct us on how far we should repress our instincts and how far, alternatively, we should weaken the superego. The therapist, however, does not exist in isolation. As a functioning member of society, the answer she gives reflects its norms. Moreover, if the patient is to function within society, he also must follow its norms; he must repress his impulses accordingly. Knowing how much repression is "normal" for society does not, however, tell us whether this amount is too much or too little. We cannot simply take our standards from our social milieu, since societies, like individuals, suffer neuroses and even breakdown. Thus, according to Freud, the structures that define the self have their social parallels. Communities, in possessing them, have their corresponding possibilities for becoming unbalanced. There is, for example, a collective superego. In Freud's words: "[T]he community, too, evolves a super-ego under whose influence cultural development proceeds" (Freud 1962, 88). Its origin is "similar to that of an individual. It is based on the impression left behind by the personalities of great leaders" (88). Like the parents of a child, their influence is prolonged by being internalized. The resulting "cultural" superego mirrors the individual superego in that it also "sets up strict ideal demands, disobedience to which is visited with the 'fear of conscience'" (89). Once again, there is the possibility of a downward spiral involving repression and aggression. To see a contemporary example of this, one need only regard the progressively increasing repression of women in certain countries in the last few decades. Regarded as objects of sexual temptation, they have been increasingly forced to cover their persons. In some regions, this has extended to their faces. The prohibition has even been extended to banishing them from most public places. The aggression and severity of the collective superego in such areas is all too apparent in the murder of the women violating its strictures.

How can we know whether the repression we engage in is too much or too little? Where shall we turn for assurance in our attempts to negotiate between the demands of the id and the superego? Given that the required guidance need not be exemplified in the society we live in, where shall we find it? What is needed is a sense of ethics that is not, like the superego, simply an expression of the social order, but rather something that can serve as its critique. This requires a standpoint that is both inside and outside of the social order. Without its being inside, we have the tyranny of reason we saw in Plato. Without its being outside, we have no perspective to judge society. Only if we combine the two can we bring closure to our reflections on ethics. Thus, once again our review of the history of ethics points to a task that our subsequent chapters must accomplish. To see more precisely what this will involve, we have to consider Aristotle's and Mill's efforts to see society as a source of ethical norms.

Aristotle and Mill

Good Character

The attempt to think freedom as part of the world leads us to define the self in worldly, nontranscendent terms. This denial of transcendence leads, however, to a certain circularity of reasoning in our attempt to derive standards for our conduct. This is particularly apparent when we take these standards from society. We begin by asserting that moral standards can be derived from an analysis of society and its functioning. We behave correctly when, following its norms, we "fit in" with society. Yet in analyzing society's functioning, we come to the conclusion that it is not something transcendent. We cannot think of society apart from the individuals making it up. It therefore seems that the validity of societal norms must be derived from an analysis of the functioning of the individuals within society. The attempt to derive standards for their functioning, however, returns us once again to consider the larger whole—i.e., the society individuals form.

The Aristotelian variant of this circle involves his conceptions of our character, our habits, and our ability to perceive the situation we find ourselves in. For Aristotle, character is an organ of perception— somewhat like an eye or an ear. Its objects, however, are not sensuous but moral. To "see" the good you need a good character. You would not, for example, ask a drunkard how much alcohol one should drink at a party. His habitual drinking has ruined his perception in this regard. Good character, Aristotle observes, is made up of good habits. We acquire our habits by repeated action, i.e., by training. This training, which our parents begin and which continues through our friends and our formal education, is social. It need not, however, always produce a good result. Not all people in society—indeed, not all societies—are good. We can, for example, characterize individuals or societies as "self-indulgent." Granting this, a parent must ask, "Which habits should I train my child in?" Similarly, the grown-up who engages in similar reflections has to ask what habits he should encourage in himself. These questions cannot be answered without a vision of what constitutes a good society. Yet how can we have such a vision apart from the sense of what constitutes a good individual? Ultimately, then, one has to know what a good person is in order to know which habits to suppress and which to encourage. To see this, however, you need good habits. You yourself, in other words, need to have the proper character in order to see what is good and what is not. Thus, knowing the good depends on having the proper character and having the proper character depends on knowing the good. With this, the circle is complete. You need the proper character to see what habits you should acquire. But only if you acquire them will you have the proper character.

Aristotle's entrance into this circle of reasoning can be understood in terms of a contradiction present in Plato's *Gorgias*. On the one hand, we have the fact that no matter how persuasive Socrates seems to be, Callicles remains unmoved. Defeated in his arguments at every turn, he still will not agree. At the end, he simply refuses to continue the discussion. On the other hand, we have Socrates' belief that to know the good is to will to do it.[17] This implies that we are bad because we do not know the good. Since we only act badly out of ignorance, it also follows that "all wrong-doing is involuntary" (Plato 1971, 120). But, if this were the case, Callicles, having heard the truth, would have been moved by it. Learning the good, he would have been transformed by it; he would, in the course of the dialogue, have become good. Yet no such transformation occurs in this or other similar dialogues.[18] Why does Plato, in spite of this, continue to maintain that the will always follows knowledge? An answer can be found in the priority of intellect to will implied by this position. For Plato, the preeminence of intellect is based on the ontological priority of the *eidei* or ideas. If these pure intelligible units are "the very being of to be," then being and intelligibility are the same. Will and desire are, accordingly, banished to the realm of what is not really real— i.e., to the realm of the shadows and images on the lowest level of Plato's divided line. In the *Republic*, this realm is pictured as a cave where prisoners are condemned to gaze on the flickering shapes of shadows projected on a wall. The realm of the ideas, by contrast, is depicted as the sun-filled world of realities outside of the cave (*Republic*, 514a–17a). As Plato's descriptions make clear, a certain relativity of standpoint is implicit in the relation of the two realms. If I am in the cave, the standpoint of willing is prior. The intellect, which has nothing certain to grasp, is devalued. What moves the will is, thus, not knowledge, but desire. The "I will" is an expression simply of the "I want." In the sunlit realm, by contrast, the will becomes a function of knowing.[19] This is particularly apparent in the *Gorgias*, where Socrates asserts that the tyrant, for all his power, never really does what he wills in acting as he pleases. It is only when a person acts from knowledge that he can be said to will what he does (Plato 1971, 52). Knowledge, however, is a property of the sunlit realm. From its perspective, Callicles never wills wrongly. He never wills at all, since he has never left the cave.

There is something clearly unsatisfactory in this response, since it does not really explain Callicles' imperviousness to knowledge. Why does Callicles, in spite of Socrates' arguments, never see the right and wrong pointed out to him? Aristotle's answer to this question is twofold. It consists, in the first place, in devaluing the role of knowledge in moral conduct. For an act to be ethical, certain conditions, he writes, must be met. It must be an act "of a certain kind." In addition, the agent must have "certain characteristics as he performs it; first of all, he must know what he is doing; secondly, he must choose to act the way he does, and he must choose it for its own sake; and in the third place, the act must spring from a firm and unchangeable character (Aristotle 1962, 39; *Nic. Eth*. 1105a. 31–34). For Plato, the first of these conditions is decisive: the agent must act from knowledge. For Aristotle, the last is the most important. Against Plato, he asserts, "[F]or the mastery of the virtues, . . . knowledge is of little or no importance" (1962, 39; *Nic. Eth*. 1105b. 1). The reason for this is that it is not knowledge that makes one virtuous, but the "repeated acts" of virtue that give one "a firm and unchangeable character." In an apparent reference to the characters who argue with Socrates, he adds: "[M]ost men do not perform such [virtuous] acts, but by taking refuge in argument they think that they are engaged in philosophy and that they will become good in this way." Such men would rather discuss the nature of the good than do it. In this, he adds, they are like the "sick men who listen attentively to what the doctor says, but fail to do any of the things he prescribes" (1962, 40; *Nic. Eth*. 1105b. 12–15).

The point of this critique is that studying ethics does not make you ethical. You can know the good and still not bring yourself to do it. The only thing that will make you just is doing just acts. The same holds for being self-controlled. Your character as self-controlled is formed by the acts in which you control yourself—i.e., by your repeated actions of not giving way to your passions and desires. This is because your character is essentially made up of your habits. What characterizes a person are his habitual ways of acting—i.e., of desiring, perceiving, judging, reacting to impulses, and so on. These are the person's "holdings"—i.e., his more or less permanent possessions as he moves from situation to situation.[20] Shaping his character, they determine whether his reactions to a given situation are moral. For Aristotle, then, "moral virtue (ethike —ἠθική) . . . is formed by habit" (Aristotle 1962, 33; *Nic. Eth.* 1103a. 16). With this, we have the second aspect of Aristotle's explanation of Callicles' inability to see the good. Having devalued the role of knowledge in accounting for moral conduct, he replaces it with character. People are good because they have good characters. Since habits compose character, there is here a substitution of habit for knowledge in guiding the will. Callicles cannot see what Socrates points out to him, because he has the wrong habits. His habits make him incapable of willing the good. Both assertions follow from the fact that character is a kind of organ of perception. Some "fundamental principles," namely, those of morality, Aristotle asserts, "are apprehended by a sort of habituation" (1962, 18; 1098b *Nic. Eth.* 3–4). You must have the right habits to grasp them. Callicles does not. Thus, he cannot grasp principles like justice or fairness. As a consequence, he cannot conform his will to them.

One way to see what Aristotle is getting at is to note with William James that our goals shape our perceptions. For example, when we are writing, paper appears "as a surface for inscription." If, however, we wished to light a fire, it would appear "as combustible material" ("Reasoning," James 1948, 355). The same paper, in fact, can be "a combustible, a writing surface, a thin thing, a hydrocarbonaceous thing, a thing eight inches one way and ten another, a thing just one furlong east of a certain stone in my neighbor's field, an American thing, etc., etc." (355). The paper's sense depends on what I am doing; and what I do depends on what I want. This "teleological" determination of perceptual meaning by my "interests," James observes, is ever present (357). To translate it into moral terms is to observe with Aristotle that "people choose the pleasant and avoid the painful." Pleasure and pain, in fact, "pervade the whole of life" (Aristotle 1962, 273; *Nic. Eth.* 1172a. 23–24). Choosing, we follow our pleasures.[21] Since what we do is determined by them, the disordering of our pleasures is also a disordering of our action. This, however, is also a disordering of what we perceive. The appearance of the world, for example, to someone obsessed with greed is such that the objects and situations that don't fit in with his obsession pass him by. He simply takes no notice of them as he tries to accumulate more and more wealth. In a real sense, one cannot argue with this person. He cannot see the contrary evidence one might provide. In terms of what he sees, he lives in a different world. As Aristotle expresses this, "as soon as a man becomes corrupted by pleasure or pain, the goal no longer appears to him as a motivating principle" (1962, 153; *Nic. Eth.* 1110b. 17). He

cannot be moved by it, since the "sort of habituation" that would allow
him to see a "fundamental principle" such as justice or fairness is missing. Aristotle is here referring to the habituation that comes from repeatedly associating pleasures with virtuous acts and pains with their
opposites. It is the sort of habituation that parents engage in as they
reward some acts and punish others. When this early "moral" education
succeeds, it produces a person who acts well habitually. His actions, in
Aristotle's words "spring from a firm and unchangeable character."
Possessed of a good character, he *follows his pleasures* and does the good
acts associated with them. Doing them, his world makes apparent the
fundamental principles and goals of ethics. Callicles' problem, regarded
in this light, is nothing less than a "wrong" childhood. He lacks the
moral training necessary to follow Socrates.

Circular Thinking

If Plato collapses will into knowledge, Aristotle does the reverse.
In the realm of practical action, he makes knowing a function of willing.
The willing that is determined by pleasure appears as desire. Desire, for
Aristotle, determines the way the world appears to us and, hence, determines our moral knowledge. The disordering of our desires is, thus, also
the disordering of this knowledge. It is, in the practical realm, the end of
certainty. In Plato, the independence of knowledge is ultimately based
on the independence of the ideas—those supremely knowable realities
that are the foundation of the world. The autonomy of reason is conceived in similar terms. Aristotle, however, denies that the ideas have any
separate existence. There is, for example, no justice "in itself" or courage
"in itself" to which reason can appeal. Even if there were some form or
idea of the Good "in itself," an appeal to it would be "pointless" in
ethics (Aristotle 1962, 12; *Nic. Eth.* 1096b. 21). Such a form, Aristotle
writes, "cannot be realized in action or attained by man" (1962, 13; *Nic.
Eth.* 1096b. 34).[22] This denial means that Aristotle, in describing our
moral conduct, cannot avail himself of Plato's conception of our self-
alterity. Reason, for Aristotle, does not stand against desire. It does not
divide the self so as to open up a space for the "ought." This is because
the evidence we reason from depends on our perceptions, which, in turn,
depend on our character, i.e., on the habits of action and thought that
characterize us as persons. These, however, depend on what we desire—
i.e., on the pleasures we have been habituated to feel when performing
various actions.[23] Thus, if to be just is to act out of "a firm and
unchangeable character," the just action is performed almost automatically. As springing from our fixed character, it is a habitual, nonreflective

action. The person performing it does not take a stand against desire. Instead, he does what is pleasurable.

This collapse of knowledge into will has its price: it results in an inability to bring closure to our reflections on ethics. On the level of the individual, we enter into a circle of reasoning where a person's knowledge is taken as determined by his habits, and these, in turn, are taken as determined by his knowledge, i.e., by the way the world appears to him in his habitual, day-to-day life. Such "knowledge" fixes him ever more deeply in the habits that, in turn, reinforce what he "knows" about the world. On the social level, we add to the circle of knowledge determined by habit the fact that a person's habits are determined by the training imposed by society. The circularity this entails involves the relativity of the standard of the "good man." Aristotle advises us to take the "good man" as a norm for our conduct. Doing so, we train the young accordingly. By virtue of this training, the young acquire the habituation that determines their moral perceptions. Such habituation will allow them to recognize the "good man" who, thus, will serve as their standard for training the young when they are adults. All is well, if the process started out correctly, i.e., if the young have been correctly trained by us. Of this, however, they cannot be certain. The habituation that determines their character—and, hence, their moral perception—is largely accomplished by the time they become adults. The same holds for us with regard to the training we received from our own parents.

Aristotle's assertion that in "its essential nature virtue is a mean" seems to get us out of this difficulty by offering us an independent standard (Aristotle 1962, 44; *Nic. Eth.* 1107a. 7). For example, independently of any training we might have had, courage is always the mean between cowardice and recklessness. Similarly, self-control is inherently the mean between being self-indulgent and being insensitive. The same holds for the other virtues, such as generosity (the mean between extravagance and stinginess) and friendliness (the mean between being obsequious and being quarrelsome). If we find ourselves at one of these extremes, then, as Aristotle advises, "we must . . . draw ourselves away in the opposite direction" and so "reach the middle" (1962, 50; *Nic. Eth.* 1109b. 5). The difficulty, however, of judging our own position remains. As Aristotle observes, where we are with respect to the mean determines where we judge the mean to be. In his words, "a brave man seems reckless in relation to a coward, but in relation to a reckless man he seems cowardly. Similarly . . . a generous man [seems] extravagant to a stingy man and stingy in relation to an extravagant man" (1962, 48; *Nic. Eth.* 1108b. 19–20). This implies that it is only when we are *already at the mean* that we can know with real certainty that we are where we ought to be. We

can, of course, attempt to determine where we are relative to the mean
by asking our friends—but this assumes that they are at the mean. If
they are not, their judgment is as unreliable as our own. The same holds
when we use the norms of society to judge our conduct. Once again we
find ourselves in the circle of training and perception with the lack of
closure described above.

Lack of closure is also apparent in Aristotle's account of practical
wisdom. Practical wisdom is defined as a "capacity of deliberating well
about what is good and advantageous for oneself . . . not deliberating
well about what is good and advantageous in a partial sense . . . , but
what sort of thing contributes to the good life in general" (Aristotle
1962, 152 *Nic. Eth.* 1140a. 25–27). Such wisdom involves both seeing
what is good for oneself in this general sense and reasoning how to attain
this. As Aristotle emphasizes, the deliberations of practical wisdom do
not involve knowledge of "things that cannot be other than they are"
(1962, 152; *Nic. Eth.* 1140a. 33). These are either things that always are
or things that are past. Neither can change. It will always be the case, for
example, that a triangle has three sides and that Socrates was born before
Plato. Statements of these facts count as knowledge in the strict sense
since, once known, our possession of them is secure. The object of practical deliberation, however, is precisely what can change. At issue is what
we should do, i.e., what changes we should bring about. If knowledge in
the strict sense involves either eternal or past objects, deliberation's concern is with the future, understood as an object of possible desire. Such
an object is a "not-yet"; it is something I can bring about if I choose.
Since it does not yet exist, I cannot, strictly speaking, know it. Similarly,
I cannot perceive my possession of what I do not yet possess. It is only
desire that places me in relation to the event of its possession. Desire,
here, is the faculty by which I apprehend this not-yet. How can I
"know" if I should make it actually present? How is practical wisdom to
be guided in its choices, given that the future it contemplates is not
accessible to knowledge strictly speaking?

Aristotle's answer to this question returns us to the circle of reasoning described above. Practical wisdom in its deliberations is guided
by mind or intelligence. The term Aristotle uses for "mind" is *nous*
(νοῦς); it is taken from *noeo* (νοέω), which can signify to "conceive," but
also can mean to "perceive." Both senses are present when he writes that
mind grasps the "primary terms and definitions" involved in our deliberations "as well as [the] ultimate particulars"—i.e., the particular facts of
the case (Aristotle 1962, 166; *Nic. Eth.* 1143b. 1–5).[24] Grasping these,
mind functions as the "eye of the soul." Now, according to Aristotle,
this "eye" can become corrupted by bad habits. If it is, practical wisdom

collapses into mere cleverness (1962, 170; *Nic. Eth.* 1144a. 30–35). My skill at deliberation then becomes reduced to a cleverness at figuring out how to get what I want—irrespective of whether it is good or bad. Thus, to be practically wise, I have to be good. In Aristotle's words, "wickedness distorts and causes us to be completely mistaken about the fundamental principles of action. Hence, it is clear that a man cannot have practical wisdom unless he is good" (1962, 170; *Nic. Eth.* 1144a. 35–37). Being good, I am at the mean. Being at the mean, I am at the place where I can see what is essential for leading a good life. The difficulty, however, is: How do I apprehend whether I am at the mean? If I am at the mean, I have the right habits. Should I then attempt to get to the mean by making sure that I have the right habits? Yet if I do not know if I am at the mean, do I really know which habits to encourage and which to suppress? The practical wisdom that might guide me here is itself guided by mind or intelligence. This "eye of the soul," which allows me to see the end, is, however, reliable only if I am already good. As Aristotle asserts, "whatever the true end may be, only a good man can judge it correctly" (1962, 170; *Nic. Eth.* 1144a. 34). The good man, however, is the person having the right habits—i.e., the person already at the mean.

For the modern reader, this account of practical wisdom is circular. An Aristotelian, however, might respond that the accusation of circularity misses the point. Aristotle's ethics is not ultimately a matter of norms or rules for guiding our conduct. It rather describes a state—the state of being a "good" person. The rules he gives regarding the mean are not prior to this state, but rather ways of characterizing being at the mean. The status of such rules is, in other words, rather like that of the forms. For Aristotle, the forms or ideas have no independent existence apart from their instantiation. Thus, just as there is no "good in itself," independent of good things, so Aristotle's descriptions of ethics all depend upon there being good persons. Hence his assertion that "our ability to perform such [virtuous] actions is in no way enhanced by knowing them, since the virtues are characteristics" of the good person" (Aristotle 1962, 167; *Nic. Eth.*, 1143b. 23–24). The relation between virtue and knowledge is, in this respect, rather like that between being healthy and having a knowledge of medicine. Being healthy is a state that is naturally prior to our knowledge of it. Without health, there would be no corresponding medical knowledge of what constitutes it. The same holds for being morally good. Knowledge presupposes the possession of this state. The lack of separation between the state and its knowledge leads, admittedly, to a certain circularity of description. This, however, cannot be helped. It is inherent in the nature of the case.

The difficulty with this defense is that it makes a virtue of an obvious problem. Even if we grant that medical knowledge presupposes health, the point of such knowledge remains that of correcting an unhealthy state. As Aristotle writes, "[W]e are not conducting this inquiry in order to know what virtue is, but in order to become good, else there would be no advantage in studying it" (Aristotle 1962, 35; *Nic. Eth.* 1103b. 27). This objective demands that, not being good, we nonetheless can learn what the good is and how we can become good. The objective, thus, presupposes that we can separate the state of moral health (or lack thereof) from our knowledge of this state. It requires, in fact, that practical reason have a certain transcendence.

Expressed in terms of our self-alterity, the transcendence of practical reason is a transcendence of our self-presence. Our presence to ourselves transcends us by virtue of the alterity of the others that are in us. As part of us, they shape the way we appear to ourselves. As other than ourselves, they allow us to see ourselves from another, external perspective. For Aristotle, we have the presence of others without this alterity. In his account of the duality of our nature, others are present in the habits we have acquired in becoming socialized. On the deepest level, they are present in the pleasures I pursue and the pains I avoid insofar as these have been socially determined. Through such habituation, I have my social being. What pertains to me, independently of others, is only my ability to be habituated. I am "equipped by nature" to receive the virtues, understood as those habits that make me choose rightly, because I can feel pleasure and pain and because these feelings can be shaped by habits (Aristotle 1962, 33; *Nic. Eth.* 1103a. 25). In this account, my internalized others are not really other than I in the sense of affording me the resources to escape my situation. They do not offer me the self-separation through which I can judge or resist pleasure.[25] Still less do they give me a sense of the "ought" that allows me to judge the training I have received. The same can be said of the account John Stuart Mill gives of our self-alterity. What Mill does, in fact, is radicalize the nontranscendence implicit in Aristotle's position. Engaging in the same attempt to conceive our self-alterity in worldly terms, he cannot explain our ability to critically assess the world that has shaped us. Like Aristotle, he cannot, as a consequence, bring closure to his account of moral conduct.

Selfless Happiness

Aristotle begins his ethics by asserting that happiness is the highest good in life. It is what all men strive for and what any account of ethics must aim at. The virtues are, in fact, those habits that, in allowing one to choose well, assist one in attaining this end. Mill begins his ethics with a similar set of assertions. There is, however, a crucial difference. While the goal for Aristotle remains by and large the good functioning and happiness of the individual, what is important for Mill is the happiness of everyone. The utilitarian standard for the moral worth of an action is, he writes, "not the agent's own greatest happiness, but the greatest amount of happiness altogether" (Mill 1979, 11; *Util.* II). This means that "the utilitarian standard of what is right in conduct" requires that one measure one's happiness against "that of all concerned." Since each person's happiness is to count equally in this evaluation, utilitarianism requires a remarkable selflessness in the pursuit of happiness. One must, as it were, stand outside of oneself and regard this pursuit impartially. In Mill's words: "As between his own happiness and that of others, utilitarianism requires him [the agent] to be as strictly impartial as a disinterested and benevolent spectator" (1979, 16). Separating himself from his private interests and regarding the collective effect of his possible acts, the moral agent chooses the action that maximizes the happiness of everyone.

Implicit here is a certain tension between one's own happiness and that of others, one that might be developed into an account of the "ought." Mill could have seen the "ought" as an imperative that arises from regarding one's pursuits in the light of their consequences for the general happiness. At its basis would be a sense of our self-alterity framed in terms of the opposition between our own and others' happiness. Mill, however, opens up this prospect only to close it off in his attempt to answer the question: "Why am I bound to promote the general happiness?" (Mill 1979, 26; *Util.* III). His reply undercuts ultimately the sense of the "ought."

According to Mill, it can properly be asked of a moral standard, "What is its sanction? What are the motives to obey?" or, more specifically, "What is the source of its obligation?" (Mill 1979, 26; *Util.* III). Apart from the "fear of disfavor" of others if we disregard their interests, "the ultimate sanction of all morality" is, he answers, "a subjective feeling in our own minds" (1979, 28). This "internal sanction" is "a feeling in our own mind; a pain, more or less intense, attendant on the violation of duty" (1979, 27). Mill, of course, is aware of the objection that if the sense of duty is just a subjective feeling, then "when the feeling ceases, the obligation ceases" (1979, 29). His answer, however, is not to reach for some nonsubjective standard to judge the feeling. Instead, he urges us to strengthen the feeling through habituation. This occurs by associating pleasure with those actions that take account of the general happiness and pain with those that disregard it.[26] This education will generate in an individual a feeling of unity with the rest of mankind "which, if perfect, would make him never think of, or desire, any beneficial condition for himself in the benefits of which they are not included" (1979, 32).

Implicit in this response is an answer to a second objection Mill considers: if the ultimate sanction of morality is a "subjective feeling," and if feelings can be shaped by habituation, is there any definite content to the moral faculty that rests on feeling? As Mill observes, "[T]he moral faculty . . . is also susceptible, by sufficient use of the external sanctions and of the force of early impressions, of being cultivated in almost any direction, so that there is hardly anything so absurd or so mischievous that it may not, by means of these influences, be made to act on the human mind with all the authority of conscience" (Mill 1979, 30; *Util.* III). The very malleability of feeling thus makes it an unreliable guide in ethics.[27] What occasions the sting of conscience (as a feeling) may, in fact, be a moral act. To counter this objection, Mill assumes that there is a natural basis for the feelings underlying utilitarianism. Because of this, they will eventually predominate. This "firm foundation" is the "social feelings of mankind—the desire to be in unity with our fellow creatures, which is already a powerful principle in human nature and happily one of those which tend to become stronger" with "advancing civilization" (30). Thus, to live in society, one must at least abstain from injuring others—particularly one's equals. Positively regarded, "society between equals can only exist on the understanding that the interests of all are to be regarded equally" (31). If the advance of civilization is, as Mill believes, the advance of equality, then this understanding (and the consequent social feeling) can only increase. The same result can be drawn from the need to cooperate. As civilization becomes more complex, people are increasingly "familiar with the fact of co-operating with others and proposing to themselves a collective and not an individual interest as the aim . . . of their actions" (31). With this, once again comes an increase of the sense of "unity with our fellow creatures." This sense is, in fact, increasingly inculcated, since civilization requires it. With this, we have Mill's answer to the question of why I am bound to promote the general happiness—why, in fact, if I have to choose, I must prefer it to my own happiness. To the point that I am bound, there really is no choice. My socialization is such that if I do not choose the general happiness, I will feel the pain of conscience. In other words: I desire to be happy and I will not be happy if I do not (if need be) choose the general happiness over my own. Indeed, if my socialization has been "perfect" I will not distinguish between the two.

This account may well explain why some people *are* moral; but does it explain why they *ought* to be moral? What "ought" to be the case can serve as a standard for something only if it is distinct from it. As a standard, it must have a certain independence vis-à-vis that for which it is a standard. Thus, if I have an independent sense of the general happiness, distinguishing it from my own, I can take it as a standard I ought to promote. Mill, however, collapses this distinction in making "the ultimate sanction of all morality" an individual, subjective feeling. At this point, general happiness is not something I aim at—i.e., an object of my will. It is, rather, a description of my state insofar as my desire for happiness has been completely socialized.

This objection can be put in terms of Mill's defense of the thesis that happiness is not just what all men desire; it is, in fact, the only thing they desire. For Mill, "happiness" signifies "pleasure and the absence of pain" (Mill 1979, 7; *Util.* II). Thus, for Mill, the thesis amounts to the assertion that desire is always directed to "pleasure and exemption from pain" (1979, 38; *Util.* IV). Now, to take the training of the desires as the training of the will is to assume that a person always follows desire. Against this, as Mill notes, the objection can be made "that will is a different thing from desire." Indeed, at times, it is adverse to it (35). Mill replies that although this may be now the case for "a person of confirmed virtue," it was not always so. Will, originally, was not distinct from desire. It became distinct through the force of habituation. Thus, originally I desired something and acted to obtain it. I continually did this, the habit of desiring and attaining some end becoming confirmed in me. At present, the habit of action continues even when the desire is absent. It is at this point that the action appears as the result of my will. As Mill states the conclusion: the "distinction between will and desire . . . consists solely in this—that will, like all other parts of our constitution, is amenable to habit, and that we may will from habit what we no longer desire for itself" (38). This means that "Will is the child of desire, and passes out of dominion of its parent only to come under that of habit" (38). Given this, we only imagine we have "freedom of the will."[28] What we have, in fact, are ingrained habits. Thus, even though "a person of confirmed virtue . . . carries out his purposes without any thought of the pleasure he has," it is still the case that he is directed by pleasure. His act is simply the habit of pursuing some pleasure that continues even in the absence of that pleasure.

This description of the will is a self-conscious reversal of Kant's attempt to base morality on freedom. According to Kant, it depends on our free choice whether a personal talent or a possession will be used for good or for evil. This, he writes, implies that nothing "can be taken as good without qualification except a good will" (Kant 1964, 61; 1995a, 393). The ultimate good in the Kantian account is, then, not pleasure, but rather the will that wills rightly. Mill, in making the will a function of habit, obviously cannot assert this. As he notes, "that which is the result of habit affords no presumption of being intrinsically good" (Mill 1979, 39; *Util.* IV). It all depends on the desire that was its parent, the desire which, when it becomes a habit, appears as the will. If the desire is "good," i.e., if it leads to pleasure or the absence of pain, then the will is good. In fact, "nothing is good to human beings but insofar as it is either itself pleasurable or a means of attaining pleasure or averting pain." This holds even for "the will to do right." In Mill's words, "this state of will is a means to good, not intrinsically a good" (1979, 40). It is good only if it leads to general happiness or pleasure.

Mill's use of habituation to collapse the duality of will and desire immediately undermines the concept of the "ought." As a practical command, the "ought" presupposes that my will can be directed, not by what is, but by what I conceive ought to be realized. If, however, will is simply a habit of desiring, how can I "will" to change this habit? How do I use my will to move from "what is"—that is, my current pleasures, habits, and character—to something better? Considered simply as a habit, my will is not intrinsically good. Neither is my moral faculty, given that it is "capable," through habituation, "of being cultivated in almost any direction." How then can I *know* or *do* the good if I have bad habits or desires? Mill's answer is that others will train me. This, however, simply raises the question of how they will know which habits they ought to train in me. In fact, however, the "ought" is out of place in this reduction of will to habit. Habits, once formed, operate automatically—i.e., without reflection. As such, they are determined by our actual state, not by the state that reflection shows we "ought" to be in.

More Circular Thinking

Once again we face a lack of closure in our attempt to determine norms for conduct. For a utilitarian the overriding norm is that of general happiness (or pleasure). We should train people in the habits that will increase this. The difficulty comes when we try to pin down what we mean by this increase. For Mill, the answer involves taking everyone's happiness as equal. This, he asserts, is "the first principle of morals" (Mill 1979, 60; *Util.* V). The "greatest happiness principle . . ." he writes, "is a mere form of words without rational signification unless one person's happiness, supposed equal in degree (with the proper allowances made for kind), is counted for exactly as much as another's" (60). As he quotes

Bentham, "[E]verybody [is] to count for one, nobody for more than one" (60). This counting each as a unit signifies "that the truths of arithmetic are applicable to the valuation of happiness, as of all other measurable quantities" (61, n. 4). While taking everyone's happiness as equal allows me to give a measurable sense to happiness—i.e., to speak of the "greater" or less "happiness" of a multitude of people—it still does not answer why people's happiness should be regarded as equal. I cannot say that I ought to do this because, living in a democratic society, I have been socialized to do so. How do I know that this socialization is correct? Most societies do not assume such equality. In the long stretch of history, very few have assumed "the equal claim of everybody to happiness," a claim, according to Mill, that "involves an equal claim to all the means of happiness" (61). The general experience of the last century, with its totalitarian ideologies, does not argue any general tendency towards such equality. The twentieth century, with its destructive wars and periodic genocides, offers mixed evidence for Mill's optimistic view of civilization's gradually fostering the "social instinct." Mill, of course, is not unaware of the "social inequalities" that have marked the course of history. His position is that they have been tolerated under a "mistaken notion of expediency" (62). People thought that the general happiness required such inequalities, but they were wrong. Translated into a positive concept, his position is that I ought to support the equal claim of everyone to happiness, since it is expedient in promoting the general happiness (62).

Does this mean that social expediency determines what is to count as equal? Should I, for example, say that gay marriages should be treated the same as heterosexual ones if doing so increases the general happiness? Can I claim that the rich and the poor cannot have an equal purchase on the means to happiness, since this is inexpedient in our capitalist society? Or is it the case that equality is some independent standard, one that I can use to measure expediency—i.e., to see if the current notions of it are "mistaken"? For Mill, the notion of increasing the general happiness has sense only if we treat everyone's happiness as equal. Treating everyone's happiness as equal, he claims, inevitably increases the general happiness. This seems to imply that equality and general happiness analytically entail each other. Yet what if it were the case that social happiness required an articulated whole composed of different social classes? Can we even be sure that the different groups composing a society have reconcilable claims? Isn't it at least conceivable that the gain of one group might be matched by a loss in the others so that a progress in equality might not necessarily lead to an increase in happiness? The very fact that we can raise these questions indicates that general happiness and social equality do not, as a matter of definition, imply each other. In the absence of firm criteria for either, we cannot bring closure to our attempt to define them. Instead, we have Mill's version of the circular thinking we encounter in Aristotle. In Mill, it runs: our current notions of expediency determine what counts for us as an equal claim on happiness and what counts for us as an equal claim in a given state of society determines expediency.

The Lesson

The lesson that can be drawn from this history of ethics has been previously stated. It is that in speaking of ethics, we must take account both of our being determined by our situation and our escaping this determination. Both the frame and the distinction of the self from the frame are required. To act and judge independently of the circumstances that frame us may secure our autonomy, but only at the loss of the context that is required for its sense. In Plato, this loss manifests itself in the tyranny of reason. In Kant, it leads to a separation of reason and freedom from the world, a separation that prevents both from appearing. Equally necessary is the possibility of separating ourselves from these determining circumstances. Without this, we lack the perspective to judge our situation. We cannot overcome this by simply balancing one part of the self against another, as Freud does with his id and superego and Darwin with his self-regarding and social instincts. As long as our inner alterity fails to pull us out of ourselves, i.e., as long as it does not give us a position from which to judge between these aspects of ourselves, we are left with each aspect claiming to be the standard for the other. The same limitation occurs when we see ourselves as socially determined. In the absence of any transcendent standard, we are left in a circle of reasoning involving both the self and its social frame. To escape these unsatisfactory alternatives, we have to conjoin framing and escape from the frame. We need a sense of framing that opens up the self-separation or self-transcendence that allows us to judge our situation. The question is: How are we to gain this?

With this question, we take up a history quite different from the intellectual one that has thus far engaged us. We leave behind the realm of theoretical speculation and enter that of action. Specifically, the object of our reflections will be those who rescued Jews in Nazi-occupied Europe. The extraordinary independence they showed relative to their largely anti-Semitic societies was matched by an overwhelming sense of an obligation they felt to those at risk. An analysis of their relations to those they saved will, in fact, exhibit a unique type of framing, one that opens up rather than closes off our self-transcendence.

4

Rescue and the Origin of Responsibility

Questions

The action of saving a life in a situation of mass slaughter is not called for in the normal functioning of society. Such functioning is, in fact, set up so that we are not faced with a situation of "playing God" in the sense of deciding if the person knocking at our door should live. The context, however, that demanded rescue of Jews during the Second World War was not that of normal life. Such life had been hijacked by the Nazis. "Public" morality, the morality that is expressed in the judiciary system and the other institutions of the state, regarded rescue as a criminal act, one punishable by the death of the rescuer. The organs of public opinion—assemblies, newspapers, the radio, and so on—daily confirmed this. The institutions that did not openly support the actions of the occupiers kept a prudent silence. No public condemnation of the roundup, isolation, and deportation of the Jews came from the leading academic or religious authorities. The pope, for example, raised no public protest when the Jews of his diocese were sent to Auschwitz (Cornwell 1999, 305–6). In such a climate, not many rescued. Most people kept quiet and tried to get along. Those who did rescue Jews thus found themselves largely on their own. Particularly in the East, they acted in isolation. They did not seek them out; the Jews came to them. Often at the very moment of encounter, face-to-face with the potential victim, they had to make a decision.[1]

Why did they decide to rescue? What informed their conscience? The question can be put in terms of a position that grows out of Mill's

belief that the ultimate basis of ethics is the "social feelings of mankind."
Given that society shapes such feelings according to its norms and that
such feelings, when violated, occasion the sting of conscience, the way
seems open to reducing ethics to a consideration of how society determines us. In this reductionist view, ethics is understood as a collection of
social norms. Those who act ethically express these norms in their conduct. Acting ethically, they "follow the rules." They do not lie or steal or
commit those other acts that undo the social bond. They act as everyone
does who is a "good" member of society. "Good," here, does not have a
sense independent of society. The ethics that expresses its sense is strictly
relative to the social community that frames its members. As such, ethics
cannot express a standpoint that could call society into question. The same
point can be put by noting that when we do follow its rules, the deter-
miner of our agency is, on this account, society itself. Because of this,
ethics, reduced to such rules, cannot guard us against the moral collapse of
society. It cannot, therefore, account for those who rescued the Jews. Yet
the existence of these individuals cannot be denied. We have, as a matter of
public record, extensive and well-documented cases of individual goodness in the face of societal evil.[2] If those who did rescue did not express
societal norms, what was the framework that gave sense to their actions?

This question receives its special focus when we recall the character
of the crime they resisted. The perpetrators of the "crime against humanity" attacked humanity itself. In self-consciously deciding who should be
excluded from the human community—i.e., which ethnic groups should
be exterminated and which preserved—the Nazis took up a position outside of humanity. As such, their stance exceeded the human perspective. In
terms of this perspective, it was senseless: no *human* reason can be given
for humanity's impoverishment or partial elimination. Contemplating the
Nazi genocide, our attempts at evaluation and judgment thus suffer a certain setback. In Emil Fackenheim's words, "the evil [of the Holocaust]
systematically eludes . . . thought" (Fackenheim 1988, 69). When the
senselessness of this self-mutilation was incorporated into the legal and
social codes of occupied Europe, the codes themselves become part of the
crime against humanity. The public framework that would allow humanity to recognize and react against its own impoverishment became its
victim. Yet, in spite of this, some people did act. Where did they find the
resources for their actions? How did they, in their encounters with the
Jews, escape the senselessness the Nazis sought to enforce?

Common Elements

To answer these questions, we must first look at the context of
rescue. In the accounts we have, it exhibits a number of common fea-

tures. The first and most obvious is what can only be called its traumatic character. Freud writes that an experience that is genuinely traumatic is so overwhelming "that assimilation or elaboration of it can no longer be effected by normal means" (Freud 1965, 286). Overcome by its affect, we cannot assimilate it by integrating it into the sense of our lives. Throughout Eastern Europe, the experience of the slaughter of a docile human population that had been herded into ghettos was traumatic in both its affect and senselessness. Nothing made normal sense in the situation of foreign occupation with its sudden devaluation of human life. In Lithuania, people could look out from their windows on the Jews being marched to their execution in the local forests and cemeteries. Their neighbors were the victims of an arbitrary, abnormal violence. In Poland, the inhabitants of the major cities could witness people being hung from lampposts on the streets.

In this traumatic context, people generally did not initiate rescue. They did not seek out Jews, placing their own lives and their families at risk. The Jews sought them out. Rescuing, thus, normally began with a face-to-face encounter. Some common examples will give the character of this event. A teenager, on the run in Vilnius, gets off the street by going to a doctor's waiting room. Finally, her turn comes to be examined. The woman doctor, examining her eyes, tells her she can find nothing wrong with her. Her tears well up as she tells the doctor her situation. The doctor continues to examine her, looking into her eyes, all the while saying, "Don't worry child. Everything will be fine. I will take care of you."[3] In Amsterdam, a woman waits in line with her ration card at a greengrocer's shop. Next to her, a woman whispers, "I have no distribution card, I am illegal, in fact, I am afraid." To this she replies, "Come along with me, we shall divide with you the food we have." The woman, Omi Strelitz, stays with her rescuers till the end of the war.[4] In southern France, a family of nine persons on the run from the Gestapo knocks at the door of a remote farmhouse. They are given dinner and shelter for the night. The next day the family is split up and hidden till liberation.[5] In rural Poland, a man approaches a house hung with a sign "Kill the Jews and save the country." Desperate and hoping the sign was there to protect the family, he knocks at the door. The woman of the house, realizing that he has nowhere to go, grabs his hand and leads him to a place of hiding.[6]

In each case what is at stake is a life. You can either admit the person at the door or turn him away to face an almost certain death. Given this, the person's life is in your hands. If you don't act, it is probable that *no one else will*. The immediacy of danger is such that you cannot hand on the task to someone else. Unasked for, you are confronted with a unique, nontransferable responsibility. The face of the other is, in this encounter, an appeal to preserve life. It is an appeal that makes you unique in your responsibility. Given the immediacy of the situation, there is hardly time to reflect.[7] You either have to open the door or close it and turn the Jew away.

The Hero vs. the Rescuer

Those who did respond clearly acted heroically. There are, however, several differences between the hero, who lives in normal times, and these rescuers. First, even though the hero who rushes into a burning building to save a life also acts without reflecting, the commitment he or she makes is limited in time. The hero either succeeds or fails, the act being over within a few minutes. The rescuer, however, faces an open-ended commitment. It might last several years. It might stretch on indefinitely. Particularly in the East, the rescuer *cannot know* who will win the war. Thus, the path chosen is open; it is without closure, while the risks taken are at least as great as in most heroic actions.[8] The contrast of the hero with the rescuer reveals a further distinction. Whether the hero succeeds or fails, the heroic deed is publicly applauded. It has a public presence and intelligibility. The rescuer, however, must always act in secret. By definition, if the act becomes known, it cannot continue. Publicity for the rescuer is equivalent to failure. This need for secrecy can even mean that one deceives close family members. A farmer in Poland hiding Jews had to send them to his wife's parents when his brother visited. His brother was part of a Polish Home Army group that hunted Jews down.[9] One measure of the public unintelligibility of the act of rescue is the level of anti-Semitic feeling in the surrounding society. In Poland, Jews were frequently murdered when, at the war's end, they finally emerged from hiding. Roving bands of the Polish Home Army still sought them out as they attempted to return.[10] On reaching their villages, they were also subject to attacks by the general population.[11] As a result, their rescuers frequently swore them to secrecy.[12] Even after the war, the act of rescue could not be acknowledged. It was still denied public intelligibility and acceptance.

The contrast between the rescuer and hero calls to mind Kierkegaard's comparison of Abraham and the hero. The hero, who appears as the "knight of resignation," expresses the "universal." His sacrifice, involving, as it does, the public good, is intelligible to all. Thus, everyone, according to Kierkegaard, can understand Agamemnon's sacrifice of his daughter Iphigenia. Everyone can sympathize with the cruel necessities laid on the father. The reasons of state that forced him to renounce his love for his daughter are known to all. By contrast, Abraham's willingness to sacrifice his son Isaac expresses the particular. It lacks public intelligibility. Its public expression is that he is willing to murder Isaac. The private expression is that this is a sacrifice, that Abraham is responding to God's call. This is a call made in private to him, a call that he cannot publicly explain except to say that it is, somehow, a "trial." Abraham, as Kierkegaard's "knight of faith," acts, humanly speaking, *entirely on his own*. He assumes an individual, nonsharable, nonexpressible responsibility. His relationship with God, who has given him this strange command, has drawn him out of his society. It is to God alone that he has his relationship as he travels to the place of the sacrifice. This relationship, which is of one individual to another, is absolute. It overrides all other relations. In Kierkegaard's words, Abraham "becomes that individual who, as the particular, stands in an absolute relation to the absolute." The "paradox" here is that "as the single individual, he is higher than the universal" (Kierkegaard 1985, 85). He assumes a stance above and beyond that universal, public intelligibility that characterizes ethics as a set of social relations.[13]

The same sort of stance characterizes the rescuer. The public unintelligibility of the rescuer's act is matched by the individual, nontransferable responsibility he or she assumes. In the life-threatening situation in which they act, rescuers have an absolute relationship with the person appearing at the door. This relationship is absolute because it does not express an obligation that is relative to some particular society. The agent is the person; it is not society acting through the rescuer. It is also absolute because it expresses a nontransferable, nonrelative demand to save a person's life. What the rescuer faces, in confronting the person at risk, is thus an absolute relationship that both "frames" and "deframes" him. The relation situates the rescuer, determining his actions through an unconditional demand. It also radically individualizes the rescuer, pulling him out of his particular social context, demanding that he act irrespective of it.

The Absolute Character of Life

How does the face-to-face encounter manifest this absolute relationship? What underlies its absolute demand? The immediate answer to these questions comes from the context of the rescue. This context is one of extreme risk. The person to be rescued appeals to you to save his life. The absolute nature of the appeal comes from the life that will be lost if you do not act. "Life" in this context does not designate a concept. It is not something you apprehend by abstracting a feature common to a number of individuals. It is rather the life of *this* individual, the life that founds all *this* person's possibilities. In Nietzsche's phrase, life here has the status of a universal that exists "before" things.[14] It appears as a prior condition, something that has to be given if anything else is to be given. The absolute nature of the appeal, then, comes from the fact that without life, nothing else is possible. Every action presupposes the life of the doer; every assertion, the life of the speaker; every value, the life of the valuer. Without individual life, there is no human "world" with its actions, assertions, and values. The latter absolutely demand life as their condition. Underlying the absolute demand is, then, this founding quality of life—a quality that is *present in each individual*.

This is the sense of the Jewish proverb, "The person who saves a life saves a world." The proverb comes from the Babylonian Talmud's discussion of how to exhort witnesses in a capital crime to tell the truth (Mishnah, *Sanhedrin* 4.5). The Mishnah notes that "capital cases are not like monetary cases" (Epstein 1935, 233; *Sedar Nezikin*). Giving false witness in monetary cases can result in financial loss for the defendant, which can be made up by "monetary restitution." But "in capital cases [the person giving false witness] is held responsible for [the accused's] blood and the blood of his descendants until the end of time" (233). The Mishnah explains this by referring to the creation of Adam: "For this reason was man created alone, to teach thee that whosoever destroys a single soul of Israel, scripture imputes [guilt] to him as though he had destroyed a complete world; and whosoever preserves a single soul of Israel, scripture ascribes [merit] to him as though he had preserved a complete world" (234).[15] This comparison of the innocent victim with Adam can be understood in two complementary ways. The first focuses on the consequence of giving false witness in a capital crime, the second on the uniqueness of the accused individual. In giving false witness, one is initially guilty of the life of the innocent person who is condemned. This guilt, however, extends to his potential descendants to the end of time. The reference to the creation of the first man, Adam, expands this to the guilt of destroying a whole world. The Mishnah claims that this is the reason why Adam was created: God fashioned him alone to teach us the extent of our guilt in destroying a single soul. In other words, God created humanity, not as a race of beings (as, say, in the ancient myth of Prometheus), but first of all as a single individual, to teach us that in each individual there is a whole world. Had one destroyed Adam, the destruction of all his potential descendants implied in this would stretch to the whole of humanity. The claim, then, is that in some sense everyone is an Adam, everyone potentially contains humanity, contains the totality of the human world in him. Put in terms of the founding quality of life, the assertion is that life in its human totality is present *in the individual*. The pricelessness of the individual is the pricelessness of life in its founding quality.

The Mishnah reinforces this position by arguing that since God originally created the world for the sake of Adam, if everyone is like Adam, then everyone can say that God created the world for him. Everyone, however, is like Adam in his uniqueness. As the Mishnah puts this: "If a man strikes many coins from one mold, they all resemble one another. But the Supreme King of Kings, the Holy One, Blessed be He, fashioned every man in the stamp of the first man, and yet not one of them resembles his fellows. Therefore every single person is obliged to say: the world was created for my sake" (Epstein 1935, 234; *Sedar Nezikin*). The assertion is that every person is unique like Adam. Thus, the "world" of each person, the world that comes to presence in and through this person, is also unique. As such, it is irreplaceable. It cannot be made up by the world of another person or persons, for "not one of them resembles his fellows." The legal point here is that we cannot atone for false witness in a capital crime, for no one resembles the unique person at risk in the false judgment. The biblical point is that we are "fashioned . . . in the stamp of the first man," not because, like coins, we resemble each other in our resemblance to an original mold, but because each of us resembles Adam in being absolutely first, absolutely unique. We are singular like Adam when he was first created. Creation—understood as referring to the presence of the world—is, then, for the sake of each of us. Like Adam, each person in his uniqueness can say that creation, in its coming to presence, is "for my sake." Each, then, manifests the founding quality of human life in its self-reference, i.e., in life's being, in each individual, *for its own sake*. Life here is absolute not just in the sense that it makes everything else possible; it is also absolute as *that for which* such possibilities exist.

To translate this into nonbiblical terms is to observe that there is no first principle, no Archimedean point from which we can derive the concrete phenomena of human life. Every human self acts to shape its environment. It constantly affects both the things and selves about it, apprehending and determining them according to its particular projects. At the same time, however, the self is constantly determined by them. Its action, in responding to the people and things it encounters, is shaped by their presence. This can be put in terms of the fact that self's environment (which includes its past) individualizes its agency: the environment makes it the agency of this particular person. This process, which is mediated by language, technology, and culture, *never occurs in isolation*. Every self engages in it, determining the environments that situate its others and their agency. Now, with selves determining environments, which in turn determine selves, there is clearly no first cause, no set of final determinants to the whole composed of selves and the things that support them. The resulting ensemble, in other words, is not a systematic structure with clear principles or beginnings; it cannot be subjected to a (Cartesian) foundational analysis designed to uncover these. Since it has no independent ground or foundation outside of itself, its "ground" or cause is simply itself in each of its members. This means that there is no "Adam" acting as a die or model from which could be derived the character of the persons or selves making it up. Each person has an equal claim to be an Adam. Each person is equally an initiator of the whole that is human life—that is to say in each, the founding quality of life manifests itself in a unique fashion. Each person, in being uniquely shaped by this life, can also claim to be that for the sake of which this life manifests itself. Each is, uniquely, the object of life's action.

This analysis can be summed up in a set of mutually implicit notions. The uniqueness of each individual life points to the nonfoundational nature of the whole of human lives. This nonfoundational character, in turn, implies the lack of any Adam, understood as an axiomatic principle for the whole of human lives. Because there is no Adam functioning as a die, the individuals composing this whole are unique. Furthermore, to say that the whole lacks a foundation is to assert that human life has itself as its principle. By this I mean that such life forms, with the things that sustain it, a self-grounding whole. It is absolute, then, because it is unconditioned by any principle prior to itself. This absolute character is what manifests itself in the uniqueness of the lives making it up.[16]

Mortality and the Face

In the context of rescue, this absolute character of life shows itself in the individual through his mortality. The rescue situation is one of a life at risk. In the face-to-face encounter, it is the possibility of its immediate loss that shows that life is irreplaceable. The absolute character of the appeal of the other comes, then, from his being liable to death. In the exchange of gazes, it comes, we can say, from the face as manifesting the "mortality" of the other person. This mortality is what points back to life as foundational. In a certain sense, death, as beyond life, gives us a perspective from which to view life. This does not mean that death, as other than life, illuminates itself. In grasping the face as the mortality of the other person, I do not gain a perspective on what is beyond life (another world).[17] Rather, death shows me what life is by showing me what its absence is. Without life, nothing else is possible. Death is the absence of all a person's possibilities. It is, in Heidegger's phrase, the possibility of an impossibility—i.e., "the impossibility of any existence at all" (Heidegger 1967a, 262). It is the impossibility of all a person's perceptions, projects, plans, desires, values, and so on. Death cancels the unique world these bring to presence. Thus, seeing the other person's life at risk, I grasp its founding character. I see why the person who saves a life saves a world—the unique world of the person before me.

Much of what the Jewish philosopher Emmanuel Levinas says about the face parallels the above. Although he does not explicitly speak about the act of rescue, he does offer a way to think about it. It is, for example, Levinas who characterizes "the face as the very mortality of the other person." The face here is grasped as "nudity, destitution, passivity and pure vulnerability." In this "nudity" of the face, "facing" the other, he writes, "is an exposure unto death" (Levinas 1994a, 107). It is an exposure first of all to the death to which the other person is liable. According to Levinas, an "obligation" arises from this experience.[18] "There is," he explains, "a 'facing up' of authority, as if the invisible death to which the face of the other person is exposed, were for the Ego that approaches it, his business . . . ." The person in this context is "called to answer for this death." He is called to assume responsibility for the life of the other person. In Levinas's words, "Responsibility for the Other—the face signifying to me 'thou shalt not kill,' and consequently also 'you are responsible for the life of this absolutely other Other'—is responsibility for the unique one" (107–8).

The key term in this account is the designation of the other person in his uniqueness as "the absolutely other Other." For Levinas, my responding to the other grows out of this sheer alterity. This alterity is that of death, the very death I am exposed to in my apprehension of the face as the "mortality of the other person." Death is, by definition, on the other side of everything I can think and know.[19] If "phenomenology" designates what can appear to me, if its field is what I can know as based on appearance, then death appears as "the rupture of phenomenology." This is the rupture "which the face of the Other calls forth" in exposing me to its mortality (Levinas 1994a, 107). Interpreting Levinas, we can say that it is precisely this alterity that calls me to respond. My response is provoked by this rupture or break in the known that death occasions. Anyone who has had a "close call" is familiar with the general sense of this response. A brush with death makes us consider our lives; it prompts us to ask what is worthwhile and what is not. It, thus, calls on us to "own" what we have, to take responsibility for the choices that shape our life. Behind this experience is the fact that death, in being beyond life, gives us a perspective from which to view life. Showing us its contingency, it raises the question of why we have shaped it in the particular ways we have. In Levinas's words, what we have here is a "questioning where the conscious subject liberates himself from himself, where he is split by . . . transcendence" (Levinas 1993, 127). On the one side of the division, we have the "I" that is questioned; on the other side, the questioning "I." This split, Levinas claims, "confers an identity on me" (127). This is because, in questioning myself, I bring myself forward to face my questioning. Confronting myself, I am what Levinas terms a "for-itself." I achieve my identity *for myself* as I respond. As Levinas describes this, the result is "the awakening of the for-itself (*éveil du pour-soi*) . . . by the inabsorbable alterity of the other" (32).

This alterity is, in Levinas's phrase, an alterity that is "in" me. The face of the other manifests alterity in its mortality. Yet I too can die. Because I can, the other's mortality, his liability to death, is also my own. It is my own self-alterity. In my liability to death, I exist in the self-separation, the standing outside of myself within myself, that gives me the perspective to question myself. Responsibility, in this context, is an ontological condition. The call for me to respond to the questioning is one with my being a for-itself. Thus, the other person is both totally other, and yet, in this alterity, this person is as intimate to me as my mortality. The other is as much a part of myself as the being able to confront myself that arises from such alterity. The key to this argument is that it is *through the other*—through the other's face, that is, through its nudity, its vulnerability, its exposure to death—*that I face death*. This mortality, which I experience through the face of the other, is mine through this other. It is mine as the other-than-I that is within me. I am, in my being for-myself, the responding (the responsibility) that this grounds. Such responsibility is first for my other and, through this, for myself as answerable for this person. As such, it forms my ontological condition as a for-itself. The constant, if paradoxical, claim of Levinas is that my being responsible for myself exists *through* my being responsible for the other, the very other whose otherness "in me" makes me a self.[20]

To translate this complex philosophical position into the concrete experience of rescue, it must be emended to include the point that death does not illuminate itself. It casts its light on life. Thus, the encounter with the other in his mortality, that is, in the liability to death that occurs when the Jew appears, points to life itself. The Jew's face exhibits life as threatened, as that which is at issue in my response to this encounter. The face, thus, contains in its mortality the commands: "You shall not kill," "You shall not allow killing," "You are responsible for this life before you." Here, the alterity of death illumines the alterity of life.[21] It points to life as the ground of innumerable possibilities, possibilities that, in their very infinity, are not thematizable. It exhibits life as exceeding and hence rupturing what I already know and, hence, as not capable of being reduced to any sort of stereotype.

Obligation and Alterity

With this we have a preliminary sense of the character of the "ought" or moral demand that springs from the context of rescue. The sense that we are responsible for the life before us, that we "ought" to save it, originates in two opposing elements. On the one hand, we have the sense of the powerlessness of life. The life before us is not just at risk, it can continue only if we act on its behalf. On the other hand, we have the sense of its alterity. The life in our hands is, we sense, beyond us. It exceeds us in its possibilities. What manifests itself in the other who is at risk is, in fact, a sense of life as founding and, hence, as authorizing all possibilities—including the possibility of our saving it. The resulting conjunction of authority and lack of power is felt as an invitation to substitute our power for its powerlessness. The ought that appears in this invitation has no "sanction." We cannot speak here of its motivating force being some "sting" of conscience. The result of not following it is not the loss of some obvious good—be this our Aristotelian "good functioning" or the Platonic "health" of our souls. All such sanctions reduce the "ought" to a compulsion and, hence, make it a function of the "is." The ought has its unique force precisely in the fact that the authority of its address to me is combined with a lack of power. The life at risk invites me to use my power to make up for its powerlessness. It asks that I put my power in the service of what, in its exceeding quality, authorizes it. The invitation, then, is to take up the authority of life. It is to assume the action of life's founding that the life at risk makes manifest in its powerlessness.

The alterity that grounds this sense of the ought can be expressed in terms of the totality of human life. This totality both frames and provokes my response to the ought. The totality has, in fact, a double alterity. Since it forms a nonfoundational whole, it does not give me the means for predicting its future course. Its otherness is, thus, that of exceeding my knowing in advance the particular possibilities it will realize. The second sense of its alterity comes from the fact that, as the ground of possibilities, it exceeds every possibility. As such, it cannot be thematized (understood or known) in terms of any one of them. This sense of its otherness points to human life as irreducible to any stereotype. No single possibility of being or behaving—no Adam as a die—can characterize it. My individual life, then, cannot count as its standard. It is but one expression of the possibilities of selfhood. Here, the sense of life in its alterity is that of a range of possibilities, unlimited and unpredictable, of which my life is only one member. The range of such possibilities is a frame that situates me. In exceeding me, it also provokes me, calling me into question. Facing it, I face the contingency of my life as I have shaped it. The fact that my life could have been otherwise raises the question: Why have I shaped it as I have? My being, as called forth to respond, separates itself from itself, faces itself and hereby becomes a for-itself. This phenomenon, which we associated with the experience of a "close call," is the result of our confrontation, not with death, but with the life that is manifest in the experience of mortality. This life gives me the sense of my life as framed by the alternatives that call it into question. Insofar as this life is my own, this framing is internal. It is my inner alterity as a for-itself.

A number of points can be drawn from this analysis. First of all, we can say that insofar as human life has this exceeding quality, so does the questioning that springs from it. It is also characterized by a nonpredictability and an irreducibility to any stereotype. Thus, the experience of someone at risk catching one's gaze poses questions for which there is no ready answer. You cannot say why you have this expression of selfhood rather than the one that faces you. In the contingency of life that the situation manifests, you cannot say why this person is at risk and you are not. A further point is that in this very contingency, we find the situation demanded by the previous chapter. The face-to-face encounter combines the opposing elements of framing and transcendence. It frames you in the sense of situating you as one of a number of possibilities. In provoking the question of why you express this rather than another possibility, it also gives you the self-transcendence that allows you to stand back and judge your situation. This judgment is not in terms of your society, i.e., your particular defining situation. The terms that frame your judgment, which are those of life itself, exceed your situation. As an example of this exceeding, we can take the statement of Dr. Antoni to Helena Bibliowicz. He said to her, "If they find you they will kill you, and they will kill me, my wife and daughters. I have a commitment to God Almighty to save the suffering Jew, but I do not know if I am right to do this. I go to church. I cry to God to find out what to do. He does not tell me. So I decide to save you."[22] What is exceeded here is Dr. Antoni's situation as given by his family and the silence of God in his church. What exceeds this is the demand of life to "save the suffering Jew." This exceeding is a self-separation. In deciding to rescue Helena, Dr. Antoni distinguishes himself from the person waiting for an answer from God, the person whose first commitment is to his family's life. Provoked by the exceeding quality of life in the person at risk, the rescuer faces himself and becomes a for-itself. A final point concerns the fact that this is done in the context of the questions raised by the other. Given that the response to these questions is never adequate, neither is one's being-for-oneself. An adequate response would imply that the self that was called to respond was not exceeded by the question put to it. This, however, would imply that the self-separation that makes possible the "for-itself" was not an ongoing ontological condition. Self-separation is, however, what makes a person a human self. As such, it also makes the person open to the "ought." This is because the inadequacy of one's being-for-oneself yields the ethical tension that separates the "is" from the "ought." It marks the divide between the situation that defines a person—family, friends, professional associations—and the questioning that exceeds this. The demand inherent in this questioning maintains, by virtue of this excess, its status as an "ought."

Empathy and the Question of Reason

It is possible to express the above points in terms of our earlier understanding of empathy as incarnation. To do so is to take the invitation of the face as a call to incarnation. The face, in inviting us, summons us to take up the standpoint of the person facing us. Its call is to let ourselves imaginatively be shaped in our flesh by the other's defining situation. Such shaping involves the dual quality of the face that manifests this summons. On the one side, we have the face as flesh—that is, the face as manifesting vulnerability, passivity, and need. On the other, we have the face as the eyes regarding us—that is, the face that manifests a subjectivity that takes up the world from another standpoint. Together they yield the sense of subjectivity as subjected to need, as liable to death if its essential needs are not met. This is the face as the "mortality" of the other. To take up this standpoint is take up such mortality. When the person we face is in need, taking up his standpoint assumes his need. The result is the experience of our own selfhood in the interruption of its enjoyment. To the extent that my self-presence includes the other who is in want, his presence is felt, in Levinas's phrase, as the "bread that is torn from my mouth." My self-experience is, in this context, shaped by two sets of needs. The set that is met results in enjoyment; the set of needs that is not disrupts this.[23] Such disruption poses questions that I cannot readily answer. In taking up the standpoint of the other in want, I cannot answer why I should eat and the other starve. In my empathy with the other at risk, I cannot explain why I should live and the other die.

As already noted, my identity involves these unanswerable questions. I exist as a human being that is a for-itself by taking up the standpoint of the other. This involves my being called to make a response that is never adequate. An adequate response would presuppose my having an undivided nature. Only if I were exclusively either myself or the other could I say why "I" should live. This can be put in terms of the paradoxical character of the invitation of the face. As subjectivity, the face summons me to take up its standpoint. As flesh, it exceeds my ability to do so in any exclusive sense. The alterity of flesh is that of bodies in their apartness, their sphere of what cannot be shared. It is what makes the bread that I consume unavailable to the other. The empathy that tears this bread from my mouth does not overcome, but rather presupposes, bodily alterity. Thus, instead of making me one with my other, it divides my selfhood.

In doing so, the incarnation of empathy raises the question of reason. To ask for a reason is to ask why a thing is as it is, i.e., why it is this way *rather than* that. We can only do this if we can conceive the thing as an alternative, as a "this" rather than a "that." To do so, however, both the "this" and the "that" must be conceived as possible (as opposed to necessary). It is, in other words, our grasp of a thing's lack of necessity—its grasp as something that could be otherwise, that could, in fact, *not* be—which moves us beyond its givenness to inquire into its ground. It moves us to ask *why* it is given as we experience it. Now, it is just this lack of necessity in my selfhood that I grasp in the invitation of the face. Confronting me with both the "this" and the "that," understood as possibilities of selfhood, empathy opens up the question of their ground. Dividing me, it opens up a "space" for this question.[24] It makes me ask why these alternatives are as they are, i.e., the reason or ground for their being such. This question, precisely because it cannot be answered, is a permanent feature of my being. My inner alterity, as based on empathy, is the ongoing origin of the question of reason.[25]

With this, we have the basis for the constant association of reason and others that we encountered in the history of ethics. Reason is, from the start, intersubjective, since the experience of contingency that raises its question comes from our inner alterity. At its basis, then, are the others we encounter in empathy. Presupposing empathy, reason also assumes the existence of embodiment and need. Its original ground is the sense of contingency that the other's need occasions when it interrupts our enjoyment. On the most fundamental level, the question of reason is why the bread I enjoy is in my mouth rather than in the other's. Given this, we cannot say with Plato that reason's relation to appetite and the body is one of ruling through the coercion and repression of desire. Such a "rule" assumes that reason would be better off were the body with its wants altogether absent.[26] In fact, however, without the body we would not reason at all, since the question of reason would not be raised for us. Without the body, there would, in fact, be no inner presence of others to raise the question. The dependence of reason on others leads to a further implication with regard to Plato. It signifies that we cannot, as Plato did, equate freedom and sovereignty (see above, p. 54). As Hannah Arendt writes, "Sovereignty, the ideal of uncompromising self-sufficiency and mastership, is contradictory to the very condition of plurality" (Arendt 1958, 234). But the freedom that is based on reason requires this plurality. The ultimate ground here is the inner alterity that others open up. Reason requires this. So does freedom in its basic sense of being able to distance oneself from, and hence escape being determined by, one's situation.[27]

The fact that the question of reason is raised by others allows us to assert that ethics involves more than responsibility—i.e., more than just responding to the other. The necessity for something further comes from the fact that this response need not be ethical in any recognizable sense. I can, for example, respond to the need of the other by turning away. I can also meet this need inappropriately. The same holds for the sense of conscience that the other provokes in me. Just as not every response I make to being "put into question" by others is appropriate, so not everything my conscience tells me is correct. This is why ethics must include the questioning of this response. Taken as a process of rational inquiry, it requires both the "call of conscience" and our putting this call into question. Both are provided by my others. In raising the question of reason, they give it its unlimited quality. Because they exceed me, the questions they pose also exceed the responses I give. Thus, they do not just call on me to respond, they also raise the question of my response. They invite me to examine its adequacy. What moves me from responsibility to ethics—i.e., from responding to an examination of my response—is, then, the others that exceed me. My others, in framing me by situating me as one of a number of alternatives, do not just call me into question, thereby provoking a response. Their calling me into question includes my response. Insofar as their exceeding alterity is "in" me, they constantly trouble my conscience. They raise the question of its ground, its reason for being the way it is.

Ontological Conditions for Intentionality

The fact that I can respond to the need of the other by turning away raises the question of why some people rescued Jews and some did not. This question demands an answer distinct from those provided by ethics or psychology. In asking why some people responded to the call of the face, we are not raising the ethical question of whether they ought to have rescued others. The validity of this "ought" sprang from the life at risk. Equally, we are not posing the psychological question of the influences and experiences that mentally determined them to rescue others. A number of books and articles have been written attempting to pin down the "altruistic personality" of the rescuer during the Holocaust.[28] It is not clear, however, that rescue in such inordinate circumstances can be reductively explained. Psychological explanations, to the point that they are empirical, are based on an experience that is open to everybody. This is the everyday public experience that we can return to again and again—the experience that, if necessary, we can recreate in the controlled conditions of an experiment. This, however, was not the experience of rescue. It was characterized by risk and secrecy. Moral considerations, needless to say, prevent us from replicating it. Beyond this, there is the question of the applicability of the psychological profile of the altruistic personality: How well does it fit those who actually rescued? The altruist has a history, a personality that develops over time, one that comes finally to expression in a more or less fixed pattern of behavior. This is the behavior of a person who seeks others out, searching for ways to help them. By contrast, the rescuer, particularly in the East, does not seek to rescue, but rather is sought out. The Jew appears—perhaps standing at the door. Confronting him, the rescuer faces an immediate decision, one that he has probably not thought through before. Since the circumstances surrounding rescue are not those of normal life, the idea of his having developed a pattern of response for this extraordinary situation is highly problematic. Given that the circumstances surrounding rescue in the East were unprecedented, they could play no part in the psychological history of those suddenly facing them.[29] Fortunately, we do not have to consider such difficulties here. What we are after are the ontological, rather than the psychological, conditions of rescue. In asking why some people rescued while others did not, the search is not for the determining elements within a person's particular history, but rather for something perfectly general. At issue are those basic structures or conditions of our being-in-the-world that make us turn to or turn away from others. A credible ethics requires that we discern them.

The most basic fact of our being in the world is that of our organic nature. It is the fact of our being "born of woman." Initially, this involves a biological identity, the embryo's literal sharing in its mother's flesh. The growth of the fetus, its birth, and the stages of childhood development all contribute to break up this identity. Each phase overlays it with another form of alterity. This fact has obvious implications for our empathy and intentionality. It implies, with regard to the former, that we can see ourselves as others, that is, incarnate ourselves imaginatively, because our original sense of ourselves included the other. This means that empathy's grasp of the other *as other* gradually arises through the stage-by-stage breakup of this identity. With each layer of alterity, the notion of incarnation gains a new sense. The same holds for the intentionality that is our being directed towards the other. The original sense of intentionality, understood as a turning and stretching out towards something, comes from the breakup of the parent-child identity. Their biological separation originates the child's first *intentio*, the Latin term signifying a "stretching out" and "straining towards" something.[30] As the child's conception of its caregiver develops, so does the form of this original intentionality.

The phenomenologist Gail Soffer gives us a useful schema for viewing this development. She begins her account of childhood development by noting that "newborn infants behave very differently towards people . . . than towards the rest of their environment." Almost immediately, they direct themselves towards the caregiver. In her words, "[T]hey focus intensely upon the face, settle when held, turn towards voices. They also imitate facial expressions as early as moments after birth, and gestural imitations follow shortly thereafter" (Soffer 1999, 153). The reasons for this immediate bonding can, perhaps, be found in the need for the child to attach its parent to it. The infant who does not turn to its parent risks having its parent *not* turn to it. To the point that the unresponsive child is in danger of being neglected, its chances for survival are lessened. From an evolutionary perspective, it thus seems that intentionality in this primitive sense is selected for. The initial turning of child towards the face, understood as a "straining" to attach the caregiver to it, probably became part of our makeup because of its survival value.[31] Whatever its origin, it is clear that the attempt at attachment begins almost immediately. Its success yields the first stage of the parent-child relation. According to Soffer, the child initially apprehends its mother "as the completion of the system" of its states and needs. Having attached her to itself, the child experiences "the maternal face as constantly associated with being fed, held, comforted, warmed, etc." (153). The same holds for the "typical auditory, tactile, olfactory, and other sensations connected with being cared for by the mother or other caretaker" (153-54). They are felt as "responsive and complementary" to its own sensations of its needs. This experience points back to the infant's original state in the womb. This state, however, is now overlaid with a certain alterity. The mother appears as a complement to rather than a sheer identity with the infant.[32]

With the growth of the child's abilities, the second stage of their relation appears. The child now distinguishes the other from itself as a well-defined "three dimensional" presence in the world. This new sense of alterity is, however, overlaid on the first stage's sense of bodily identity. As a result, the child takes the caregiver as an extension of its bodily "I can." It grasps the other, in Soffer's words, as "a well-defined . . . pattern of behavior. At this point the other does not merely happen to respond, but can be made to respond in typical and predictable ways" (Soffer 1999, 157). The caregiver answers the infant's calls. In fact, "the infant holds sway much more effectively and can accomplish much more via the body of the other than via its own body, such as orientation of its body, movement through space, or bringing distant objects closer, etc." (158). The child, however, does not always succeed in controlling its parent or caregiver. As it enters the third stage of their relationship, it learns to differentiate the control of the other from that of its own limbs. The same holds for the sensations its body provides it. As Soffer observes, "At first the infant expects to experience sensations in the hands and feet of the other, and must learn through experience that this is not the case" (158). "It is," she adds, "the disappointment of such expectations that first gives a clear differentiation between the own-body and the other-body" (158).[33] The sense of alterity that characterizes this third stage is that of the other as having its own body and viewing the world from its own perspective. Gradually the child learns that the other does not see things the way it sees them. It learns, for example, to hold the picture book right side up when turning it so that the other can see it. The underlying identity overlaid by this new sense of otherness manifests itself in the belief that the other, if properly positioned, will see what it sees. To reverse this, the child believes that were it to take up the other's standpoint, it would actually have the other's experience. It can, in other words, reestablish the previous stage's identity of itself and the other by changing its place.

The disappointment of the expectations that are founded on this belief leads to the final stage in its relation to the other. This, according to Soffer, is the stage of "individualized empathy, an empathy of the form, 'if I were there and I were x,' where x specifies traits of the other," then I would experience what x experiences (Soffer 1999, 163). "X" here can refer to a large number of features that I do not have, but that I can perhaps imaginatively place myself in. For example, in empathizing with someone who is afraid of dogs, I might imagine what I would feel like were I to feel towards dogs what now I feel towards some animal I am afraid of. Similarly, I might empathize with a blind person's experience of the sun by closing my eyes and moving in and out of its rays. In neither case, however, do I assume that I can totally recreate the other's experience—i.e., actually reestablish through any actual shift in perspective a real identity of self and other. In Soffer's words, inherent in such empathy is "the realization that the other is not the same as the self, and does not experience the world as one in fact did or in fact could, but differently" (164).[34] The object of this empathy is, in fact, the other in his alterity. With it, the duality of selfhood that empathy brings about is complete. The other, here, is present "in" you as "other" than you with an alterity that cannot be overcome.

Whether or not the stages that Soffer describes are ultimately accepted need not concern us. The particulars of her descriptive account are less important than the general point that can be drawn from them. This is that our sense of the other develops over time from identity to difference. The movement from one stage to the next occurs when the child's sense of identity with the other shows its inadequacy. This failure motivates the constitution of a new apprehension of the other, one with an increased sense of alterity. With this comes a new sense to the intentionality that stretches out and strains towards the other. Such "straining" is, in fact, a straining to reestablish the previous apprehension of identity within the conditions of that alterity that mark the new stage. For example, when the child recognizes that the other has a distinct point of view, he apprehends the other as the "same" as himself by intending the other as the person he would be if he occupied the other's place. Equivalent attempts to reestablish identity occur in the other stages. This implies that the turning towards the other that underlies such attempts is not something a person does on occasion. It is, rather, inherent in self-development. It is built up, layer by layer, as part of a person's self-constitution. With this development of turning towards and intending the other, the sense of what it means to respond to the other also develops. The result is a corresponding growth in a person's inner alterity and ethical life. Initially, the infant has no ethical sensibility. Its sense of identity with the other is too complete. As Soffer remarks, the infant does not *attribute* his sensations to the other. Rather, "he expects to sense in the body of the other." Similarly, he presumes "that the other senses via *his* own body" (Soffer 1999, 160). Lacking any real sense of alterity, the infant can never be put into question by the other. It thus lacks a "conscience" in the sense of being called forth to face itself in responding to the other. The child's having a conscience develops along with its sense of alterity. The process ends with the sense of an otherness that cannot be overcome. The corresponding sense of empathy has the widest possible openness to alterity. This includes an openness to being called into question by it. It also includes a maximum of openness to our enjoyment's being interrupted by the other's need.

The concept of this interruption leads to a second condition of our being-in-the-world. Once again its basis is our organic being as flesh. Flesh is naturally vulnerable. It is marked not just by intentionality—i.e., a turning outward to the other. Flesh also turns inward, guarding itself against the things that would interrupt its enjoyment. In doing this, it protects itself from itself. This can be put in terms of the two essential elements of trauma: strong emotional affect and lack of sense. The body combines both. As the place of our sensuous passivity to all the degrees of pleasure and pain, it is the seat of affect. As the organic functioning that makes possible both experience and sense, it is, in its unique singularity, beyond sense. This senselessness is a function of the privacy of organic functioning. Such functioning has a uniqueness that defeats substitution. No one can eat for me. No one can take a walk or exercise for me. In general, no one can perform any of my bodily functions for me. In their very inalienability, such functions are like my death. Just as I alone must undergo my own death, my own cessation of organic functioning, so I alone must engage in the elements of this functioning.[35] My organic activities cannot be substituted for. My body, as irretrievably my own, is this inability to find a substitute. It, thus, escapes signification in the indicative sense of having a substitute stand in its place. Equally, it slips away from signification understood as meaning. My body cannot be grasped as a meaning, a one-in-many. It cannot be represented through a common feature that, in being abstracted from many examples, can stand for each of them. The inalienability of organic functioning—its essential privacy—prevents this. In doing so, it gives the body its lack of sense.

Normally, this senselessness escapes me. In everyday life, I place various senses on my body; I let one representative after another stand as its substitute. In doing so, I take my body as an object, something out there that I can gaze upon. In this "inauthentic" grasp of the body, it becomes a place-holder for a constantly shifting circle of significations. Through these, it is inauthentically apprehended as something pertaining to everyone and no one. What interrupts this is the encounter with the suffering other. His misery exhibits subjectivity in its dependence on what is ultimately not representable. The suffering I encounter, precisely because it is that of the body in its uniqueness, is sense-less. In such an instance, to accept the invitation of the face is to experience the affect of suffering as senseless. The incarnation of empathy thus assumes a certain traumatic quality. One does not, in taking up the other's standpoint, represent it to oneself. One undergoes it in its senselessness and affect. The result is the experience of one's own body as something *other* than the means of one's "I can," as other than the responsive organ of a controlling subjectivity. One gains the sense of the body as subjected to the world—that is, as vulnerable, as passive to the point of denying subjectivity. This experience of the face of the suffering other does not just tear the bread from one's mouth. Its import is that of snatching away every enjoyment, every bodily function. The body in its alterity—that is, in its standing *outside* of our abilities to do and to make sense—points to the possibility of the loss of the whole of our selfhood. In reaction to this, we have the intentionality of the self's turning away from the traumatic encounter. The self protects itself from itself—i.e., from what the other reveals about its basis as flesh—by turning from the other. It concentrates on the enjoyment that was so "senselessly" interrupted, and it attempts to restore it.[36]

Responding and Not Responding

Our intentional relations to the other are, thus, guided by two ontological conditions that have opposing effects. The first, our original bodily identity with the other, manifests itself in our continuous directedness towards the other. As we gain an increasing sense of the alterity of the other, this original identity directs our attempts to restore it through empathy. Empathy, in opening us up to the suffering of the other, exhibits the second condition: the vulnerability of our flesh. The trauma this provokes manifests itself in a self-protective response. Engaging in it, we turn away from the other, attempting thereby to silence the other's exhibition of our vulnerability. The question that naturally arises is: What decides between the two? Given that they are both rooted in our bodily being, what motivates us to turn one way rather than the other?[37]

The motives for not responding to the appeal of the face during the German occupation are obvious enough. The whole power of the Nazi state, with all its ruthless brutality, was employed to prevent people from rescuing others. Yet, in spite of this coercion, some answered the appeal. Many, of course, did not. The same divided response occurs in normal life, when some people stop and give money to a street beggar and others, stereotyping him as a social parasite, an alcoholic, or worse, look past him and walk on. Stereotyping also played an essential role in people's unwillingness to rescue Jews. The Jew in the Polish stereotype had exploited Poland for years. It was assumed during the war that he was hoarding gold.[38] In the Ukraine, the Jew was regarded as a Bolshevik, and hence as responsible for the Stalinist terror. Such stereotyping is the opposite of the face-to-face encounter, since, in it, I determine the other according to my categories. Doing so, I deny that the other can be other than my conception of him. So regarded, stereotyping is a denial of the alterity of the other. It is, thus, a silencing of the other as calling me into question. Equally, it is a denial of my need to respond to such questioning. Thus, insofar as I deny the other his uniqueness, I deny my need to respond uniquely—to respond as an individual to the individual who stands before me. In other words, I do not feel the need to transcend the social norms that set the stereotypes. Instead of encountering the person, I think the stereotype and close the door. Doing so, I deny the uniqueness of human life. My action belies the Mishnah's assertion that there is no "Adam" who functioned as a die, i.e., that everyone is like Adam in being unique.

This division between the stereotype and the face-to-face encounter does not mean that mixed cases, where both elements were present, did not occur. Such cases are of particular interest, since they often show the two elements working against each other. A case in point can be found in the account of Andreas Sheptitski, the Greek Catholic archbishop of L'vov (then Lwow in Galicia, Poland) who provided refuge to Rabbi David Kahanna. One day, finding the rabbi in his library, he opened the New Testament and asked him to read aloud the passage he pointed to. The rabbi read: "His blood be on our heads and those of our children." The archbishop then asked if the present events were not a fulfillment of this prophesy. The rabbi looked at him, but maintained a prudent silence. Later that evening, the archbishop summoned the rabbi to his chambers, asking him for his forgiveness. He explained that their earlier encounter had been weighing on his heart, and he could not sleep. The interview ended with the rabbi forgiving him.[39] One can see this result as the outcome of the conflict between the motivations springing from the rabbi's gaze and the biblical stereotype, with the influence of the former finally gaining the upper hand.

The effect of this sort of stereotyping can be put in terms of Freud's division of our instinctual life into two basic forms: those of the love and death instincts. As we cited Freud earlier, the aim of the first is "to establish ever greater unities and to preserve them—in short to bind together; the aim of the second is, on the contrary, to undo connections and so destroy things" (Freud 1989, 18). From an evolutionary perspective, it is relatively easy to imagine their formation. The aggressive tendencies of the death instinct were, in part, selected for by the need of our primitive ancestors to defend the tribe from outsiders. The love instinct, with its aim of binding people together, performed an equally useful service within the tribe. The more intimate the kin relation, the stronger is its force. Radiating outward from the parent-child bond, its binding force is felt throughout the group.[40] In Freud's account of their "economy," the two instincts hold each other in check. This means that the more the one is absent, the greater is the force of other.[41] Now, when I stereotype the other, I reduce this person to a fixed set of categories. At the extreme, I objectify him as I would a thing. I take him as completely open to inspection and description in his unchanging "typical" nature. So regarded, stereotyping can be seen not just as denying the alterity of the other. Paradoxically, its denial of the other person's otherness is also the positioning of the other as an outsider. This is because the ultimate outsider is not even human. He is just a thing, a sheer givenness with no alterity, no resistance to the categories we happen to impose on him.

Given that the death instinct directs itself against the outsider, the stereotyping that positions the other as an outsider makes him liable to its action. Stereotyping, thus, precedes genocide. The elimination of a person *because* he is a member of a group presupposes that the stereotypical features of the group capture him entirely.[42] By contrast, the face-to-face encounter, in undermining our categories, undoes this instinct. When I accept the invitation of the face, I encounter the other in his alterity. This other, in his alterity, is "in" me. He is my alterity. He is my standing-outside-myself-calling-myself-into-question. He is "in" me as the very thing that allows me to be a for-itself. I am a human self insofar as I question my categories. Now, the relation to the other underlying this questioning involves the love instinct. In its intimacy and alterity, my relation to the other recalls the origin of my directedness to the other: namely my status as a child in the womb. The child in the womb is the "first" other in the sense that it is the other at its origin. The intimacy of the parent-child relation continues when, after birth, the parent becomes the infant's "first" other. This initial relation directs the subsequent development of the child's empathy. The restoration of the relation is the object of the successive stages of the child's grasping the other as "like" itself. Now, the initial relation was one where the force of the love instinct was at its height, where, as a consequence, it was most opposed to the death instinct. To restore it, then, is to undo the death instinct. To put this in terms of the obligation of life, we need only note that this relation, at its origin, is that of sharing flesh and, hence, life.

Thus, the turning toward the other in empathy recalls the demand that springs from life. It calls us to authorize life's founding quality by participating in its preservation.[43]

A moral imperative can be drawn from this analysis. Given that stereotyping undoes the obligation springing from the encounter with life at risk, it should be prevented. This can be expressed in terms of the experience of the tension between the "is" and the "ought." What yields this tension is the exceeding quality of life. In containing more than any individual can possibly exemplify, life calls into question the choices a person has made. It raises the question of whether he "ought" to have acted as he had—i.e., made those choices that constitute his "is." The tension, then, is a result of our being framed by life and its possibilities. It is the result of the "in-placeness" of our being, that is, of our being situated as one of a number of possibilities, the very one we are called forth to answer for. The being "out of place" that exists as the opposite of this denies both the exceeding quality of life and ethical tension springing from it. Stereotyping results in such "placelessness" by reducing the life that confronts us to a limited number of "typical" qualities. Rather than placing us, this life becomes something we place, something we fit into our pregiven categories. In this, we assume the attitude of standing outside of life. It stands before us as an external object of our judgment.[44] The moral imperative of preventing stereotyping, thus, becomes one of avoiding this being out of place. Positively, it is that of maintaining our being "in place" by preserving the alternatives that frame us.

An ethics that works out this imperative is one that assumes that we have a moral life only insofar as we can be for-ourselves. It also assumes that we can be for-ourselves only in terms of a frame that situates us by exceeding us. To proceed from these assumptions to an actual ethics, we must begin by confronting the basic questions of good and evil. Concretely, this means speaking of them in terms of our being "in-place" or "out-of-place."

5

An Ethics of Framing

Good and Evil as Ontological Categories

Normally, when we use the terms "good" and "evil," we take "good" to be what is useful or "good for" achieving some given subjective purpose or desire. The "evil" or the "harmful" is the opposite of this. It is what prevents our achieving our goals. There is, however, a difficulty in limiting ourselves to such meanings: they make good and evil relative to us. Taking such terms as "values," the usage implies that without us—i.e., without our inclinations and needs—things are valueless. Kant exemplifies this view in his devaluation of both man-made and natural objects. The things we make, he observes, depend on us—ultimately, on our desires—to come into being. As for natural objects, they have, he writes, "only a relative value as means [for our purposes] and are consequently called things" (Kant 1964, 96; 1955a, 428). As Kant states the general conclusion: "All the objects of inclinations have only a conditioned value; for if there were not these inclinations and the needs grounded on them, then their object would be valueless" (95; 1955a, 428). The world, in this essentially utilitarian view, is intrinsically without value. Making goodness relative to us, we eliminate the notion of *being* good as an objective, ontological category.[1] Yet, as Aristotle notes, "we do not make all our choices for the sake of something else." If "good" always meant "good for," then every end we achieved would point to the next. The process would "go on infinitely so that our desire would be futile and pointless" (Aristotle 1962, 4; *Nic. Eth.*, 1094a. 2–21).

Kant attempts to avoid this difficulty by positing the person as an "end in himself." The person is that for the sake of which all other things are sought. Yet as Arendt observes, such a term is either a "tautology" or a "contradiction in terms." As the first, it applies to all ends. As the second, it points to the fact that "an end, once it is attained[,] ceases to be an end"—i.e., a goal that guides us. An end that is accomplished is no longer a not-yet, but rather "an object among objects" (Arendt 1958, 154–55). A person, however, is not an object. Given that we are already persons, it is also unclear how in a Kantian sense we can be considered as ends (or goals) to be achieved. To call a person an "end in himself" thus cannot point to his being an "end" like other objects. This is particularly evident since a person does not have "value" in the way that things do. Things for Kant have value only insofar as they are "good for" something else. Viewed in such terms, however, the person is "valueless." As an end in himself, he is not good "for" anything else. One may with Kant assert that he has an infinite worth, but this worth is without context. His pricelessness puts him beyond any measure. In attempting to speak of good and evil in terms of value—i.e., in terms of subjective valuation—we thus face the difficulty of trying to base value on what is beyond value. We begin by saying that without the person, none of the other objects in the world have value. Intrinsically, they are valueless. We then assert that the person, as an end himself, has no value in the basic sense of having some definite worth that might function in a system of exchange. Thus, from the perspective of the things that do so function, the person is valueless. From the perspective of the person, however, such things are valueless. As is obvious, two different senses of value are at work here. Kant's designation of the person as an "end in himself" is a "contradiction in terms," as Arendt points out, precisely because it is their unstable amalgam.

To avoid these difficulties, we have to take good and evil as ontological categories. We must see them as descriptive of the way things are, independently of whether this suits our inclinations or needs. In other words, rather than measuring goodness according to our desires, we have to measure such desires according to a goodness that is prior to them. To do so is to assert that they can be called "good" according to the categories that apply to the world that situates both our desires and their satisfactions.

In-Placeness and Out-of-Placeness

As already indicated, the categories we require are the ontological ones of being "in-place" and "out-of-place."[2] To start at a completely nonsubjective level, we can define being-in-place as being part of a relatively stable system of things and forces. A planet, for example, is "in-place" as part of a solar system. "Being-good," taken as an ontological category, refers to its being part of this system, i.e., its participating with other things in the system's balance of forces. Revolving about its sun, the centrifugal force that would make the planet spin out (the force springing from its inherent tendency to proceed in a straight line) is opposed by the centripetal force of gravity. As Newton showed, the law of gravitational force is just such as to make possible the balance of the two forces. Were the gravitational force between two bodies not inversely proportional to the square of the distance between them, no stable orbits would be possible. Bodies would either fly off or else spiral into each other.[3] If the "good" of the planet is its being in place as part of this system, the opposing category of ontological "evil" is the destruction of the conditions that made this possible. This can be caused by something "out-of-place"—e.g., some large gravitating body—entering the system, disturbing its balance, and causing the planets either to spiral into the sun or fly off into space. The result would be the loss of the diversity that the organized system made possible. Instead of different planets with different masses, angular velocities, and distances from the sun composing an interrelated system, the planets would either be consumed by the sun or else move through space as unrelated objects. "Evil" here designates both the loss of order and the lack of diversity. Its causes are the "out-of-placeness" of the intruding object and the lack of balance caused by its "excessive" presence—a presence that introduces a level of force that the system cannot tolerate.

Moving to an animate level, evil can be understood as arising from the introduction of an out-of-place plant or animal. Its success in its new environment leads to an overwhelming presence that upsets the environmental balance, causing a loss in bio-diversity.[4] Examples of the destruction this can occasion are quite numerous. Thus, the escape of European rabbits in Australia in 1862 led to an immense explosion in their population that was disastrous for the local fauna. The Asian tamarisk, introduced into the American semideserts, had a superior ability to find water, which resulted in its sucking its environment dry. Eurasian zebra mussels, carried to the Great Lakes on the hulls of tankers, multiplied to the point that they clogged the surrounding waterways (Watson 1995, 28). In each case, the sudden introduction of a foreign species resulted in a loss of the local species. What remained was simpler and less diverse. When this loss of diversity becomes extreme, the possibilities of recovery through evolution are severely diminished. In such cases, the materials that evolution has to work with—i.e., the differences between competing species and individuals—are simply not there. As the naturalist Lyall Watson describes the result: "The process of evolution requires . . . something to work with, some purchase to give leverage on life. . . . Every loss of diversity represents a loss of organic vigor and a corresponding reduction in possibilities of interconnection and cooperation. And the loss is progressive. As diversity fades, so do the chances for change and eventually the system breaks down altogether" (44–45).

When a foreign species does succeed in disrupting the local environment, it generally has no natural predators. As foreign, it has not evolved with the local inhabitants. They, thus, have not had the chance to adapt to it. This can be put in terms of Darwin's assertion "that the structure of every organic being is related, in the most essential yet often hidden manner, to that of all the other organic beings, with which it comes into competition for food and residence, or from which it has to escape, or on which it preys" (Darwin 1967b, 61). For Darwin, the individual features that make up a particular being's structure, from the shape of its legs to the type of eyes it has, are actually a set of indices. Each points to the specific features of the environment in which it functions. Insofar as they shape the organism, the environment can be considered as functioning through it. Since this environment includes other organic beings, each can be considered not just as determined by the world that shapes it, but also as part of this world insofar as it functions as a determinant for the beings of *its* environment. The organism's being-in-place is its functioning in this system of mutual determinations. It includes the internalization through its own bodily development of its external situating context. In-placeness, thus, involves the organism's definition and limitation by this environment. Both appear, for example, "in the structure of the teeth and talons of the tiger; and in that of the legs and claws of the parasite which clings to the hair on the tiger's body" (61). Such features define the organism. They also limit it to a specific prey and to a strategy that works with regard to specific competitors.[5] The fundamental limitation is that of the environment that functions through it. An organism's success cannot have been such that it would have destroyed this environment since such destruction would have resulted in its own elimination. In other words, the very evolutionary processes that produced a species, in presupposing the organisms that situate it, placed limits on its action with regard to them. Now, the foreign species has, in its very out-of-placeness, no such limitations. Its definition is, in terms of its new environment, not a limitation. Thus, if it can find food, if it lacks local predators, and if the circumstances of its release are lucky,[6] then it may well overrun and ruin its new territory. The result may be similar to, for example, the denuded "goatscapes" of

Antigua and St. Helena caused by the release of goats on what once were forested and well-watered islands (Watson 1995, 37–38).

If evil manifests itself in a catastrophic loss of diversity—that is, in an environmental degradation so severe that the means for recovery are impaired—goodness shows the opposite characteristics. It manifests itself in diversity. An increase in diversity is, as Darwin continually observes, an increase in life. Experimentally this is shown, he writes, by the fact that "if a plot of ground be sown with one species of grass, and a similar plot be sown with several distinct genera of grasses, a greater number of plants and a greater weight of dry herbage can be raised in the latter than in the former case" (Darwin 1967b, 85). The principle here is that "the greatest amount of life can be supported by great diversification of structure" (85). Behind it is the fact that each species exploits the environment in a unique way. Doing so, it does not so much compete with its neighbors as increase its numbers by filling the different ecological niches its environment affords. Each unique species, however, also enriches this environment. Its actions increase its diversity and hence the places within it where its neighbors can gain a living.[7] Naturalists offer us many striking instances of this. Darwin, for example, having observed that "humble bees alone visit red clover," also notes that "the number of humble bees in any district depends in a great measure upon the number of field-mice, which destroy their combs and nests." But "the number of mice is largely dependent on the number of cats." Thus, we can tie the presence of cats to that of red clover (59). If the latter is the chief food of the local dairy, one might even extend this connection to the production of milk. Lyall Watson gives a similar example, connecting otters to the presence of fish. Otters eat the spiny sea urchin that feeds on the kelp that "provides an essential nursery area and vital habitat for local marine life." Trapping the sea otter thus has "disastrous consequences for near-shore fish and fisheries" (Watson 1995, 41). The loss of this species is rather like that of pulling a keystone from an arch. Corresponding to the collapse of the arch and the loss of order this implies, we have the destruction of the kelp forests and the marine life they support.

Darwin, reflecting on such interrelations, compares the activity we have exercised on nature through selective breeding with the action of evolution. He writes: "Man can act only on external and visible characters: Nature, if I may be allowed to personify the natural preservation or survival of the fittest, cares nothing for appearances, except in so far as they are useful to any being. She can act on every internal organ, on every shade of constitutional difference, on the whole machinery of life. Man selects only for his own good: Nature only for that of the being which she tends" (Darwin 1967b, 65). The reference of "the being which

she tends" and its benefit seems at first to be to some particular organism. It is for its good that natural selection seems to work. Yet, once we
bear "in mind how infinitely complex and close-fitting are the mutual
relations of all organic beings to each other and to their physical conditions of life," the reference becomes highly ambiguous (63). If, in fact,
every being is ultimately determined and defined by every other, the
"being" tended by nature can only be nature itself understood as the
whole web of relations and entities. Goodness, defined in these terms, is
a function of the being-in-place that is both a ground and grounded by
this whole. Each species has its goodness in terms of a whole that forms
the context in which it plays its role. This role is that of tending nature
itself. It involves the multiplication of places or niches that life can
occupy. The goal of such "tending" is, in other words, life itself in its
maximal possible diversity.

What sets the human world off from the merely animate world of
nature is the sense humans make of it. This sense, as manifested in
speech and reason, is both individual and cultural. Good and evil, understood as in-placeness and out-of-placeness, involve the maintenance or
destruction of the contexts that allow us to make sense. A couple of
examples will make this clear. For an individual, the senselessness and
overwhelming affect of a traumatic event can disrupt the ability to make
sense of life. In spite of the fact that the event does not fit in with his
normal experience, the individual is riveted to it by virtue of the affect it
occasions. It calls up feelings that the individual cannot master even
though their very violence makes it impossible to ignore them. Its out-
of-placeness, thus, disrupts what Freud calls the ego's "synthetic function"—the function by which it interprets and makes sense of the world
and its affects. It cannot synthesize, i.e., put the event together with the
other affecting elements of its world. Given the "synthetic nature of the
workings of the ego," the disturbance of this functioning is the ego's disruption.[8] The result of the overwhelming presence of the out-of-place
event is, then, a loss of psychological balance, which occasions a corresponding mental disorder. On the collective level, out-of-placeness
appears in the destruction of one culture by another—for example, the
destruction of the aboriginal cultures by Europeans. In such cases, the
result of European colonization was not just a transformation of the
land through enclosures and destruction of habitats—a change that
deprived the inhabitants by and large of their original means of supporting themselves. Concomitant with it was a disruption of the contexts of
sense by which the natives interpreted their world. Thus, once the land
was divided up and enclosed for farming, the aboriginal hunter-gatherer
activity became impossible. The inhabitants could, consequently, no

longer understand themselves within this context. The men, for example, could no longer see themselves as hunters or pastoralists, given that all the suitable land was enclosed by the colonists. Foreign missionaries, who often traded medical aid and other material advantages for professions of belief, had a similar effect on their religious self-understanding. It changed its terms of reference, often in surprising and inappropriate ways. The body, for example, became reinterpreted as the "flesh" that was liable to corruption and sin. In North America, the forcible removal of native children to residential schools continued this cultural disruption. These children were forbidden to speak their native language, thus preventing them from transmitting its special senses. The cumulative effect of this imposition of non-native cultural and religious outlooks was not necessarily their adoption. Their inappropriateness—as belonging to a different social context and situation—often ruled this out. The result was simply the collapse of their own interpretative categories—including most prominently the ones by which they judged good and evil. At the extreme, then, the natives suffered a breakdown in their ability to make sense of and, hence, function in their new situation. With this came the phenomena of abuse. In the disorders of sexual, spousal, drug, and alcohol abuse it is possible to see a cultural parallel to the "goatscapes" mentioned above. A similar impoverishment of the environment had occurred—one that manifested itself in the bleakness of the human context of sense.

Joseph Conrad's Account of the Hiddenness of Evil

The collapse of the context of sense does not just affect natives. The newcomers are also caught within it. It makes them unaware of the destruction they are causing. The best description of this remains Joseph Conrad's novella, *Heart of Darkness*, a fictionalized account of his experiences in the Congo. Its story revolves around Kurtz, described by its narrator, Marlow, as "a soul that knew no restraint, no faith, and no fear . . ." (Conrad 1989, 108). Kurtz, until his last moment, failed to recognize the evil that positioned him within the "heart of darkness."[9] Such evil is both individual and collective; it includes both Kurtz and the "Company" he works for. The novella can be taken as an attempt to describe evil, its theme being the lack of restraint that is its most obvious marker. This lack of restraint is intimately tied to the difficulty of recognizing evil. The evil that is unrecognized can increase unchecked. Its very growth results in the destruction of the contexts of sense that would allow its recognition. What we have, then, is a self-reinforcing process in which lack of recognition and lack of restraint increase each other, the result ultimately being the destruction of one culture by another. What we confront is, in fact, the human parallel to the overwhelming presence of the out-of-place organism that destroys a local environment. The context that could have restrained this organism has been left behind. Its elimination of the local fauna forecloses the possibility of their adaptation and, hence, resistance to its encroachments. Similarly, the lack of restraint on the part of the Europeans begins with their externality to the contexts of sense they find themselves in. Their destruction of this context prevents it from ever calling their actions into question. The result, then, is the self-concealment of evil. Evil, taken as an overwhelming destructive presence, generates its own hiddenness by destroying the contexts of sense that would allow it to be recognized.

Conrad's description of this process begins with a reminder of the Roman conquest of Britain. The Romans, Marlow declares, "were no colonists; their administration was merely a squeeze and nothing more, I suspect. They were conquerors. It was just robbery with violence, aggravated murder on a great scale, and men going at it blind. . . . The conquest of the earth, which mostly means the taking it away from those who have a different complexion or slightly flatter noses than ourselves, is not a pretty thing . . ." (Conrad 1989, 31–32). The Europeans in the Congo, he implies, are engaged in a similar venture. They, too, are "going at it blind." Their blindness is a function of the externality of their situation. Like the Romans in Britain, they enjoy an overwhelming technological advantage over the natives. The isolation this power affords is combined with a near-total ignorance of the local culture. Kurtz, the extreme example of this combination of externality and power, thinks of himself as a god. He writes in a report composed for "the International Society for the Suppression of Savage Customs," "we whites from the point of development we had arrived at, 'must necessarily appear to them [the natives] in the nature of supernatural beings—we approach them in the might of a deity.'"[10] While he believes that with "the simple exercise of our will we can exert a power for good practically unbounded," his actual relations with the natives are destructive. The one "exposition of a method," found in a note later appended to the report's last page, is "exterminate the brutes" (86–87). In fact, this process of extermination was ongoing from the beginning. The dominant impression of Marlow's "two-hundred-mile tramp" to the Company station is one of "a solitude, a solitude, nobody, not a hut." He does, however, pass "through several abandoned villages." All their inhabitants had fled the advancing whites (48). Such destruction is the only thing that the blind power that Kurtz represents is capable of. Like the out-of-place organism that is unrestrained by the local fauna, the Europeans, in Conrad's account, eliminate the natives.

That Kurtz cannot, till the end, grasp this is a result of evil's self-concealment. Its destruction of the context of sense that would allow it to appear gives evil its uncanny quality. Facing it, we face not presence but absence, not sense but nonsense. Marlow's account is haunted by this fact. At a certain point in his tale, he exclaims in exasperation: "Do you see the story? Do you see anything? It seems to me I am trying to tell you a dream—making a vain attempt because no relation of a dream can convey the dream-sensation, that commingling of absurdity, surprise, and bewilderment . . . , that notion of being captured by the incredible which is of the very essence of dreams" (Conrad 1989, 57). What frustrates his attempt to present a clear narrative is the absurdity of what he is describing. Events occur without any clear purpose. For example, as he travels down the coast of Africa, his ship encounters "a man-of-war . . . shelling the bush" (40). He relates, "In the empty immensity of earth, sky, and water, there she was, incomprehensible, firing into a continent. Pop, would go one of the six-inch guns; . . . a tiny projectile would give a feeble screech—and nothing happened. Nothing could happen." Given that the shore was empty, "there was a touch of insanity in the proceeding . . ." (41). The French ship was firing at an invisible enemy while its own men "were dying of fever at the rate of three a-day" (41).

The same pattern of death and senselessness marks his further encounters. At the trading station at the mouth of the river, he comes across a collection of abandoned objects including "a boiler wallowing in the grass" and a "a railway-truck . . . with its wheels in the air." Their utter lack of utility matches the purposeless blasting of a nearby cliff. He remarks, "They were building a railway. The cliff was not in the way or anything; but this objectless blasting was all the work going on" (Conrad 1989, 42). Again, illness haunts the proceedings. In the shade by the falls, Marlow stumbles on a collection of dying natives: "Black shapes crouched, lay, sat between the trees leaning against the trunks, clinging to the earth, half coming out, half effaced within the dim light, in all the attitudes of pain, abandonment, and despair." Left to their own devices after they had sickened, "they were dying slowly" (44). Their painfully thin shapes matched those of the black prisoners that had just passed him by. "Black rags were wound round their loins, and the short ends behind waggled to and fro like tails. I could see every rib, the joints of their limbs were like knots in a rope: each had an iron collar on his neck, and all were connected together with a chain . . ." (43). They are carrying baskets of earth up the hillside in an activity as senseless as the incomprehensible blasting. This combination of senselessness and death repeats itself in his encounter with the Company's impeccably dressed accountant. In his ramshackle office, a dying company agent has been placed in the corner. Exhibiting a "gentle annoyance," the accountant remarks, "The groans of this sick person . . . distract my attention. And without that it is extremely difficult to guard against clerical errors in this climate" (46). The natives outside are also a cause for his distress. As Marlow relates his conversation, "'When one has got to make correct entries, one comes to hate those savages—hate them to the death.' . . . 'When you see Mr. Kurtz tell him that everything here'—he glanced at his desk—'is very satisfactory'" (47).

What exactly is "satisfactory"? The reader is not told. The glance at the desk suggests that the reference is to the accounts he is keeping. This focus allows him not to see the death that is before him nor the senselessness of the Company's enterprise. Again and again, this lack of sense or purpose is driven home. Conrad writes, for example, of the company's upriver outpost: "There was an air of plotting about that station, but nothing came of it, of course. It was as unreal as everything else—as the philanthropic pretense of the whole concern, as their talk, as their government, as their show of work" (Conrad 1989, 54). What is truly uncanny is the fact that those engaged in it do not see it. Marlow sees them "strolling aimlessly about" the station's enclosure. He relates: "I asked myself sometimes what it all meant." But the best he can come up with is the simile of a pointless pilgrimage: "[T]hey wandered here and there with their absurd long staves in their hands, like a lot of faithless pilgrims bewitched inside a rotten fence." Supposedly, they were after "ivory." Its word was on their lips. "You would think that they were praying to it. A taint of imbecile rapacity blew through it all, like a whiff from some corpse" (52). Yet even the notion of ivory fails to explain what goes on about him. These pilgrims never leave the station to start their pilgrimage. Their desire for it is an "imbecile rapacity." With the mention of the "corpse," senselessness and death are again associated.

To recognize something as itself is to place it within the categories that mark the boundaries of its sense. In general, we grasp what we can make sense of. To turn this about, to escape sense is to escape our grasp. So regarded, Marlow's descriptions of the senselessness of what he sees can be taken as attempts to describe this escape. They may be regarded as Conrad's effort to describe the *non*recognition of evil. In *Heart of Darkness*, evil escapes our grasp through its senselessness—the very senselessness that it occasions. This nonrecognition extends to the death that has been constantly conjoined with the enterprise's lack of sense. Thus, the deaths of the natives and agents seem to pass unnoticed. At most, they are occasions of annoyance. In the absence of sense, they simply contribute to "that commingling of absurdity, surprise, and bewilderment" that Marlow describes as characterizing a dream. A dream is marked by a lack of reality. Nothing "really" corresponds to it. Marlow, however, is not dreaming. He is awake. His remark points to the fact that the difficulty he faces in telling his story is not just its lack of sense. He is frustrated by a corresponding lack of being. Normally our apprehensions of sense and reality occur together. If we cannot make sense of our experiences, that is, if we cannot make them fit together so as to see them as presenting a self-consistent situation, then their referent is also lost to us. A lack of sense makes us assert we are dreaming rather than encountering a reality. Marlow's account exemplifies this in its dreamlike character. His account is constantly undermined by the vertiginous feeling that as we get to the heart of the matter, we find less and less of substance. Our encounter is simply with absence.

Conrad uses a number of striking images to make this point. The station manager, for example, is described as "a common trader" whose only ability was to inspire "uneasiness." How could such a perfectly ordinary individual be in charge of a station that, from the natives' perspective at least, must appear more like a concentration camp than a commercial venture? Marlow relates, "He had no genius for organizing, for initiative, or for order even. . . . Perhaps there was nothing within him. Such a suspicion made one pause" (Conrad 1989, 50). The suspicion is that at his heart there is an absence rather than a presence. Marlow's unease comes from the fact that there is nothing there to see. As Marlow describes the experience of talking with him: "He sealed the utterance with that smile of his, as though it had been a door opening into a darkness he had in his keeping. You fancied you had seen things—but the seal was on" (51). What is the "seal" and what is "sealed" by it? The suggestion here is that the "nothing within him" is both. In its nonbeing, it conceals itself. It is both seal and sealed. The same lack of substance appears in the description of the manger's confidant as "a papier-mâché Mephistopheles." Like a papier-mâché figure, this devil conceals an absence. As Marlow says, "[I]t seemed to me that if I tried I could poke my forefinger through him, and I would find nothing inside but a little loose dirt, maybe" (56).

Kurtz, at the very heart of the darkness that Marlow is trying to describe, appears as both a voice and a nothingness. Deathly ill when Marlow encounters him, he still preserves his eloquence, his capacity for creating a "splendid appearance" through his words. Marlow describes him as "a shadow insatiable of splendid appearances, of frightful realities, a shadow darker than the shadow of the night draped nobly in the folds of a gorgeous eloquence" (Conrad 1989, 116). In Kurtz's case, the nothingness within and the terribly destructive power of his company's enterprise form an active unity. His nothingness, precisely in his command of language, appears all-consuming: a devouring emptiness. In Marlow's words, "I saw him open his mouth wide [to speak]—it gave him a weirdly voracious aspect, as though he had wanted to swallow all the air, all the earth, all the men before him" (99). The political implications of this combination of eloquence and nothingness are not hard to find—particularly with our experience of the dictators of the last century. Conrad in 1902 was not unaware of them. He has a journalist, who knew Kurtz, describe him to Marlow: "'[B]ut heavens! how that man could talk. He electrified large meetings. He had the faith. He could get himself to believe anything—anything. He would have been a splendid leader of an extreme party.' 'What party?' . . . 'Any party' . . . 'He was an—an—extremist'" (115).

The Holocaust and the Limits of Rational Intelligibility

The remark that Kurtz could have been the leader of any party points to the fact that the power of his eloquence does not lie in the content of his essentially senseless ideas, but rather in his being an extremist. The two, in fact, are combined. His extremism is his standing outside of a situating context of sense. Such senselessness lames the ability to withstand his eloquence, thereby increasing its power. This may be put in terms of our initial remarks about crimes against humanity. These crimes exceed, by their very nature, our attempts to make sense of them. Their senselessness is, in fact, a function of the extremism of the standpoint they embody. This standpoint is outside of the normal context in which people make sense of their lives. To the point that its position is outside of humanity itself, it escapes human sense altogether. This very senselessness, we remarked, is what disabled people's judgment of the Holocaust. Its extreme evil concealed itself by virtue of its being out of place.

The senselessness of the Holocaust prompted Hans Jonas to remark paradoxically, "[M]uch more is real than is possible." Normally, we say that the possible is greater than the real. In limiting the real to what we can make sense of, the possible simply sets the bounds to what can (but need not) be realized. Yet, in attempting to account for the Holocaust, this order is reversed. Describing its "how and why," one is confronted by the incredible, by what seems to exceed the possible taken as the realm of sense. As Emil Fackenheim writes, citing Jonas' remark:

"To explain an action or event is to show how it was possible. In the case of the Holocaust, however, the mind can accept the possibility of both how and why it was done, in the final analysis, solely because it was done . . ." (Fackenheim 1988, 64). In our inability to account for the "how and the why," we confront the sheer purposelessness of the enterprise. Its senselessness (its lack of any sufficient "reason why") shows itself in the insufficiency of the attempts to explain it.

In making this point, Fackenheim runs through the standard explanations. Suppose, for example, we say that the Nazis believed their propaganda regarding the Jews. We could then assert that "The Nazis wished to save Germany . . . from what they considered to be the 'Jewish virus'" (Fackenheim 1988, 63). The difficulty here is that Germany was itself sacrificed when it came to a choice between defending the country and destroying the Jews. In pursuit of the latter, essential workers were gassed, and trains were diverted from the front to continue the deportations to Auschwitz.[11] All this bespeaks an essential madness. Should we then reach for psychological explanations? Must we say that the Holocaust happened because Hitler was disturbed? In Fackenheim's formulation: "Were the German people led—did they let themselves be led—first to victory, then into catastrophic defeat because Hitler had a love-hate relation to his mother? Were six million actual 'non-Aryans' and many additional honorary ones butchered and gassed because the Führer hated his father and thought of him as a half-Jew?" (64). The very formulation of the question reveals the difficulty. There is an immense disproportion between the cause and the effect. To overcome it, we have to suppose that the Germans themselves were disturbed. The Germans, however, were not alone. Hitler had his allies—Croatia, Hungary, Austria, Italy, and Spain, to name a few. Even the Catholic Church under Pius XII afforded him a crucial recognition through its Concordat.[12] Were they all unbalanced? In Fackenheim's words, "Must one—may one—extend such psychopathic hypotheses beyond Hitler to the German people, to much of Europe, to large parts of the world?" (64).

One can, of course, say that rather than being mad, the Germans were manipulated. The actions of those who supported the final solution were not really their own. In the infamous phrase, they were "just following orders." Yet, as Fackenheim asks: "[A]re there *no* limits to *being* manipulated?" What does this say about the bureaucrats, generals, soldiers, academics, clerics, officeholders, and so on who actively or passively contributed to the solution? Were "there none equal to the power of the manipulators" (Fackenheim 1988, 64)? The chief manipulator was Hitler himself. The dilemma, as Fackenheim notes, is that if we pursue this route, "we at once falsely endow this individual with a diabolical omnipotence that is beyond all humanity and, equally falsely, ascribe to all those ordered and inspired by him an all-encompassing manipulability that is beneath all humanity." The problem here is that "between these two extremes, Man is lost" (65). He is either more or less than the recognizably human. Hitler, however, with his mass of petty resentments and shopworn ideas, hardly qualifies as a superman.[13] As for those beneath him, they were not automatons. They were human beings like ourselves. As we know from our own experience, there is in every being-manipulated a *letting oneself* be manipulated. Belief comes not just from without, but from within.[14] Did these people persuade themselves that they were indeed saving Germany from "the Jewish virus"? Did they continue in this belief even when it meant sacrificing Germany? With this, we return, as in a circle, to the difficulty of our original explanation. To do so, however, is to begin this circle again. The very circularity of our explanations points to their insufficiency. Each one leads us on to the next. Each regarded by itself reminds us of Marlow's description of the company agent as a "papier-mâché Mephistopheles." None of them has the substance that can stand examination. The result, then, is that there is no anchor for our explanations. The Holocaust's defining character thus seems to be its inexplicability. To the point that it exceeds the bounds of sense, it exceeds any attempt to integrate it into any intelligible framework.

The Limits of Philosophical Rationality

Fackenheim writes that "to confront the Holocaust . . . is to face the fact that the precise point which marks the limits of penultimate rational intelligibility marks the end also of ultimate or philosophical rationality" (Fackenheim 1988, 65). His claim is that the Holocaust escapes any ultimate philosophical explanation. A philosopher who accepts this still can ask why this must be so. What does this failure reveal about philosophical rationality? Can we give a philosophical account of the failure of philosophical rationality to deal with evil in its most exemplary manifestation?

This manifestation is marked by a lack of sense and a corresponding lack of substance. In Conrad's novella, the search for evil—for the "heart" of its darkness—leads to absence, to a void that is at once self-concealing and all-consuming. In the Holocaust, when we turn to Hitler, we meet a similar lack of substance. Instead of encountering a superman, we find what has been described as an "'almost inconceivable spiritual, moral and human inferiority'" (Fackenheim 1988, 65). In both cases, our thought confronts "what is not"—that is, what can only be negatively characterized. Philosophical rationality, however, is first and foremost the thought of "what is." Taking its origin in Parmenides' speculations, it has by and large heeded his admonitions about the two "ways of inquiry":

> [T]he one way, that it is and cannot not-be, is the path of Persuasion, for it attends upon Truth; the other, that it is-not and needs must not-be, that I tell thee is a path altogether unthinkable. For thou couldst not know that which is-not (that is impossible) nor utter it; for the same thing can be thought as can be. (Parmenides 1966, 269)

The injunction here is to think about the "it is," not about the "is-not." The latter cannot be grasped. The correlation between thinkability and being means that the "is-not" can neither be philosophically known nor uttered. From the beginning, then, the limits of philosophical rationality are those of being.[15]

The modern expression of this position occurs in Heidegger's account of disclosure. For Heidegger, we disclose "what-is" through our projects. Such projects uncover both what and how a being is. Thus, my project to build a fire reveals paper as combustible. My project to write a letter shows it to be a surface for writing. In each such action I also reveal my own being. I show myself to be the one building a fire or writing a letter. Heidegger puts this point in terms of his definition of us as "care."[16] Care is our being responsible for our being. This means that our being is an issue for us (Heidegger 1967a, 325). It is the result of our projects, of the choices we make in deciding not just what we will do but (as inherent in this) what we will be.[17] This last is the crucial and underlying issue in every project we undertake. Each action, Heidegger argues, is ultimately for our sake. Its ultimate motivation is the concern we have for our own being. Given this, the world we disclose through our projects has an intelligibility that presupposes this concern.[18] The beings within our world have the sense of the "in order to."[19] They appear as the means for achieving our projects. Thus, paper appears to me as combustible when I use it in order to build a fire. I build it for my sake, i.e., in order that I be warm. Without this concern, it would not be there for me.[20] Even the thought of it as "missing" requires that it relate to my goals.[21]

In such a framework, as is obvious, purpose is everything. Both sense and being rely on our ability to respond to the question: "Why are you doing that?"[22] Philosophical rationality traces this to our own being—i.e., to the care we have for it. This, however, is precisely what is denied to us when we regard the Holocaust. As already noted, Germany was itself sacrificed when it came to choosing between defending the country and destroying the Jews. In pursuing it, the Germans manifested a *lack of care* for their own being. The death marches at the end, when the camps had to be abandoned and the war was clearly lost, were completely useless and, hence, in Heidegger's terms, senseless. In such terms, we have to say that nothing was disclosed by them. If we take "truth" in Heidegger's preferred sense of "unhiddenness," this lack of disclosure is a lack of "truth." Nothing is made manifest here. To turn this about, we have to say that such actions reveal not being, but its absence. Philosophical rationality is stymied by a void surrounded by nontruth.

Heidegger, as is well known, observed a complete silence regarding the Holocaust. Having equated philosophy with ontology (the science of being), one may speculate that he found nothing in the event to consider.[23] In its exceeding both "truth" and "being" (as he defined these terms), the Holocaust exceeded what his philosophy could grasp. So regarded, his failure to speak about the Holocaust may be accounted for by his philosophy. An explanation, however, can also be sought in the circumstances of his life—e.g., in his decade-long involvement with the Nazi movement.[24] Thus, the suspicion remains that this silence is self-serving. Yet when we turn to the philosophical tradition he criticized, our search for philosophical intelligibility does not advance. Ancient and mediaeval philosophy seem equally incapable of coming to terms with evil.

The essence of its position is summed up by Augustine in his attack on the Manichaean belief that good and evil (light and dark, God and Satan, spirit and matter) are the names of opposed powers locked in struggle for the world. Evil, he argued, is not a positive character. It is a lack, an absence of goodness. In his words, "[E]vil is nothing but the removal of good until no good remains" (Augustine 1961, 63). In itself, it is simply a nothingness.[25] In the Middle Ages, this position became incorporated in the doctrine of the transcendent properties of being. These are the properties of being irrespective of where it is found. Every being is not just existent. To the point that it is, it is one, true, and good. Conversely, to the point that it is not, it lacks unity, truth, and goodness. "Truth," here, does not so much signify disclosedness as a correspondence of a thing to its exemplar. A "true" man is a person who fully instantiates the form or essence of what a person ought to be.[26] In such an instantiation, he has his unity. He participates, as it were, in the self-identity of the form he instantiates. This participation and correspondence is a human being's goodness or excellence as a person. Goodness is not a matter of usefulness. There is no hint here of the pragmatic basis of Heidegger's account.[27] Goodness is simply one of four equivalent ways of characterizing what is. To the point that something can be characterized by one of these predicates, they all apply to it. To lack any one of them is to lack all of them.

If we grant this, then to the extent that something is evil, it lacks not just goodness but also being, unity, and truth. Its lack of being will give it the substanceless character of a dream. By virtue of its lack of unity or self-identity, our experience of it will be marked by a lack of focus, an inability to pin it down. The same holds for our attempts to get at the "truth" of it. It will constantly elude us, its evasions appearing to us as "lies."[28] Of course, to assume that they are such is to assume something is there to which they do not correspond. Yet, given that evil also lacks being, this itself appears as a deception. It is part of evil's self-concealment.[29] As such, it reminds us of Marlow's description of the station manager's smile as a "a door opening into a darkness he had in his keeping." Did the smile conceal something or was there nothing there to conceal? The answer of "philosophical rationality" that there is "nothing there" implies that we are at its limits, i.e., that we cannot use its concepts to grasp what is within.

The "Givenness" of Evil

Such thoughts on the limits of philosophical rationality imply that ethics, if it is to come to terms with evil, must move beyond the traditional ontological concepts that mark Western philosophy. The "is-not" of evil cannot be grasped or described by either the Heideggerian or Augustinian accounts of being. For Levinas, in fact, no ontological account is adequate. "The 'quality' of evil," he writes, "is . . . non-integratableness itself." As such, we cannot position it in any account of what is. It simply cannot be synthesized, i.e., integrated through the use of appropriate categories into some greater ontological whole. In his words: "Evil is not only the non-integratable, it is also the non-integratableness of the non-integratable" (Levinas 1998, 128).[30] If this were literally true, then it could never be given or described in terms of what is. The "out-of-placeness" that we have used to categorize it would neither be an ontological nor a descriptive category. It would be a designation of an absence that left no trace behind. In fact, however, this category points to evil's special type of givenness. The nonappearing of evil is an active self-concealment. In such action, it gives itself as out-of-place, i.e., as what cannot be placed. Phenomenologically, it appears with the givenness of what cannot be given, of what cannot be integrated into the context of appearing.

The best way to see this is through some examples. As Fackenheim observes, a "single incident," occurring during Eichmann's trial in Jerusalem, was sufficient to demolish the claim that there were no independent actors in the Holocaust, only an escalating "system." He writes: "The accused had preserved a stolid composure throughout his trial. One day the room was darkened and pictures of Eichmann's victims were flashed on the screen. Secretly, a camera was trained on him in the dark. Believing himself unobserved, Eichmann saw what he saw—and smirked."[31] This minor detail gives what refuses to be given in the context of Eichmann's defense. It points to a hidden complicity of the doer and the deed, a complicity that positions Eichmann as something more than a "cog in the wheel." Conrad's *Heart of Darkness* is filled with a host of similarly revealing details. There is, for example, the "gentle annoyance" of the accountant with the "groans" of the dying agent in his badly constructed office. There is the contrast of his impeccable appearance—"high starched collar, white cuffs, a light alpaca jacket, snowy trousers, a clear necktie, and varnished boots" (Conrad 1989, 45)—with the rags wrapped around the loins of the prisoners outside the shed. What appears in both cases is a concern for human misery that should be present but is not. The "is not" of the lack of concern unsettles the description. A similar unease is felt when we are told of a painting made by Kurtz "representing a woman, draped and blindfolded, carrying a lighted torch" (54). The description makes us ask: For whom is the torch lit? How can she light the way for (or lead) anyone in her "stately" progress if she herself is blind?[32] The unease we feel here is over the absence of sight. It is through the addition of such details and the questions they raise about what should be but *is not* present that we gain a sense of the evil that pervades the whole enterprise. Marlow's descriptions never directly point to it. There is never an unmasking that directly exhibits the sense or meaning of evil. Instead, he proceeds by indirection. As Conrad describes his storytelling: "To him the meaning of an episode was not inside like a kernel but outside, enveloping the tale which brought it out only as a glow brings out a haze, in the likeness of one of those misty halos that are sometimes made visible by the spectral illumination of moonshine" (30). It is in the descriptions of the surrounding details, rather than in the plot, that the meaning unfolds.

Grasping the absent by the halo, that is, by the details that frame what should be present but is not, Conrad describes evil in terms of its self-concealment. The very uneasiness his descriptions provoke points to the absence behind the appearance. This uneasiness is itself a giving of what cannot be given. In Marlow's tale, then, the journey down the Congo to find Kurtz is a voyage into the "heart of darkness"—not in its storyline, but in its relating of what seems to be both inappropriate and incidental to the enterprise. It is, in its telling, an attempt to "see" the "is-not" of evil by describing it through its surrounding halo. Evil, here, is recognized by what should be present but is not. To describe the giving of the absent is precisely to call attention to the "smirk" of Eichmann, to the "gentle annoyance" of the accountant, to the unease occasioned by the empty "smile" that sealed all the station manager's remarks, etc. In each case there is a disturbance of presence, an inappropriateness that points to a tearing of the context of sense. To be sensitive to this is to be aware of the giving of the absent; it is to grasp the peculiar "is not" that characterizes evil in its self-concealment.[33]

Stereotyping and Good Sight

Pascal, in his *Penseés*, describes two different types of mind. The first, the "geometrical intelligence" (*l'esprit de géométrie*) proceeds deductively from a small number of definite principles. These principles are "remote from ordinary usage." Yet once we grasp them, we can reason securely. The second, the "subtle intelligence" (*l'esprit de finesse*), proceeds by regarding a host of details. Its "principles," Pascal writes, "are so subtle and so numerous that it is almost impossible that some will not escape notice" (Pascal 1960, 264). He adds, "They are scarcely seen; they are felt rather than seen; there is the greatest difficulty in making them felt by those who do not of themselves perceive them" (265). What is required for this mind is "good sight." (ibid., p. 264). Having this, we "see the matter at once, at one glance and not by a process of reasoning . . ." (265). In Marlow's tale, we have in its wealth of details the results of such "good sight." To read it is to experience an education of our sensibility, a training of the *esprit de finesse* that allows us to grasp the absent by the present.[34]

What we are actually being sensitized to see is the situating frame, the context in terms of which we interpret what we see. Eichmann's "smirk" is revealing in its inappropriateness. It does not fit in with the context of the trial and the pictures of his victims. Similarly, the annoyance of the accountant is out of place in the presence of the dying agent. Such out-of-placeness points to the action of evil, which is that of undermining the context in which such elements would appear as inappropriate. For the accountant, this action is complete. He does not see the inappropriateness of his keeping an accurate account of an essentially senseless enterprise. The self-concealment of evil manifests itself in his remark that "everything here . . . is very satisfactory" (Conrad 1989, 47). In grasping the context, we apprehend the inappropriateness of this remark. Doing so, we see what should be present, but is not. The absence that we are brought to regard—here, the accountant's lack of concern for the agent—is the givenness of evil in its quality as "that which is-not." The categories of being-in-place and being-out-of-place, while acknowledging what Levinas rightly calls the "non-integratable-ness" of evil, capture this regard. This is because out-of-placeness refers to and is framed by the in-placeness it disturbs. Thus, the "good sight" that allows us to grasp the "in-place" is essential if we are to regard the "out-of-place." Without it, we do not have the context for grasping the "is-not" of evil.

Stereotyping is, of course, the opposite of "good sight." In its refusal to look beyond what fits a pregiven set of concepts, it limits what we can see. It thus makes invisible the context that could call these concepts into question—i.e., the context in terms of which they might be deemed inappropriate. Thus, for the accountant the natives are all "savages." They and the dying agent are seen only as disturbing factors—obstacles to his keeping accurate accounts. They cannot call into question the appropriateness of this action—i.e., question its lack of fit with the misery that forms its context. For this, a face-to-face encounter would be necessary. But such an encounter is precisely what stereotyping prevents. It prevents him from actually facing the dying man within or the natives outside. If he could face them, his categories could be called into question. The blinders they impose could be lifted. In other words, just as stereotyping closes off good sight, so the face-to-face opens us up to it. Situating us within a context that includes our alternatives (those, e.g., represented by Marlow, Kurtz, the agent, and the natives), it confronts us with the exceeding quality of life. In doing so, it opens us up to a set of "principles" that, in Pascal's words, "are so fine and so numerous that a very delicate and a very clear sense is needed to perceive them" (Pascal 1960, 265). When we do perceive such principles, we apprehend the being-in-place that is determined by their locating context. The action here is the opposite of evil, understood as an out-of-placeness that destroys the context of sense. The action of evil ends with the type of paradox Fackenheim uncovers as he moves between the paltriness of Hitler and the virulence of the evil he released. The context that would relate the two, that would make sense of this relation, is not present. To make it present, the evil would have to be undone. One would have to undo the Holocaust relation by relation, substituting, in each case, an actual encounter for a stereotype. Since, however, we cannot undo the past, the senselessness of the relation between Hitler and the evil he engendered (as between Kurtz and the "horror" he caused) remains. The most good sight can do is to regard this lack of sense, to catch sight of it as the camera did in recording Eichmann's smirk.

Tolerance as an Ethical Ideal

To draw a practical ethics from the above requires that we speak of goodness, not just as the opposite of evil, but as a positive, practical ideal. There are a number of ways to express this ideal. In Darwinian terms, it appears in the way that each species places others, each helping to provide the niches in which others can flourish. Thus, the cat is crucial to the success of red clover and the humble bee; similarly, the otter is required for the flourishing of the marine life that lives within kelp forests. For Darwin, these examples point to "Nature" in its action of seeking its own good through the diversity of its species. The Darwinian ideal this manifests is that of maximizing life by promoting diversity of structure. The greatest possible diversification consistent with the order involved in species placing species is the "good" towards which "Nature" tends in its seeking the benefit of each organism. "Nature," for Darwin, is simply a personification of "natural preservation or survival of the fittest"; it is shorthand for the action of evolution. The ideal it embodies, however, is not limited to natural processes. This is shown by the theological cast Leibniz gave this ideal in the seventeenth century. In his *Monadology*, he states that the mind of God, in its "ideas," contains "an infinity of possible universes." There must, he argues, have been a reason sufficient "for him to select one rather than another" to exist. This reason is found "in the fitness or in the degree of perfection" of the one chosen. God, in other words, always chooses the best. Thus, given that each "possible thing" has "the right to claim existence in proportion to the perfection which it involves," the universe that actually does exist must have "the greatest possible perfection." (Leibniz 1962, 262–63; §§53–54). It achieves this, according to Leibniz, by having "the greatest possible variety, together with the greatest order that may be" (263; §58). Order comes from God's "adapting" each substance to every other, such that each gives a "reason" or cause for what occurs in the others (262; §52). Variety comes from the plurality of different substances involved in this web of mutual determination. Each works to position all the others as uniquely situated perspectives on the whole (263; §56). To translate these Leibnizian and Darwinian ideals into human terms is to see them in relation to the contexts of sense—social, religious, economic, and so on—that are specifically human. So regarded, the ideal becomes one of the "fullness" (or filling out) of the possibilities of being human through the maximum of cultural diversity consistent with social harmony.

To see "tolerance" as an ethical expression of this ideal, we must turn from its negative sense, which ranges from suffering or enduring evils to the forbearance or sufferance of what one actually does not approve. The various "edicts of tolerance" of the seventeenth and eighteenth centuries embody the latter sense. They were formulated to permit the practice of sects that were distinct from the officially approved religion.[35] "Tolerance," in its *positive* sense, embodies the Darwinian and Leibnizian ideals of diversity and order. Taken in its original Latin sense of "supporting" or "sustaining,"[36] it can be understood as the attitude that actively sustains the maximum number of compatible possibilities of being human. As such, it is a condition for our advance towards the ideal of human "fullness." To call such "fullness" an *ideal* points to the fact that no given state of humanity is to be regarded as completely filling out the possibilities of being human. Rather than being identifiable with any actual state of humanity, such fullness is, rather, a goal for an ongoing process. At each stage of the advance towards the goal, the current possibilities of being human permit new intentions to arise that point toward the realization of further possibilities. The accomplishment of human speech, for example, opens up a whole range of further possibilities—civil society, commerce, and so on—to the possibility of being actualized. Each of these, when actualized in some particular way, points, in anticipation, to further potentialities. Thus, printing opens up the possibility of mass literacy, which, in turn, opens up the cultural possibilities that depend on this. Each advance towards the goal can be seen as providing a context of sense out of which arise the intentions towards the next advance. Such contexts can be seen as analogous to the ecological niches species provide for each other in their ongoing evolution. Each niche, once opened, can be taken as a possibility waiting to be realized. It forms an intention within the process of natural selection as it tends towards greater and greater complexity.[37]

While tolerance in the human sense is not implicit in natural selection, it is inherent in the ideal of human fullness. It appears when we acknowledge our finitude in attempting to embody this ideal. An individual can realize one aspect of human fullness—i.e., realize one possibility of his being—only by neglecting others. He cannot simultaneously train to be a weight lifter and a sprinter. Having engaged in a specific course of action, his finitude prevents him from engaging in others.

Thus, the ideal of human fullness demands more than himself. Its progressive realization through finite individuals is necessarily collective. To embrace this ideal, I must, then, affirm the other and his (or her) possibilities. This affirmation, as Edmund Husserl pointed out, is not an adoption. Mutual tolerance does not require that we affirm *as our own* one another's goals. Rather, as Husserl writes, I affirm "his ideals as his, as ideals which I must affirm in him, just as he must affirm my ideals—not, indeed, as his ideals of life but as the ideals of my being and life" (MS. E III 1, p. 7). The same point holds with regard to different societies. Societies are "not egotistical"—i.e., *not intolerant*—he writes, if they can affirm one another's "particular goals and particular accomplishments" (MS. A V 24, p. 4).[38] This point follows automatically from our finitude. As finite, individuals and their societies can pursue only limited sets of goals. Both, however, can tolerate others in the pursuit of their goals. Negatively, this implies not interfering with their pursuit. Positively, in the sense that actively promotes the ideal of human fullness, it implies "sustaining" and "supporting" such pursuit insofar as it leads to the maximum realization of compatible possibilities.

Intolerance, as the opposite of tolerance, promotes, not progress, but rather retreat from the ideal of human fullness. It does this by attempting to narrow (or, at least, hold static) the meaning of being human. Since the advance towards human fullness implies the affirmation of others as other—i.e., as expressing alternative ways of human being and behaving—intolerance, as the opposite, blocks this advance by a corresponding denial. Engaging in it, I deny the humanity of the others expressing such alternatives. The following dialogue from *Huckleberry Finn* in which Huck explains to his aunt Sally why he is late, provides an example of this attitude.

> "It warn't the grounding—that didn't keep us back but a little. We blowed out a cylinder head."
> "Good gracious! anybody hurt?"
> "No'm. Killed a nigger."
> "Well, it's lucky; because sometimes people do get hurt." (Clemens 1977, 216).

The stereotyping implicit in this racist remark is obvious: only whites count as "people" for the aunt. Engaging in intolerance, we do not recognize others in their alterity. Stereotyping these others, we view them through our pregiven conceptions. What we already "know" determines what we will accept as human. What fails to satisfy this, we dismiss ahead of time. As history shows, such an attitude can lead to genocide when widespread. With the destruction of a people, the context of sense they embodied also goes. When, for example, the Jewish communities of Eastern Europe were destroyed, the possibilities of being and behaving—of interpreting the world from their situated standpoints—also vanished.

The result of the Holocaust was, in fact, a permanent foreclosure of possibilities—an actual regress from the ideal of human fullness. In a certain sense, the possibility of such foreclosure is inherent in human finitude. An individual, because he is finite, must forego some possibilities when he actualizes others. Of course, since he is part of humanity, such possibilities, at least in a generic sense, are not permanently lost. Someone else is always free to take them up. When, however, humanity closes off a possibility for itself, it cannot appeal to another collectivity to make good this loss. There is no collectivity beyond itself. As for itself, its own finitude is shown by the fact that it has not the resources to make good this loss. It is, itself, only a contingently situated, finite totality of individuals. The possibilities these individuals actualize are not the totality that could be actualized. They represent a limited, contingent set of resources, one that its past actions have either enriched or diminished. Their diminution is, however, precisely the impoverishment of the context of sense from which the intentions to add to their store must arise.

An essential dimension of human finitude arises from the type of whole it forms. Its nonfoundational character is such that humanity's powers to determine itself are always limited. As noted earlier, the whole is one of individuals determining environments that, in turn, determine individuals. Such a whole has no first cause, no initiating set of agents that could serve as levers for our action. In other words, since humanity does not form a systematic structure, with clear principles and beginnings, it is not amenable to the kind of precise control that could restore its losses. Were the individuals and groups composing humanity essentially identical and, hence, replaceable, such losses could, of course, be made good again. Its nonfoundational nature, however, is such that there is no "Adam" that can be posited as a model for the persons composing humanity. Positively, this signifies that every person is unique and, hence, irreplaceable. So are the ethnic groups that these unique individuals form. Negatively, this irreplaceability signifies that *we have not the resources* to make up their loss. It is, in fact, only on the average that humanity in its possibilities makes good the loss of a single individual. It cannot restore the unique combination that was the person. When an entire ethnic group is lost, its resources are even more limited. To think that the loss of a people is not permanent is, in fact, to take up the attitude that tends to promote such loss. Humanity can be conceived as a set of manipulable determinants only from a standpoint external to humanity. Within humanity, one is caught within its web of mutual determination. The independence required for complete control, thus, demands the adoption of an external, objective relation to the human whole. The out-of-place-ness here assumed is, of course, that of Kurtz or the Nazis. The attitude it characterizes is also a human possibility. It points, however, not toward humanity's restoration, but rather toward its impoverishment.

As the mention of Kurtz and the Nazis indicates, tolerance does not embrace all possibilities. Only those possibilities that do not permanently exclude other possibilities fall within its purview. This means that, as a *positive*, practical ideal, tolerance embraces as values to be realized only certain possibilities: those that permit the actualization of further possibilities within the horizon of being human. Those whose actualization results in harm, in the narrowing of an individual's potentiality for humanity, it forbids as a *negative* command. If it did not forbid them, it would contradict itself. It would be directed to the goal of fullness of human being and, at the same time, embrace actions contrary to this goal's realization. A few common examples will make this clear. Tolerance, understood negatively as a prohibition—ultimately, as a prohibition of intolerance—forbids lying and theft. The first, to the point that it is collectively actualized, undermines the possibility of speech to communicate verifiable information. Thus, lying undermines those human possibilities, such as civil society, that presuppose this possibility. Theft, when collectively actualized, has a similar effect on the possibility of possession and, hence, on the possibilities, such as commerce, springing from this. Insofar as lying and theft cut off such possibilities, they result in a narrowing of human potentialities and are actually acts of intolerance. Most of the standard rules of morality are in fact directed against such narrowing. Engaging in the acts prohibited by them, we do harm to our neighbors in the sense of preventing the development of their possibilities. Similarly, the injunction to treat others as we would like to be treated is actually a command that allows us both to participate in the mutually enriching expansion of our potentialities.

As directed towards this expansion, tolerance is not a static notion. Its structure at any given time is determined by the stage of our advance towards the ideal of human fullness. The possibilities present at a given stage determine what is compossible with them. They also set what must be overcome insofar it retards this advance. At the present time, for example, the achievements of information technology lead to an ever increasing process of economic and cultural globalization. To the point that the uniformity this imposes undoes the richness and diversity of human being, it represents a danger for humanity. The same holds for the abilities that have been developed for genetic manipulation. They open the possibility of imposing a biological uniformity on humans and the species we depend on, which would represent a regress in terms of the ideal. In each case, what gives sense to the stance humanity adopts are the compatible possibilities that compose the human frame. They set the limits on what can be sensibly intended (or proposed as a goal), and what cannot. It is, for example, senseless to propose the sacrifice of humanity in terms of some transcendent goal, as senseless as proposing the replacement of humanity with some new redesigned form. In each case the objective exceeds any possible context that could give it an intelligible human sense.

The overall imperative here is that of not making choices one cannot provide a context for. One should not, for example, engage in heroic medical intervention to save an infant without also committing an equal effort to supply it with the caregivers and support the infant will need when it leaves the hospital. The latter provide the necessary frame in which the medical act makes sense. The absence of such a frame is the reason why medical ethicists are so often called upon to make impossible decisions. What is lacking is neither skill nor knowledge, but rather the context in which these can be successfully employed. No "practically oriented" ethics, no professional skilled in its practice, can compensate for a systematic lack of medical or social resources. Going to such a professional for a quick solution (an instant answer) to a systemic problem manifests an attitude that is itself problematic. When, for example, it is asked whether a hospital should spend its scarce resources on infant crib monitors or on an indigent child who desperately needs a costly operation, the question may not just turn on the value of present life versus that of future infants. It may also conceal a demand for a cost-benefit or "economic" response, in which the ethicist is called upon to decide the "best" economic allocation of scarce resources. By definition, such a response must ignore the uniqueness of the individuals involved. But attending to this uniqueness is precisely what an ethical response requires. Its imperative is that of providing the context in which alterity and singularity can appear. This requires "tolerance" in the sense of bearing or supporting the costs that this involves.

The definition of goodness in terms of "in-placeness" thus leads to the imperative of providing places. The ethics that follows from this attempts to do justice to the necessity of framing, i.e., placing human being. Does it also match the need humans have to escape from the frame, that is, transcend their context in order to judge it? To answer this, it is necessary to show how our transcendence is inherent in the human frame itself. At issue here is the frame as the origin of our freedom.

6

Freedom and Alterity

The Out-of-Placeness of Freedom

There is a ready objection to the description of good and evil in terms of the environmental categories of "in-placeness" and "out-of-placeness." It is that "out-of-placeness," rather than characterizing evil, is essential to ethics. This is because the possibility of ethics is that of freedom. To be free, however, is to be "out-of-place." It is, in Sartre's words, the "possibility, which human reality has, to secrete a nothingness which isolates it" (Sartre 1966, 60). This "isolation" is our separation from our environment. Because we can escape its determination we can ethically appraise and act to change our situation. Given this, we cannot assert that "in-placeness" is a sufficient basis for ethics. Ethics involves judging the frame we have been placed in. Thus, animals are "in" nature, framed by their environment; yet we cannot say that they are ethical. Neither can we say that "goodness," defined in environmental terms, has an ethical component. What is lacking is freedom, the very freedom that separates us from nature.

The philosopher Luc Ferry formulates this objection in terms of our unnaturalness. He writes:

> [M]an is the antinatural being par excellence. . . . This is how he escapes natural cycles, how he attains the realm of culture, and the sphere of morality, which presupposes living in accordance with laws and not just with nature. It is because humankind is not bound to instinct, to biological processes

147

alone, that it possesses a history, that generations follow one
another but do not necessarily resemble each other—while the
animal kingdom observes perfect continuity. (Ferry 1995, xxviii)

What distinguishes man is his freedom. In Ferry's words, "His humanitas
resides in his freedom, in the fact that he is undefined, that his nature is to
have no nature but to possess the capacity to distance himself . . ." (5).
This capacity allows us to have culture, history, and so on. Instead of
simply repeating the biologically determined patterns of the past, we can
distance ourselves from our predecessors, judge their achievements, and
advance culturally. The fact that animals cannot do this shows that the
inner distance implied by freedom and required for cultural advance is
not part of nature.[1] That it is not is also shown by the distinction between
acting freely and being determined by an "interest." Nature acts according to interests. Thus, animals act prompted by the advantages that their
circumstances offer. Freedom, however, consists in the ability to abstract
from interests. As Ferry notes, in reference to Kant, "it is . . . the ability
to separate oneself from interests (freedom) that defines dignity and
makes the human being alone a legal subject" (32). Being such a subject
requires "a refusal to allow oneself to be limited to any particularity"
(15). It requires the self-distancing that permits us to view ourselves from
the perspective of a law applying to everyone.[2] Doing so, we disregard
the interests that arise through our particular situations. We consider ourselves as subjects, not of our environment, but of a universal law. Now,
the fact that we can do this leads to what is, arguably, Kant's central
insight: As free beings, the only thing that can bind us to follow the
moral law is ourselves. Ethics, in other words, is a matter of self-limitation.[3] Thus, we need ethics precisely because, unlike the animals, we have
escaped the control of nature. Having distanced ourselves from it, we are
not subject to its laws or constraints. Ethics, then, does not just demand
for its possibility the separation of the self from nature. As self-limitation,
it is a necessary response to the freedom that accompanies this.

   In essence, then, Ferry's objection is that, rather than being a
matter of fitting in with some pregiven circumstances, ethics implies a
radical subjective autonomy. Its possibility is that of the subject that has
freed itself from any frame in which it might appear.[4] At least in outline,
my answer to this is apparent from the preceding chapters. I do not deny
the necessity of freedom, but only the characterization of it as out-of-
placeness. The independence and autonomy of the subject, rather than a
manifestation of placelessness, is a function of the subject being framed
by its others. Human subjects abstract each other from "nature" in the
Kantian sense. What makes this abstraction possible, what sets human

subjects apart from the animal world, is language. An inherently inter-subjective phenomenon, language is essential to the way in which we frame each other. It is what makes the alterity implicit in human life capable of freedom.

Freedom and Causality

Ferry's objection is based on the distinction Kant draws between nature and freedom. The response to this objection will thus be clearer if we grasp the difficulty this distinction conceals. Essentially, it involves the fact that "nature" for Kant designates the appearing world, a world that he takes as causally determined. Everything appears within "nature"; within it, however, nothing occurs without being caused by something else. Freedom, taken as the ability to act independently, is thus limited to the nonappearing world. This, according to Kant, is the "noumenal" world, the world as it is in itself. The self that is part of this world—the noumenal, nonappearing self—is the self that is free and, hence, capable of moral action. The difficulty here is not just in our recognizing a moral agency that can never appear. It is that our positing of nature as causally determined depends upon such recognition. Its conception implies others like ourselves, i.e., subjects that enjoy an autonomy similar to our own.

To see this, we may begin by asking why Kant assumes that the appearing world is causally determined. Kant's response is that we make this assumption in order, as it were, to get out of our heads. We need it to move from assertions that are merely true for us and our subjective flow of perceptions to those that can claim an objective validity. Suppose, for example, I regard a house. As Kant writes, "[M]y perceptions could begin with the apprehension of the roof and end with the basement, or could begin from below and end above." This subjective flow of perceptions is particular to me. It depends, for example, on the way I turn my head. To transform it into more than this, I need "a rule that makes the order in which the perceptions follow upon one another a necessary order" (Kant 1955c, 221; B238). If it is a necessary order, then it does not just pertain to me and my private experience. Everyone else in viewing what I see will experience the same sequence. The point is that being in a common objective world presupposes a common temporal ordering of our perceptions.[5] Thus, when I assert that an objective event has occurred, I presuppose that the sequence of perceptions by which I grasp it is the same as that experienced by others who see it.[6] A common sequence gives us a common, objective sense. It can be common, however, only if its ordering is necessary rather than random. Causality enters into this picture because Kant, following Hume, defines causality in just these terms. Phenomenologically speaking, the assertion that A causes B is simply the claim that the perception of A is always followed by that of B. For Kant, this means that I take their sequence as having a "necessary order." Thus, to assume a common, objective world is, for Kant, *also to assume* that its objects are causally determined. The upshot is that in the objective world nothing can be without its cause. Everything must have its "sufficient reason." Such necessity, of course, is not apprehended like a thing. It is not some object in the world. It is rather an interpretive stance or "category" I assume in relating my perceptions to a common world.

Kant's motives for developing this position are well known. He wants to show "how the science of nature is possible" (Kant 1955d, §§14–39). Natural science proceeds by making a few crucial experiments and then assumes that the causal sequence that is shown to obtain always holds when the same conditions are found. A strict empiricism, by contrast, would assert with Hume that the successful repetition of the experiment makes its outcome probable, but hardly necessary. This follows because everything established by experience can, by the same token, be overthrown by experience. Thus, there is no guarantee that the next experiment would not overturn our earlier results. Science, of course, asserts that its assurance follows not just from the repeated experience of a sequence of events, but from an actual insight into their cause. Hume, however, undermines this by pointing to the fact that we never actually "see" the necessity that is supposed to underlie causal connections. Our actual experience is simply that of sequences of appearances. Thus, as Kant himself admits, "No one will say that a category like causality will be intuited through sense and is itself contained in appearances." Consequently, the question Hume raises is: "How, then, is the . . . application of the category to appearances possible?" (Kant 1955c, 180; B177). Kant's answer is that, rather than being something that we experience, the category is what we impose on experience. It is, as noted, an interpretative stance we assume in talking about an objective world. Thus, when we transcend the mere subjective flow of our perceptions to speak about the world "out there," what we do is take each of its objects as an event, that is, as something determined in its present character by the events that preceded it. The stain on the ceiling, for example, is grasped as the result of a leak in the roof; the overturned chair is viewed as a result of someone having upset it. In each case, we take the present appearance as necessarily determined by what temporally preceded it— whether we happen to see this or not. So determined, the appearance has a definite temporal position. It is understood as a member in a necessary sequence of appearances, one open to everyone's inspection (Kant 1955c, 170–71; B239–40). Since, of course, we cannot see what others see, in the sense of looking through their eyes, we cannot actually verify that others experience the same perceptual sequences that we do. From Kant's perspective, however, this is beside the point. Causality, taken as a category, is not something we arrive at by consulting other subjects. It is, rather, something we assume in positing an objective world, the world "out there" in which our other subjects are placed. Understood as "nature," this world consists of the totality of what appears, its appearance being regulated by universal causal laws. Behind science's confidence in its experiments is, then, the fact that no objective experience could ever undermine this sense of "nature." This is because what does not conform to the category of causality cannot be taken as an objective experience. As soon as we fail to see appearances as events—that is, as definitely positioned in objective time by what preceded them—they lose their claim to be more than our private perceptions.

The point of Kant's argument is not just to secure science from Hume's skepticism. It is also to secure human freedom by reducing causality to an interpretative category, one that applies to appearances (to their necessary order) rather than to things in themselves. The result is a double transcendence of the subject "in itself." Ontologically, the subject's transcendence of the appearing world is based on its not being subordinate to the interpretative categories required to posit a common world. In itself, the subject is prior to them, serving as their origin. As prior, it escapes the interpretations that would situate it as part of a common world. It cannot be considered as framed or particularized by the objective environment it shares with its others. This ontological transcendence is mirrored by its ethical transcendence. As distinct from the appearing world, the subject can separate itself from the interests arising from it. Universalizing its maxims, it can see if they are consistent or inconsistent. It can, for example, see at once that if everyone made a false promise, such promises would not be believed. In guiding its conduct by such rational insights, it reveals the essential role that reason places in its ethical transcendence. This is because such transcendence is essentially a matter of its ability "to act in accordance with laws of reason independently of natural instincts" (Kant 1964, 127; 1955a, 120–21). Free subjects can do this precisely because "the laws of their operations" are not the causal laws "that govern their appearances" (1964, 127; 1955a, 121). The laws of their operations are those of reason. As such, they are distinct from the causal laws. Thus, as already noted, logical relations have to do with the formal contents of assertions. While we can specify the logical consistency of propositional contents independently of their temporal ordering, the laws of cause and effect describe the temporal relations that determine events (see above, p. 63). Here, as is obvious, the transcendence of freedom is one with that of reason. I am free, according to Kant, to the degree that I act in accordance with the laws of reason. Contrariwise, to the degree that reason determines my conduct, I am free. This mutual implication of reason and freedom forms for Kant the content of my ethical selfhood. For such selfhood, reason, as determinative, has a practical effect.

Achieving this selfhood involves the subject's "thinking itself into the intelligible world," the world in which reason is operative (Kant 1964, 126; 1955a, 118). This world, however, is not one that appears. "The concept of the intelligible world is, thus," Kant admits, "only a point of view which reason finds itself constrained to adopt outside of appearances in order to conceive itself as practical" (1964, 126; 1955a, 119). The difficulty with adopting this point of view has already been noted. It is that the supposed practical effect of reason—that is, its exercising a real causality in our affairs—is by definition excluded from the world of appearances. Thus, as soon as I take up the interpretative stance that allows me to assume that I do experience objects "out there," I exclude such rational agency from the field of appearances. Such agency is, however, my very selfhood. The laws of its operation pertain to me as a thing-in-itself. Given this, I must presuppose it, not just with regard to myself, but also with regard to all other subjects that I take to be like me. Now, such subjects are precisely those whom I presuppose in my thought of a common world. This is because the supposition of a common world is based on assuming that I am not alone in the world, but that there are others *like me*, viewing it as I do. The fact that I must assume that my sequence of perceptions is the same as theirs, i.e., that a necessary ordering informs our apprehension of this world, means that the world that we do apprehend stands under universal causal laws. As such, however, it excludes the subjects that I must assume in its positing. Thus, the interpretative stance that takes nature as causally determined hides from me the other subjects that this stance presupposes. Given this, why should I assume them? What permits me to exclude the possibility that there are no others, that I am, in fact, alone? The specter of solipsism that here arises signifies that Kant's account of our ontological and ethical transcendence presupposes what it cannot provide: the presence of our others. Without subjects like ourselves, we cannot posit the appearing world as causally determined; without this determination, the sense of our transcendence with regard to it breaks down. Lacking this sense, we cannot maintain the dichotomy between nature and freedom that is at the basis of Ferry's objection.

The question that this analysis leaves us with is that of the common world. How do we understand it as including the subjects its sense presupposes? For such subjects to appear as part of this world they have to give themselves as vulnerable to its assaults, as subject to the effects of its causal agency. Yet, they must, as transcendent, also give themselves as not being able to be given in such terms. They must, in other words, show themselves as incapable of being interpreted according to the categories that we impose in assuming a common world. The very notion of subjects' being given as not being able to be given seems impossible from the Kantian perspective. For Kant, the nongiven (or noumenal) in *founding* the given hides itself. If, however, the nongiven were *founded by* the given, common world, then its nonappearing would be a function of this world's givenness: the appearing, common world would give the nonappearing as not being able to be given. What is implied here is, then, a reversal of the relation of subjects to this appearing world. For Kant, the appearance of the common world is explained in terms of the functioning of a hidden subjectivity. Such subjectivity is ontologically and morally prior to this world. The reversal would take the common world in its givenness as first, and subjects in their inability to be given as founded on this. In other words, it would explain the hiddenness of subjects—understood as their transcendence and freedom—in terms of the appearance of the common world. Given in terms of this world, subjects would, through the very appearing of the world, give themselves as escaping its appearing.

Hiddenness

What is called for in the above reversal is an analysis of hiddenness in terms of appearance. What objectively appears is the world that I share with my others. My original sharing was with the flesh of my mother. In this original identity, we cannot really speak of a shared world, since the alterity implied by the notion of commonality is not yet present. Even after birth the alterity of my first other—my mother or my caregiver—is not apparent to me. Thus, as earlier noted, I initially take this other as simply the completion of my system of states and needs (see above, p. 113). My caregiver appears to me to be an extension of my "I can." It is only gradually that I distinguish between the control of my own body and of that of my caregivers. The breakup of this original identity of child and caregiver has a triple effect. It yields my *sense of the world as common* to myself and my others. This sense develops along with my understanding of these others. I can, for example, gain a sense of a world that is common to adults and children only when I have some grasp of these states. Coincident with this, the breakup also yields my *sense of intentionality* in its original meaning as a stretching out or straining towards something. Originally, this straining is towards the other as the object of all my needs. Its effort, as we saw, was to reestablish the original identity. This effort continues, with appropriate modifications, as my sense of the alterity of my others develops. Now, by virtue of its origin in subjective need, intentionality has a characteristic feature in all its subsequent developments, in all the extensions of its intending beyond the original caregiver to objects in general. Engaged in it, the subject is there at the object of its intending. With this comes the *sense of the subject's hiddenness*. What is hidden is not the object of intentionality, but rather the subject who engages in it.

This characteristic is behind the fact that when I face another person, I am aware that the contents of her consciousness are not my own, that they are, in fact, hidden from me. When we both regard a common object, I usually assume that the sight that fills our consciousness is roughly the same. If I doubt this, I can ask her, and adjust my viewpoint. I cannot, however, see what she sees when she faces me. Because I cannot see myself, the content of her consciousness seems to form a hidden sphere. When I then say to myself, "I am a subject just as she is," I assume that I also have such hiddenness. Of course, relative to this person, I do. Facing her, I see what she cannot see—namely herself. But this realm of privateness is not really shut off, not something apart from the common world. In this world we both appear. What is actually at work here is my own self-hiddenness. My positing that the other has a hidden sphere is based on the fact that I cannot see myself. This self-hiddenness, mediated through the other's facing me, makes me posit myself as hidden from the other. Hiddenness, here, is not shut off from appearing, since its basis is the stretching forth of the intentionality, the directedness towards objects, that first makes things appear. As intentional, consciousness is inherently transcendent. Originating in our bodily needs, needs that are fulfilled by the presence of the object, intentionality evacuates consciousness in favor of the object. The result is that what fills intentional consciousness is not itself, but rather the object intended.[7] Because of this, every act of perception hides the perceiver. Every act shoves the perceiver into the background even as it moves the object into the foreground.

As Merleau-Ponty noted, this foreground-background structure is essential to consciousness. In fact, it *is* consciousness in its intentional structure.[8] This is because this structure, having originated in bodily need, is based on our embodied being-in-the-world. Our body's senses are primarily directed outward. Turning our heads, focusing our eyes, and moving closer to get a better look are all tied to bringing an object into the foreground. When we turn away from it, it sinks into the background as another object occupies our consciousness. Given our embodied finitude, we can only turn in one direction at a time. The other directions form its horizon. They indicate the possibilities of our bodily "I can," that is, the set of bodily abilities that relate us to the world. Such abilities allow us to be in the world in the sense of having bodily projects. Inserted by our bodies into the world, we use them to manipulate its objects to satisfy our needs. Every such project involves our own hiddenness. For example, someone is knocking and I walk to the door. Perceptually, it is not I myself but the door that fills my consciousness. My thought runs ahead of me and sees me there at the door already reaching with my hand to open it. Already, in intention, awaiting myself at the goal, I thrust my present situation into the background.

The above implies a certain reversal in the sense of intentionality. It implies that rather than being a movement from an essentially private subject to a public object, it is actually the reverse. Intentionality begins with the object taken as what is (or will be) publicly available. Its origin is what transcends the private in its being there for everyone. This is because our being-in-the-world is primordially public. This public quality is implicit in the sense of hiddenness just developed. At its basis is the lack of any private content in the self-evacuation (the self-transcendence) of the perceptual act. If we start with such self-transcendence, we have to say that first we are out there among the things, and then we posit the private sphere from which we suppose our intentions originate. In other words, given that our being there (our *Da-sein*) is originally with the object of our intentions, it is our withdrawal into hiddenness—a withdrawal originally accomplished in childhood—that stretches out this thereness to yield intentionality in the traditional sense. Thus, our intentions transcend our private sphere because they begin outside of this. Their starting point is not, as Kant thought, a merely subjective representation. It is our being-in-the-world outside of ourselves. The selfhood we do transcend is, in this context, a hiddenness in the world we are "in," a hiddenness that owes its origin to the intentionality that directs us to this world.

It is possible to express this relation of self and world in biological terms. Biologically regarded, selfhood is sometimes supposed to be a matter of brain function. In this pound and a half of gray matter lie all our memories, intelligence, ambitions, and projects—in short, the totality of what is a self. All this, we are told, is present in the brain. Yet as long as we remain with this reductionist account, the nature of its presence in the brain seems inexplicable. This is because, biologically regarded, the brain is similar to a large secreting gland. Its pathways, the neurons, are long thin tubes "along which waves of chemical change pass . . . " (Dawkins 1995, 15). The effect of this "chemical pulse" is either to increase or decrease the firing (the sending off of chemical pulses) of the connected neurons. This is all that seems to happen as long as we limit our focus to what is occurring within our heads. Such a limitation, however, ignores the fact that the human brain along with the rest of the body is "in" the world. Having evolved in response to the world, its functioning cannot be understood apart from it. When, however, we regard the brain in terms of the world that is outside of it, we cease to regard it as simply a secreting gland. We have already placed it in an interpretative context that exceeds its structure as a series of chemical pathways. It now shares in the aboutness, and possesses the intentionality of an organism whose functioning must be understood in terms that exceed itself. In this, of course, it is not unique. All organisms evolve in terms of the world. Their functioning, insofar as it is directed to fill their bodily needs, is attuned to it. Since need is directed outward, they function with regard to what is not themselves. Thus, what they are "about" as they engage in their activities transcends their physical being. Inherently transcendent in having a world, they possess a primitive intentionality in being engaged in it. When and if in their evolutionary development they become conscious, their consciousness will share this aboutness. It will be intentional. It is only when we localize the brain's functioning in its physical structures and limit our attention to its chemistry that we lose the intentionality that is the point of this functioning. We do so because we lose the world, which is where intentionality must begin, given its basis in need. Abstracting from the world, we are in a situation analogous to someone examining the transistors of a radio and attempting to discover its function from its structure alone. In point of fact, the orchestra it receives is no more "in" the radio than the world is "in" my brain. The functioning of both involves, rather, their being-in-the-world. It begins with this.

The Visible and the Invisible

For the child, the sense of being-in-the-world starts with the caregiver. Initially, its intentionality begins with its straining towards the latter. The withdrawal into hiddenness that accompanies this gives the child its first sense of self-hiddenness, its first sense that it cannot see itself. This sense both begins with the other and is compensated for by the other. At the beginning, the infant expects "to experience sensations in the hands and feet of the other." Even later, the child assumes that the other can see through its eyes. Thus, it fails to turn its picture book about when "showing" it to the other (Soffer 1999, 158). When experience disappoints these expectations, the child learns that the other sees what he does not (namely himself), while he sees what the other does not (namely, the other). Together these imply that he can compensate for his lack of self-perception by relying on the other's perception of him. This is a strategy that serves us throughout our lives. Such reliance, however, involves us in a new hiddenness. To see this, we must first observe with Merleau-Ponty that "to see the other's body is to see my body as an object" (Merleau-Ponty 1968, 225). I need the other to gain an objective sense of myself. I can see my hand, but I cannot see my backside. To complete my body image I must acquire a sense of this from the other—originally from my caregiver. He has a backside, I must have one too. It is, in fact, the sight of the caregiver that originally brings a wholeness to the body that the child can only grasp in parts.[9] The other does not just allow me to grasp the integrity of my body as something that can be viewed in the round (something that has simultaneously both a front and a back). The other is also crucial for my sense that this body is capable of objective motion. As Merleau-Ponty observes, "[M]y body is never *in movement perspektivisch*, as are the other things" (224). I can leave other things behind. As I do, they become smaller. In their own change of position, they show first one perspective and then another. I cannot, however, leave my own body behind. It remains "here," never departing in space from me. To get a sense of its having an objective motion, of transiting in space like other objects, I must pair my body with another person's body. I must transfer to myself the sense of the other's moving from one position to another in the world. Thus, I need the other both for the sense of my being objectively out there in the world and as capable of objectively transiting it. Such being-in-the-world is never solipsistic. Its sense always presupposes the givenness of the other.

This presupposition involves me in a kind of alternating hiddenness. On the one side, I have the immediate sense of my body as mine—this is the body whose movement is "not perspectival." Broadly speaking, this is the body of the "I can," the body that I directly experience in my ability to move myself. On the other side, I have my body's sense as there in the world, as objectively present and moving within it. Now, the body in its first sense is invisible with regard to the second. My body's incapability of departing from me means that it is incapable of the perspectival unfolding that would allow it to objectively appear. Similarly, the body in this objective sense is invisible with regard to its first, immediate sense. In the sphere of what Husserl calls "my own" (*mir Eigenes*)—the sphere of the contents of *my* consciousness—I never leave the here. A movement from here to there in such a sphere cannot be made. The result of these two senses is an alternating invisibility or hiddenness, one that depends on the perspective we take. What we have, in fact, is the presence of the invisible in the visible. We are in the objectively appearing world because we are never alone. But this being-in-the-world is fissured. It conceals an invisibility, which is that of the body in its immediate presence. The body of "I can" cannot appear within it.

It is possible to interpret Kant's phenomenal-noumenal distinction in terms of this fissuring. If we make the perspective of the objective world our exclusive focus, making it the only access to the appearing world, then the invisibility of the "I can move myself" can be seen as the invisibility of freedom. Here the world, stripped of its self-movers, is made up of things that move only because others move them. It is the world of "nature" in the Kantian sense, a world in which every motion necessarily points back to an external mover. In such a world, I may see another person as a causal agent moving objects. In this, her causal agency is apparent. Yet I cannot see how this person could move herself. Objectively, the most I can imagine is a little person within her moving her. Since this fiction is untenable, I have to say that the assumption of her self-movement points to the nonappearing, noumenal realm, the realm in which I place her freedom. I can, of course, reverse this perspective. I can take the standpoint of the "I can move myself" my exclusive focus. When I do this, I have no problem grasping the self-movement of the other. The difficulty is that from this perspective "nature" disappears. All movements are interpreted as self-caused. Thus, this perspective makes me assume a universal animism.

Both perspectives are obviously one-sided. As already noted, the common world requires both standpoints. Thus, to place myself and my "I can" in space, I require the other. This other must be like me. He must, consequently, possess the freedom of the "I move myself." Of course, once I do place myself in the common world I share with my other, we both become objectively present in the world. The grasp of the common world marks the transition from the "I move myself" to the "I transit space" like other objects out there. To make it, of course, I need to transfer to myself the sense of the other person as also "in" space, the other as part of the objective world. Such an other, however, is not free but rather causally determined. He is in a world whose positing as objective assumes that there are no self-movers. The inference is that to enter the objective world, I need both perspectives. I have to grasp the other as both caused and free. The same holds for myself insofar as I enter this world by transferring his sense to myself.

There is, in fact, a dual transfer of sense, one that goes on simultaneously and continuously. I transfer my sense of freedom (my "I can") to the other to grasp him as a subject like myself. I also receive from him my sense of being an object in an objective world. As a result, we take on the dual sense of being both subjective and objective. We appear as both free and as caused, as both hidden from and present to the objective world. Thus, I take the other as vulnerable to the assaults of the world, as capable of being crushed by it. Yet I also take him as a free agent, as able to employ its causality to accomplish his purposes. Initiating a causal chain, he moves objects by moving himself. While his moving objects is apparent, his self-movement is not. Such movement, since its external cause is not apparent, conceals an essential hiddenness. In his appearing agency, *the other thus "gives" himself as not being able to be objectively given.* This giving points to his necessary role in the constitution of the objective world—the very world in which he cannot be given. In this world, he is "like me" in being both present and hidden. His nonappearing freedom does not conflict with his appearing agency—his ability to cause changes in objects. It is simply a function of the way bodies appear to their possessors. It marks the divide between the "owned" body that cannot appear perspectivally and yet can initiate action and the body that is taken as transiting space "out there." They are not two bodies, but rather one and same body viewed from the two standpoints required to constitute the objective world. This is the body that allows what from the first perspective is an independent self to appear from the second perspective as exercising its causality "in" space. The essential point here is that the resulting objective hiddenness of this self's agency is inherently intersubjective. It is not something prior to or extraneous to the intersubjective world. It is built into its constitution.

The Temporal Structure of Alterity

The two perspectives required for the intersubjective world correspond to two types of temporality. The temporality that corresponds to the "I move myself" begins with my registering my impressions as I move. Each impression is present to me as a now. Each is registered as a successive, content-filled moment. The pattern of what I register, once committed to my memory, allows me to anticipate as I go about my familiar tasks.[10] Suppose, for example, I reach for a glass. As my arm moves towards it, the fingers of my hand extend to its anticipated shape. My arm extends to its anticipated distance. Grasping the glass, I apply just enough strength to lift its anticipated weight. Knowing how to do this involves having the correct anticipations. This involves remembering and projecting forward my past experience as an anticipated pattern. In the performance of this action, each anticipation is matched by a corresponding perception. When the match is perfect, the action proceeds effortlessly, the flow of bodily and visual impressions being just what I expect. Over against this inner time consciousness of registered, remembered, and anticipated impressions, we have the temporality that corresponds to the objective world. While inner time is determined by the "I can," objective time measures objective movement. It corresponds to my body placed in space through my others—i.e., my body seen as transiting space. The moments of objective time are thus intersubjectively present. Rather than being given immediately through my registering my impressions, they are given through timepieces—be this the position of the arms of a clock, or the sun in the sky, or the shadow on the sundial. The presence of such moments is spatial. It is a question of the position of objects in objective space when I happen to inquire what time it is.

For a Kantian, objective time implies the necessary order of perceptions required for assuming a common world filled with things like timepieces and astronomical objects. It is the temporality of the causality of "nature." Inner time, by contrast, corresponds to the *I can move myself this way or that* and, hence, to the *I can experience sequences of perceptions this way or that*, e.g., see the house starting from the roof or starting from the basement. To the point that it dispenses with necessary sequences, inner time corresponds to my freedom. For Kant, one temporality rules the other out. I must abandon the perspective of inner time in order to enter the objective, common world. In fact, even in the realm of "inner sense," my freedom, given its noumenal character, cannot appear. By contrast, the view that I am advocating sees the common world as presupposing others and, hence, their inner temporality. Given this, we have to say that both forms of temporality are at work in its constitution. In the common world, inner time gives itself as not being able to be given. It gives itself as something that, from the perspective of the common world, appears as a disruption of the given.

The disruption occurs because the temporality of the "I can" is based on elements that cannot appear in the objective world. Everything I view in this world is, as I view it, "now." "Out there" in space, time is present only through my interpretation of the position of bodies. I look at my watch, regard the position of its hands, and say, "Now it is one o'clock." When I look again, I say, interpreting the change of position of the hands, "Now it is two o'clock." I thus can say, "An hour has passed." I do not, however, see this past hour "out there." To have a sense of pastness, I must turn inward and remember what has passed. I cannot, however, do this with regard to my other. Out there in space, he is simply now. His past as remembered by him is not available to me. Neither is his future taken as a projection of this past, i.e., as an anticipation based on what he has already experienced. Insofar as the self-determination of his "I can" requires memory and anticipation, it thus cannot appear in objective space. The result of this nonappearing is that the other is and is not a unity of sense for me. He is such a unity insofar as I grasp him as an appearing object, i.e., unify his appearances under a given set of categories, including that of causality. He is not such a unity insofar as the inner determinants of his action—his past and his future—cannot appear. While his objective being in space seems to open up the possibility of predicting his behavior, these nonappearing determinants undermine this possibility. The most I can do to compensate for their hiddenness is to project my past and anticipated future on him. Thus, anticipating his action, I can reason: this is how I have behaved when I was confronted by a similar situation. Since he is like me, he will probably behave the same way. This attempt at predicting his behavior is, of course, never completely successful. If it were, the other would be my double. He would not be "like" me. Behaving exactly as I do, he would be me. The actual experience of the other is, then, that of his giving himself in space as not being able to be so given. It is one of synthesizing an objective unity of sense that continually shows its inadequacy. I experience the other as disrupting this unity.

Since my sense of myself includes my relation to the world "out there," this inadequacy also affects it. My inability to make objective sense of the other is experienced as a gap in the sense of my surrounding world, as a tear in its unity. The unity of the world is, however, correlated to my own unity. Framed by the world, that is, by the senses that position me within it, I have my being as a spatio-temporal center. Spatially, I am a "here." I experience myself as a point from which distances are measured. About this, the world unfolds in its perspectivally arranged patterns. Temporally, I am "now." I experience myself as a shifting temporal center between my remembered past and my anticipated future. All of the senses I synthesize are correlated to this double centering. Their disruption is its disruption.

To see this, we have to observe that synthesizing sense begins with our making sense of our perceptions. This involves our taking them as perceptions of objects out there.[11] I do this by taking the perspectival patterns that fill my remembered past and projecting them forward into an anticipated future. Suppose, for example, I notice in the shadows under a bush what seems to be a rabbit. As I move to get a better look, its features seem to become more clearly defined. One part of what I see appears to be its head, another its body, still another its tail. Based upon what I see, I anticipate that further features will be revealed as I approach: this piece of light and shade will be seen as part of the rabbit's ear; another will be its eye; and so forth. If my interpretations are correct, then my perceptions should form a part of an emerging pattern that exhibits these features, i.e., that perceptually manifests the object that I assume I am seeing. If, however, I am mistaken, at some point my experiences will fail to fulfill these expectations. What I took to be a rabbit will dissolve into a flickering collection of shadows. I will, in failing to anticipate correctly, have failed to make sense of my perceptions. Now, to the point that I do succeed in making sense of my perceptions, I correlate them to my being as a center. They fit in with the past that lies behind me, the past that positions me on its leading edge. They confirm the expectations that, lying before me, compose my anticipated future. My perceptions do so by continuing the perspectival patterns that position me as the spatial center of my world. My failure to anticipate correctly, thus, does not just undo the sense that I have been trying to make of my perceptual experience. It also strikes at my being as a center.

In the case of another person whose actions I can never completely anticipate, this failure becomes an ongoing experience of decentering. My experience of the other as other is, in fact, this experience of decentering. It is the intentional evacuation of my experiencing consciousness in his favor. As other, he acts out of a distinct spatial center; he has his distinct past and future. As such, he is present to me as an inner distance that dislodges me from "my" world. His presence thus makes it impossible for me to be a center unambiguously defined and fixed by an environment. Thus, the fact that the determinants of his action—his memories and anticipations—do not appear prevents me from reducing the anticipated future to my projections of my past. His presence, in other words, is that of the future in the sense of the new.[12] It is that of the contingency and openness of the future. My experience of the alterity of the other is, consequently, an encounter with the openness of the frame that defined me. Insofar as it calls into question this frame, the experience is a kind of deframing.

This deframing is also my freedom insofar as it brings about the inner distance that separates me from my environment. The secreting of the "nothingness" that, in dislodging me, frees me does not point to my out-of-placeness, my "isolation" from the world and my others.

Equally, it does not indicate the existence of a noumenal world. It is not a function of what can never appear, what, in Kantian terms, is absent even in the realm of "inner sense." It is rather a function of the others who, in framing me, deframe me, that is, abstract me from "nature" in the Kantian sense.

In this context, the hiddenness of freedom results from the two perspectives required for the presence of the intersubjective world of nature. It comes from the hiddenness of the one in the other. Thus, just as the lived body of the "I move myself" cannot appear perspectivally, i.e., appear as the body that transits space, so my memories and anticipations cannot appear in space. This holds true even though the constitution of space, taken as the frame of what lies "out there" common to subjects, presupposes others like me—i.e., subjects who possess memory and anticipation. The fact that the constitution of the objective world of clocks and necessary causal sequences requires them means that this world always suffers disruption. The others that do appear within it, as they act on the basis of their memories and anticipations, disrupt its unity. Doing so, they delocate one another, abstracting each other from nature. The resulting break in its causal sequences does not rend its fabric because the subjects who accomplish this are built into this fabric. The objective world of nature presupposes them.

What is ultimately presupposed here is embodied subjectivity. As stated earlier, flesh lies at the basis of the inabsorbable alterity of the other. Thus, being called into question by the other demands corporeality. To put this in terms of the alterity of temporality is to note the dependence of time on flesh. Temporal synthesis begins with its receptivity, i.e., with the lived body as the place of the "impress" of impressions. Each such impress is registered as a content-filled now. Through the retention of such nows, we have our memories; through their anticipation, we project our futures. Given this, we have to say that with each new birth of human flesh, time begins. The alterity of flesh, the fact that each of us from birth has a distinct lived body, thus yields temporal alterity. With distinct bodies are given distinct sets of impressions and, with this, distinct pasts and distinct projected futures. The result is the other's givenness as not being able to be completely given by the senses that I, making use of my past and projected future, impose on my world. The other calls this sense into question by disrupting it. He does this through the alterity of his body, i.e., through its being an alternate source of temporality. The common time of the objective world, in being correlated to both our bodies, conceals a hiddenness that disrupts and makes possible this world.

Language and Hiddenness

The above returns us to the observation that the alterity of the flesh is the indispensable condition for raising the question of reason, the question of why this rather than that. Corporeality, however, is not a sufficient condition. Reason, in the sense of logos, implies language. On a self-conscious, reflective level, the question of reason is posed and answered through speech. Thus, the face of the other person that calls me into account is not mute. As a human face, it is capable of language. Its alterity, in putting me into question, includes this capacity. It includes a demand that I explain myself in terms that my other can understand and accept.[13] Language, then, is the specifically human response to the decentering of the self by the other. We respond by speaking, by using language to bridge the gap between our own and the other's experience. Doing so, we construct the intersubjective world on a specifically human level. This helps us overcome our mutual hiddenness. We can speak about our past and our anticipations. We can, if we choose to, reveal our motives. Yet it also introduces a further level of hiddenness, one specifically correlated to the possibilities of concealment that language affords.

To say that the intersubjective world is linguistically structured is to point to the fact that its objects are clothed with the common meanings language provides. This provision occurred in our learning our language. Our initial life projects—such as learning to eat at the table—were accompanied by a constant commentary from our caregivers. Each new object or activity was introduced to us with a verbal description. Now, as the child learns to speak, a remarkable phenomenon arises: soon it also learns to lie. In this, it shows itself capable of both truth and falsity, of both openness and hiddenness. Because it can lie, its words cannot automatically be taken as revealing what it has "in mind." Thus, the very thing that opens this mind up to me—the child's learning to speak—brings about the possibility of its concealment. In fact, the sense of the child's mind as a place of hiddenness, of privacy, now appears. In adult life, I get this sense each time I begin to mistrust another's words. The thought that they are concealing his intentions makes me regard the latter as hidden. I say to myself, "I don't know what he is thinking," making his intentions part of his interior, hidden life.

When the suspicion of lying makes me posit an inaccessible life, I thus do so on the basis of language. Language, however, is intersubjective. It is part of our being-in-the-world along with others; it is part of the way that they "frame" us. Given this, the hiddenness of intentions that I posit on its basis must be inherent in our common world. One way to see this is to recall how we reveal the objects of the world through our intentions (see above, p. 135). Making sense of our perceptions begins with our taking them as perceptions of some object. What determines the perceptions we do have of the object is, however, not some abstract intention directed to the object per se. It is the use we intend to put it to. If, for example, my intention is to write, then this paper appears to me as "what you write upon." Its sense unifies the series of perceptions I have as I write on it. If it is to start a fire, then the paper appears as "combustible." In this case, I have a very different set of perceptions of it and a different unifying sense. In both cases, however, the object's sense is set by its instrumental character. The sense that appears is that of the object as a means to accomplish my projects. As the psychologist William James noted, the appearance of objects is a function of the projects that determine the perceptions I will have of them.[14] In fact, as Heidegger stresses in his reworking of James's insight, it is only in terms of such projects that the world appears at all, i.e., as articulated into objects with disclosed properties.[15] Thus, what gives this articulated world its common cast is the interweaving of our projects. This makes the senses of its objects intersubjective and hence capable of being expressed by a language that is inherently intersubjective. Yet language does not just express the senses of the world as given by similar sets of projects. Insofar as the same object can be the goal of different projects, its disclosed sense can be multiplied. As intersubjective, language itself is open to this multiplicity. In describing an object, the words it uses are not limited to the single meaning that this object must bear. In the very multiplicity of the meanings available to it, language, rather than being the unambiguous recorder of intentions, has the ability to conceal.

Subjectively regarded, this concealment points back to me, to my intentions. The different senses of the object lead back to the different possible projects that can disclose it. Thus, when you doubt my words, you doubt that I will actually engage in the behavior (the project) that they promise. Objectively, however, the place where the different senses of the object are hidden is the world. It is because the intersubjective world affords multiple possibilities of behavior, each with its own intentions, that we can speak of its objects having different senses. Here the question of our hiddenness concerns these different possibilities of behavior. How are they inherent in this world? What is the feature of the common world that in concealing multiple possibilities allows us to conceal ourselves? The answer is implicit in the fact that our being in this world is mediated by language. The objects within it are drenched in linguistic meanings. We learned these by participating, actually or imaginatively, in the different projects of our others. The result is that to

apprehend the world through language is to see it as implicitly containing multiple possibilities of behavior, possibilities that are expressed by
its multiple senses. Mediated by language, the objects of my world have,
in fact, a sign-like character. Like the words that express them, their primary referent is the range of possibilities they afford me. My openness
to these possibilities is my freedom. It is my having the world as a field
of choices. This freedom is not within me. It is out there in the world—
i.e., in the possibilities it offers to me. The same holds for my hiddenness. When I speak, I reveal myself as open to the possibilities of the
world that I share with my others. *Their multiplicity is simultaneously
contained in the openness of my language.* It is, in fact, essential for its
communicative function. It is also essential for my use of language to
evaluate different choices. This openness, however, is also a concealment
since, *given my finitude, I cannot simultaneously realize their multiplicity.* Speaking, then, I reveal myself as open to more than I can reveal. I
give myself as not being able to be given.

This inability is my privacy; yet it follows from my being in communication with others and their possibilities. So regarded, it is actually
a capacity. My ability to conceal myself is a capability founded on the
constitution of a common world. Along with my freedom, it is a function of the possibilities it affords me. Open to them, I confront real
choices. With the reduction of such choices, my agency (my organic "I
can") remains, but it becomes impoverished in a human sense.
Increasingly like the agency of animals, it becomes more and more determined by my natural environment. What transforms this agency into
freedom are my others in their alterity, i.e., in their stocking the world
with the range of the possibilities that our language exemplifies. The
same transformation grounds the hiddenness of this agency, since it
makes it impossible for me to manifest all that I am capable of. This
impossibility, which is correlated to the possibility of my freedom, is not
a function of some nonappearing, invisible realm. It rests, rather, on the
richness of the appearing world.

Language and Freedom

Freedom is more than having the world as a field of choices. It also
involves the ability to stand back from such choices, to judge them in
terms of their consequences. It is, in other words, not just a *standing
open* to the possibilities of the world through language. As rational freedom, it also implies the ability through language to *stand back* and evaluate. At least two features of language underlie this capacity. The first is

that most of its nouns are general rather than proper names. For example, if someone says, "I am going to build a house," the use of the word "house" leaves undetermined what this house will be. The word, in *functioning as a concept*, involves a general notion, a one-in-many, that can be applied to a range of instances—i.e., to particular houses that can be built. Thus, to use the general term effectively, we must be able to conceptualize. We have to grasp what transcends the particular circumstances of a particular environment. We do this each time we abstract from such circumstances to grasp what is common in them. Apprehending the latter, we have the possibility of practically transcending these particular circumstances. With this comes the possibility of escaping the constraints of a particular environment. The same capability to grasp a one-in-many is behind our ability to apprehend what can be put to a multitude of uses, both good and bad. A particular implement, say a knife, can be used both to cut food and to kill. We know this because we know the different projects in which it can function. The knife, as a one-in-many, is the implement that can be put to these different uses. Grasping its identity in these different projects, we thereby perform the abstraction that allows the use of "knife" as a general term. My intent is not to delve into the mysteries of conceptualization, i.e., how we actually do this. It is rather to observe that this linguistic capability gives "human reality" a specifically human way of standing back from the world, of secreting (in Sartre's phrase) the "nothingness which isolates it." This standing back gives human agency its possibility of newness. Newness arises from the fact that the conceptual abilities inherent in language allow us to transcend rather than simply repeat the factual presence of our physical environment.[16]

A further sense of distancing and newness arises from a second feature of language. We use language not just to assert but also to argue and draw conclusions. This involves, as earlier noted, an ability to abstract from the contents of assertions so as to regard their formal relations. Using these to infer, we can draw a conclusion that was not present in the individual assertions (see above, p. 70). This ability allows a special projecting forth of the future. In it, we infer the possible consequences of an action rather than simply picture them through association. Association and abstraction are, as noted, opposites: while association works through the pairing of specific contents, inference proceeds by abstracting from them. This abstraction is a liberation in a much more complete sense than the conceptualization that gives us general terms. When we use it to work out our goals, we generate an anticipated future that is more than simply a projecting forward of the associated memories of our past.

This freedom that language affords is not total. The sensuous basis for conceptualization is given by the world we find ourselves in. Thus, without an appropriate range of experience of others and their projects, we cannot perform the abstractions that result in general terms. Limitations of experience thus become limitations of the terms available to us. The meanings they can take on can be further restricted by the practices of our linguistic community. We can be held back by the conventional usage that prevails in discussing our projects. Such limitations, however, should not be exaggerated. They are no more inherent in language than transcendence is. By virtue of the abstractions involved in its conceptual and logical structures, the linguistic community is always proceeding beyond the particular experiences and usages that define it. In this advance, the language-using self both defines and is defined by its environment. Functioning within a linguistic environment, the self becomes capable of the distancing and newness that characterizes human freedom. This freedom allows it to transcend and change its present environment and, hence, itself insofar as it has been determined by it.

A number of points follow from the above. The first is that the freedom that language conveys allows the self to have a conscience in a practically effective way. Standing back from its world, it can reject the choices offered to it. Prompted by its conscience to change itself, it can do so by changing its situation. The second point is that our capacity to distance ourselves from ourselves is what allows us to pass beyond "having a conscience," in the sense of simply responding to the other. Regarding ourselves, we can question this response. Asking whether the response is appropriate, we can raise the broader question of the correctness of what our conscience tells us. This questioning makes us ethical in the fully human sense—a sense that involves not just responding but also reflecting. Thus, as earlier observed, ethics begins with having a conscience, but cannot end with this. It must include the questioning of this response. Taken as a process of rational inquiry, it requires both the "call of conscience" and our putting this call into question. We do so when we use language to evaluate the response. This involves working through its consequences. It also can involve asking on the level of generality that language alone makes possible: What would happen if everyone responded in a similar fashion? The point here is that the standing back that language allows enables us to carry on an inner dialogue with ourselves. The self-reflection prompted by the other can thus become an explicit questioning. As a result, conscience can function on an expressly rational level. This can be put in terms of the ethical relation. The relation involves, first of all, the responding to the appearing, bodily other. As such, it is a responding to being put into question on a prelinguistic, bodily level—the level of organic need. It also, however, involves the translation of this to the level of reason. The universality implicit here frees the response from being simply a reaction determined by "interests." The result, as indicated, is the ability not just to respond to the bodily presence of the other, but also to rationally judge and adjust this response. With this, we have the genesis of what we called the "ethical tension," the tension that begins with the temporal decentering of the self. For this tension to become explicitly ethical, the self's exposure to the other as other must include language. The exposure must include the question of whether what is true for itself is also true for this other. To ask this, of course, is not just to have a conscience, but to question it. It is to be engaged in a dialogue that confronts, transcends, and returns to the other's bodily presence and need. With this, we have our response to Ferry's objection. By virtue of our making both reason and freedom part of the appearing world, we need not depart from it to describe the ethical relation. Along with our selfhood, this relation is embodied in the world. The world itself offers us the possibility of ethical transcendence.

Our relation to the world can be expressed by the statement that being is where it is at work, i.e., *is* where it functions by embodying itself. To say that color is in the eye is to assert that color is color by being at work in the eye, that is, by functioning in and through a particular bodily environment (see above, p. 41). The same point can be made about this chapter's characterization of selfhood as being-in-the-world. To define it in these terms is to see the world as the place of its actualization. The world is the place where its activity manifests its concrete presence as both intersubjective and private, that is, as both given and not able to be given. This implies that the self's transcendence, since it is founded on the world, is vulnerable to it. Since it requires an intersubjective, speaking community for its manifestation, it can be undermined by the impoverishment of language. In particular, the expressions of power that deform communication by preventing people from speaking their minds can diminish the very selfhood—the "mind"—that speech is supposed to manifest. This is because they prevent our access to the possibilities that constitute our freedom. Doing so, they impoverish our agency. Limiting our choices, they also limit our possibilities for concealment. The implication here is that the safeguards of selfhood are to be found in the human rights that defend speech and action against the encroachments of arbitrary power. The universality of such rights does not point to subjectivity as some uniform quantity. It is not in any sense tied to Kant's concept of the autonomous self—the self that, in transcending its environment, is identical to every other self in the "kingdom of ends" (see above p. 62). Such rights are rather conditions for the privacy of selfhood in its particularity. They are founded on the recognition that its inaccessibility is a function of the public realm. As such, it is something that can be lost.

As the news of the world often shows us, there are communities that suffer breakdown. There are societies that—given their history of dictatorship—have great difficulties with freedom. Their attempts to restore it tend to go awry. These negative examples point to the political imperative of maintaining the public realm as a place where freedom can manifest itself. Positively, this involves fostering the richness of the intersubjective world. The task is no less than that of multiplying the mutually enriching possibilities of our being-in-the-world. This can be put in terms of the care of the self. Such care is not just a personal but also a political goal. The moral imperatives that are rooted in our onto-logical condition as being-in-the-world bear upon how we organize our-selves politically. Ancient writers took this link as a matter of course. It is implicit in Aristotle's writing his *Ethics* as a necessary introduction to his *Politics*. It is also implied in Plato's assertion that the state is the soul writ large. As Plato interpreted this, the state actually "writes" the soul. Its character determines that of its citizens. Totalitarian systems take the power to do so as a matter of course. They aim at a complete determina-tion, a total control of the person. The disasters that this has led to indi-cate that the success of the state in caring for the soul should rather be measured by the ways in which the state allows it to *escape* from the uni-formity of its action. This means that the measure of the public realm is the possibilities of hiddenness it alone can foster. Only then can the state in its "writing" the soul give it the freedom that allows it to stand back and judge its text.

What does this imply with regard to the actual structures of soci-ety? To answer this is to make explicit the link between these structures and ethics. The task here is that of moving from ethics to politics.

7

Alterity and Society

From Ethics to Politics

It is not at all obvious how the transition from ethics to politics is to be made. Often there is a surprising disjunction between the private ethical conduct of citizens and what counts as "just" or "fair" in the actions of the state. Victor Klemperer's diaries of the Nazi years bear eloquent testimony both to the private decency of ordinary individuals and the brutality of the state that had at least their passive acquiescence. A Jew married to an "Aryan," he spent the war in Dresden. In a diary entry dated 17 March, 1940, he remarks: "Vox populi disintegrates into voces populi [. . .]—I often ask myself where all the wild anti-Semitism is. For my part I encounter much sympathy, people help me out, but fearfully of course" (Klemperer 1998, 329–30).

For Levinas, this contrast between the private and the public follows from the singular character of the ethical relation. In his view, the face-to-face encounter that initiates ethics sets up a "relation with the singular . . . excluding every common measure" (Levinas 1993, 127). As such, it excludes every formulation of universal or common maxims to judge the relation. It thus stands outside of the realm of politics, which involves laws applicable to everyone. The distinction between ethics and politics, for Levinas, is ultimately ontological. While the public, political realm involves what can be thematized and made institutionally concrete as part of being, i.e., part of the existing political order, the ethical obligation that arises through the face "undermines the ontological primacy of being." This means that it "predisposes us to a meaning that is other than Being, is otherwise than being (*autrement qu'être*)" (Levinas 1984, 59). Behind these assertions is a radical conception of the alterity of the other. The other that calls me to respond is, in this call, beyond being. Being, according to Levinas, is what we posit through an identity synthesis, i.e., a synthesis in which we continuously re-identify something as the same.[1] The other, in the alterity that calls me into question, evades this process.[2] Thus, the ethical relation that results from this call can contain nothing of the "same." Its nonrepeatable uniqueness is such that it cannot be thematized. Because of this, it cannot provide those common standards (standards that are "the same") by which we might integrate it into our collective, political life.

Fortunately, the attempt to base ethics on alterity need not imply Levinas's radical conception. Alterity can be conceived as a function of flesh. As has been suggested, its irreducible quality can be seen as arising from the fact that, given the distinctness of our bodies, the standpoints of self and others can never be collapsed. To consider alterity in this way gives us a better chance of making the transition to politics. This is because an ethics based on this sense of alterity shares with politics an acknowledgment of the fundamental human condition: that of plurality. We are, given our bodies, inherently and irreducibly plural. From birth onwards, we are with others.

To see what this implies in terms of political structures, we need to review the main features of the ethics that follows from conceiving alterity in these terms. This review will not just allow us to sum up the conclusions of the previous chapters; it will also elucidate the traits of selfhood that can be translated into the political realm. Now, the first and most obvious feature of the ethics thus far developed is that it involves empathy. In its basic etymological sense, empathy is a *feeling* (a suffering or undergoing) of the world in and through another person. Flesh is our capacity to suffer and undergo. Taking myself as another in empathy, I take up the other person's standpoint, letting myself be determined by his situation. The tie here to the common notion of ethics is relatively direct. There is an immediate link between empathy and, for example, the ethics of the Golden Rule. Thus, it seems a function of normal human empathy for us to treat others as we would like to be treated. If, through empathy, we have the capacity of experiencing the distress of others, then we refrain from harming them. Positively, we treat them as we would like to be treated were we in their position. Thus, in the first instance, our guide is the negative rule: "Do not impose on others what you yourself do not desire" (*Analects* 15.24).[3] In the second, we follow the positive Confucian precept: "Try your best to treat others as you would wish to be treated yourself" (Mencius VII. A. 4).[4] The fact that variations of the rule occur in all the world's religions points to the universality of the empathy that lies at its basis. Such universality springs from our condition of plurality. We are always already with others. To work with them, we have to anticipate their actions; but this requires that we regard the world, not just from our own, but also from their standpoints. It involves our letting ourselves be imaginatively shaped by the latter. Given our lack of immediate access to their memories and anticipations, the attempt to do this is never entirely successful. Our plural condition, however, demands that we make the attempt.

To think of alterity in terms of empathy is to focus on the split in one's self-presence that empathy occasions. When I do take myself as another, I continue to be determined by my own circumstances—on the most basic level, by my bodily being. Yet insofar as I "feel in" and through the other, I am shaped by what shapes this person. The result, then, is a certain doubling of my selfhood. I am present to myself as determined by my circumstances, yet this self-presence also includes myself as an other, i.e., as defined by an alternative environment. Such duality can, of course, be quite disturbing. As earlier noted, the misery of another person can ruin my enjoyment. Interrupting my self-presence, the other person's need can be experienced as my own. Undergoing it, I can, in Levinas's words, experience the other as "the bread snatched from my mouth." Given this disquieting possibility, people often attempt to shield themselves from the effects of empathy. They turn away from the face of the other. They stereotype the unfortunate, placing them in a category that somehow makes them inherently deserving of their fate. All of this, however, requires a special effort. Our normal condition, which is that of plurality, requires the openness of empathy. This involves each of us taking into account not just the "true for me" but also the "true for others." Doing so, we face the task of arriving at agreements that we can share. This happens whenever we attempt to mediate between our own self-knowledge and what others say about us. Insofar as such others through empathy are part of our self-presence, their judgments are not external. They are inherent in our ability to question ourselves. Behind this is the fact that the standpoint of the other gives me a perspective from which I can view myself. It affords me a certain inner distance that allows me to be there "for myself." The openness to the other that characterizes empathy thus reflects itself in the very structure of my selfhood. Concretely, I am a self insofar as I am for-myself, i.e., am capable of carrying out that inner dialogue in which I bring myself forward to face the question that the other within me puts to me. At stake in my ongoing attempts to mediate between my own and my others' perspectives is, then, my unity as a "for-itself." I am, in a certain sense, the process of this negotiation. Engaging in it, I maintain the unity that allows me to carry it forward.

The move from this ontological condition to ethics occurs through the use of language. The freedom it affords me in my inner dialogue allows me to pass beyond having a conscience in the sense of simply responding to the other to a questioning of my response. It is with such questioning that the openness of empathy achieves its full sense as an openness to the other as other. Such openness asks whether the response is appropriate or not—i.e., whether or not it is a response to the other as other or to the other as simply a projection of myself. So conceived, openness is a self-evacuation of consciousness in favor of the other. It is an intentional directedness to the other as escaping me, as "hidden" in the senses described in the previous chapter. Since this directedness is based on language and its abstractions, it is also open to reason. It includes the calculation of actions appropriate to the needs of the other. The possibility of such calculation does not contradict the alterity of the other. It does not, to use Levinas's phrase, "reduce the other to the same"—thereby denying his alterity. This is because alterity is not "beyond being," but rather based on it. The "otherwise than being" that is our hiddenness is actually a function of what appears. Its origin is the flesh in its alterity— flesh understood as the basis of both need and empathy.

The above can be summed up in the notion of "con-science," understood in its etymological sense as an inward "knowing-with" the other person.[5] So defined, conscience is intertwined with the concepts of selfhood and empathy. Selfhood requires conscience insofar as we are for-ourselves only through our ability to know in and through the other. In fact, given that selfhood, in its quality of being "for-itself," includes the other and that conscience is this inclusion, the inward knowing that defines conscience actually establishes the self that is known. Conscience's link to empathy follows from the fact that my inward "knowing-with" the other person involves my taking up his standpoint, the very standpoint that allows me to know myself. Doing so, however, requires the empathy that exposes me to this person's needs. Thus, the standpoint that opens me up to the other also divides me. It makes me present to myself as alternative sets of needs springing from my own and the other's embodied being. Given the inherent alterity of our flesh, neither set can be reduced to the other, neither can be ignored. Conscience in the sense of an inward knowing-with the other thus sets me the task of having to negotiate between them. As already indicated, I am in my concrete being-for-myself the process of this negotiation.

This account of selfhood points to a new way of interpreting Plato's position that the state is the soul writ large (*Republic* 368b–69a). Given that selfhood involves an inner alterity, the state that reflects this must have its own alterity. Similarly, the mutual implication of selfhood and "conscience" points to the structures that would perform a parallel function within the state. An individual's alterity involves alternate standpoints, alternative expressions of the person's self-presence. Having a conscience begins with one expression being able to call the other into question. Is there a parallel structure that would allow the state to also have a conscience? A valid parallel would demand the consideration of social (as opposed to individual) standpoints. These standpoints, to be considered as inherent in our collective self-presence, would have to embody aspects of our human condition. Each, as a partial expression, would require the others. Incapable of reducing the others to its own perspective, each would be open to being called into question by the other expressions of what it means to be human. Inherent within our social selfhood, the alterity of such expressions would thus provide the basis for society's inner distance, the distance that would allow it to be a for-itself.

Arendt's Structures of Collective Selfhood

One can think of a number of expressions of the human condition. Its divisions into youth and age or male and female, for example, express essential aspects of what it means to be human. In choosing which aspects to incorporate into public life, we must keep in mind that they are not ends in themselves, but only means. They are suitable to the point that their institutionalized expressions allow the state to have a conscience, i.e., inwardly know itself. Having a conscience is to be regarded as the norm; alterity, in its particular forms, has its validity as the means to realize this. The choice of such means is, then, a matter of practicality. We have to ask: What are the states, natural or otherwise, that are essential to the human condition as presently constituted?[6] Which are capable of institutional structuring? As examples of such states, I am going to limit myself to Hannah Arendt's threefold division of the human condition into labor, work, and action. Other elements can be added to these without changing the argument so long as we take them as essential yet partial modes of our collective self-presence.

Of Arendt's three modes, labor is perhaps the most fundamental, since it manifests to us the natural, biological aspect of our presence. All living organisms engage in metabolism, an exchange of materials with nature. They take in its elements as food and transform them into their own structure, later expelling what they can no longer use. This process leaves no lasting products behind. Its result is simply itself as the continuance of the process of life. According to Arendt, the same can be said of labor, understood as the human analogue of this process.[7] In her words: "It is indeed the mark of all laboring that it leaves nothing behind, that the result of its effort is almost as quickly consumed as the effort is spent" (Arendt 1958, 87). Subsistence farmers, for example, labor; so do those who hunt and gather food. The effort spent in cooking and cleaning is another example of labor. In each of these instances, we have a repetitive cyclical activity that mirrors the biological cycles of nature. The point of such cycles is simply their continuance. Mirroring these, "the productivity of labor power produces objects only incidentally and is primarily concerned with the means of its own reproduction." This means, Arendt adds, "it never 'produces' anything but life" (88). Labor, insofar as it is bound to the cycles of nature, such as those of the seasons in farming, does not have in itself a beginning and an end. Rather, "laboring always moves in the same circle, which is prescribed by the biological process of the living organism . . ." (98).[8]

As essential as labor is to the human condition, it suffers from an obvious liability. The very transience that marks it means that it leaves no lasting, sheltering world behind. Everything, from its perspective, is a consumer good, something to use up almost as soon as it is made.[9] For us to have a world in which we can dwell, a world of more or less durable structures that outlast the laboring process, we have to "work" at making such structures. Work consists in designing and fashioning lasting objects—be they chairs, houses, or city squares. Since to have a world is to have a lasting human environment, such objects save the laboring process not just from transience but also from worldlessness. The world that is produced manifests to us our presence as makers. It exhibits in its concrete reality—that is, in actual objects and structures— the subjective conceptions that guide the productive process.

The limitation of this form of self-presence appears when we try to absolutize its perspective. In making, things have value if they can be used to make something else. From the perspective of the productive process, value is use-value. A tree, for example, is seen as having value if it can be used as wood, which, in turn, is valued if it can be used to fashion some object, which, in turn, has value if it can be put to some further use. If, however, everything is useful in terms of something else, nothing has any intrinsic value. There is only an endless chain of means and ends in which each thing has value only through being useful for the next.[10] In Arendt's words, if we let the utility "standards which governed its coming into being" rule the world that the productive process builds, then "the same world becomes as worthless as the employed material, a mere means for further ends . . ." (Arendt 1958, 156). This dissolution of value is also a dissolution of meaning, understood as the guiding purpose or end of an action. The unending character of the chain of means and ends results in the meaning of each action being found in the next. No member of the chain has an intrinsic meaning. If, however, we stop the chain and say that meaning is given by some achievable end, i.e., some product, then, as Arendt, notes, this end, "once achieved, ceases to be an end." Made concrete, it becomes simply "an object among objects." As just another thing, it has no longer a meaning, since it "loses its capacity to guide and justify the choice of means, to organize and produce them" (154–55). Thus, identifying meaning with the end or goal, we have to say that the meaning ceases when the product is made.

Just as the laboring process needs the perspective of work to save it from worldlessness, so work needs another expression of the human condition if the world it constructs is to keep its meaning and its value. It must, therefore, be apprehended from a perspective distinct from that which rules the productive process. According to Arendt, the required standpoint is that of "action," a term she uses for our social and political interactions (Arendt 1958, 176). Action manifests our presence as public persons, that is, as the authors of deeds having a public significance. Such manifestation involves a twofold constitution. First, deeds are constituted; then, through them, the person as their author. Language is crucial to this process, since it manifests the deeds as pointing to the person as a responsible agent. Thus, the medium through which a public person appears is neither nature (as it is for labor) nor material (as it is for making), but rather speech. Correspondingly, the first result of public action is neither our biological continuance nor some product. It is rather our deeds taken as publicly discussed and interpreted acts. In the public realm, it is assumed that a person can give a rational account of his actions, that he is responsible for them. In this realm, our acts are interpreted as manifesting the acting person as possessing reason and responsible freedom. This manifestation is through speech. As Arendt puts this, "The action he begins is humanly disclosed by the word, . . . his deed . . . becomes relevant only through the spoken word in which he identifies himself as the actor, announcing what he does, has done, and intends to do" (179). Thus, through our linguistically situated deeds, we appear as responsible agents.

Since it is based on language, this public appearance conceals a private hiddenness. As the last chapter described this: when a person speaks, he reveals himself as open to the possibilities of the world he

shares with his others. This is the common world formed by the interweaving of our projects, an interweaving by which such projects and
their senses become accessible to us. The possibilities thus made available exceed what any agent can possibly manifest as a finite individual.
Speaking, he thus reveals himself as open *to more than what he can
reveal* (see above, p. 166). The resulting hiddenness points to the inherent ambiguity of our assumption of agency. The very interweaving of
projects that makes possible language and public life also undercuts the
notion of an independent actor. Thus, public actions by definition
involve others. Without them as witnesses and partners, there is no
public disclosure of the person. Yet, as Arendt notes, the very fact that
our actions "fall into an already existing web of human relations" makes
their consequences uncertain. The web, "with its innumerable, conflicting wills and intentions," has the effect that "action almost never
achieves its [originally intended] purpose" (Arendt 1958, 184). The story
line traced out by an action thus reveals the person as "its actor and sufferer," but not as its independent author (184).[11] The true author is the
interweaving of wills, intentions, and projects that forms the social web.

How does action save the world from the loss of value and meaning
that plagues the utilitarian perspective of the productive process? In
making, meaning is external to the process. Understood as its "where-
fore" or goal, it resides in the product to be produced. As a guiding
moment, it is extinguished once the process reaches its end in a given
object. In action, however, the end "lies in the activity itself."[12] This is
because the end of action is the person it manifests. Thus, the actions that
reveal the actor are not a means to some end external to themselves. They
are rather the actuality of the actor, they are the acting person's ongoing
being-in-act. What we have here is, thus, an alternative to the means-ends
relationship that renders things valueless by always placing their value in
something else. In action, there is no higher end or value than the person
manifested through action.[13] Such a person is not a product, i.e., an end
that can be achieved at some given time. Inherent within the life of the
actor, the end is ongoing. The same point can be expressed by noting that
the meaning generated by action is, in the first instance, biographical. It is
inherent in the story line traced out by a person's deeds. In it, the person
appears as a subject, that is, as the actor and sufferer of various actions.[14]
The world that work produces has its sense and value insofar as its
actions and products are involved in this biography.

This ability of action to make meaning inherent in what we do in
no way signifies the independence of its standpoint. Its dependence follows from the fact that the authorship of action is always shared.
Because of this, the meaning it originates is never private. Action, in

other words, manifests the person as a part of the web of human relations. The person's being-in-act involves the being-in-act of others.
Thus, biography shades off into history. The limitation of the standpoint
of action is implicit in this interdependence. Insofar as authorship always
involves others, it is intertwined with the standpoints of labor and work.
The person it reveals acts in and is dependent on the world that labor
sustains and work fashions.

Labor and work exhibit the same dependence. In fact, all three
expressions of the human condition depend on and condition one
another.[15] This is why each, taken in isolation, exhibits an intolerable one-
sidedness. To avoid this, each standpoint must open itself up to the others;
each must permit its being called into question. Thus, labor cannot exist
without a corresponding sheltering world and the socio-political relations
that regulate this. Were its perspective to absorb those of work and action,
the transience in which consumption immediately follows production
would become the norm. The result would be a meaningless consumerism.
It would be a disposable society that would ultimately dispose of itself, a
society that would efface itself as it consumed its products. Similarly, productive work demands the labor that sustains the world it fashions and the
action that gives it meaning. To make its perspective dominant is to
devalue such "unproductive" labor as the nurture and education of the
young. Since those who nurture and educate do not make things, their
only value is that of creating "productive" individuals—i.e., fitting them
for the workforce. Insofar as action does not fit into this paradigm, it too
is devalued as mere "politics" and unproductive "talk." As already noted,
strictly utilitarian societies devalue even themselves, since they make
things valuable only in terms of something else.

Action, of course, does not have this drawback. This, however,
does not mean that it can exist without the perspectives of labor or
making. Action exists in a web that involves both. To eliminate labor
and making is, thus, to undercut the world in which the actor functions.
The one-sidedness of action's perspective is apparent whenever it
becomes the dominant norm. In societies where it prevails, both the pro-
ducer and laborer are devalued. Thus, in classical Athens, craftsmen were
treated with aristocratic contempt, while labor was degraded to the point
of slavery. Not just slaves, who made up a majority of the population,
were considered as incapable of action, but also the women who carried
out the work of the household were denied any public presence. This
separation of action from making and labor deprives societies of the per-
manence and organic vitality necessary for their continuance. At the
extreme, it pits the few who have the leisure to engage in political life
against the many that are excluded.[16]

The obvious conclusion of this analysis is that all three standpoints are required for proper social functioning. That they are distinct means that each offers a different perspective from which to judge the others. Each achieves its objective presence through being seen from the perspectives of these others. Together, then, they allow society to regard itself objectively. Thus, it is through their copresence that society gains the inner alterity that is required if it is to achieve its identity as a for-itself. This identity is formed insofar as it calls itself into question, that is, insofar as it is forced to respond, to explain its actions. Having such an identity and hearing the call of conscience in the voice of the other go together. For a state to have a conscience, then, the following conditions must be satisfied: It has to allow each of the expressions of the human condition to achieve its own voice. It must give these the means, through social and political action, to call the others into question. This has to be so arranged that none of these dominate, none be allowed to set the rules according to which all of them are valued. What is required, then, is precisely the sort of negotiation that takes place within the self in a person's encounter with others. There must, on the social level, be a parallel negotiation regarding the needs of each of the expressions of the human condition. In the appeal of each to the others, society must, through its institutions, hear the call of conscience and attempt to address conflicting claims through negotiation.

Plato's Error

The above paradigm presupposes a break with an important theme of Western political discourse. In its emphasis on negotiation, it refuses the standard equation of freedom and sovereignty, understood as rule. Such an equation implies that the freedom of one person or element cannot, as rule, exist without a corresponding lack of freedom or rule in others. Plato's conceptions of the individual and the state, one being the image of the other, exemplify this view. For Plato, as we saw, the sovereignty of reason is such that it uses the other elements of the soul as means to its ends (see above, p. 54). Reason's autonomy is, for example, one with its coercion of desire. Similarly, the sovereignty of action in the state, as represented by the philosopher-king, involves a similar reduction of the other elements to mere means. Rule, here, is the opposite of negotiation, since only the perspective of the ruler has any value. Such a view might be plausible for the individual if reason could exist apart from desire, if, as Socrates so devoutly wished, the soul could rid itself of the body. Similarly, it might be possible for society if the philosopher-king and the action he embodies could exist apart from the other elements of society. Since, however, both presuppositions are impossible, there is an obvious error here. Hannah Arendt puts it in terms of the condition of human plurality. As we earlier cited her: "[I]f it were true that sovereignty and freedom are the same, then indeed no man could be free, because sovereignty, the ideal of uncompromising self-sufficiency and mastership, is contradictory to the very condition of plurality. No man can be sovereign because not one man, but men inhabit the earth" (Arendt 1958, 235). In other words, given that plurality is essential to the human condition, the sovereignty of the individual is impossible. For Arendt, this impossibility arises because the acting individual with his publicly interpreted deeds can appear only through others.[17] The web of human relations, through which he becomes manifest, hopelessly entangles any question of authorship. This entanglement manifests a fact that has been emphasized throughout this book: since it is established through others, human selfhood is always plural. We are born from others. Others provide us with our language. They give us our ability to confront and call ourselves into question. The self-separation they provide liberates us from ourselves. Given that such self-separation is essential for freedom, we cannot assert our freedom (and hence our rule) apart from them.

If others do provide the space where freedom can appear, then rule or sovereignty can only be collectively realized through negotiation. Insofar as it recognizes different perspectives and needs, this negotiation takes account of the demands of empathy. The ethics that sorts out these demands on a social and political level expresses in its rules the state's response to its conscience. Good statesmanship preserves and gives a voice to the alterity that makes this possible. It constantly acts through its institutions to insure that the different elements that make up our human plurality can call each other into question. In providing a common forum for their debate, it makes possible a collective knowing-with and through the other that gives a state a conscience.

So conceived, the move from ethics to justice is not an impossible transition. It involves neither the naïveté that ignores political realities nor (as Levinas would have it) the metaphysical presumption of translating the infinite demands of the other into the multiple, finite obligations of social life. What is required is, rather, the structuring of our national (and international) relations to prevent the powers of the state and the global community from collapsing into a single expression of the human condition. The essential plurality of our condition demands the institutions that, in dividing social and political power, provide the means for the multiple standpoints of humanity to call power into question—i.e., to require that it justify itself and its exercise. That such division also increases the possibilities of our hiddenness, i.e., our abilities to escape state power, returns us to the conclusion of the preceding chapter: both our privacy and our freedom are posterior, not prior, to the public realm. Their vulnerability to the abuses of power points not just to the need to divide the latter; they also require the human rights that prevent the state from arbitrarily limiting the possibilities of speech and action. Such possibilities, in enriching the intersubjective world, give content to our freedom. As such, they do not just allow us to stand back and judge the public realm. In their very multiplicity, they also provide us with the resources, the "human wisdom," for this judgment.

Responsibility

There is a special sense of responsibility for the world implicit in the above. Our responsibility is not that of an owner or master distinct from the world. It cannot be if our transcendence of the world is founded on the world and, hence, can be undermined by it. The vulnerability this implies includes the very possibility of our being responsible. Without the world, there is neither self nor response. Given this, we have to say that we are responsible because, rather than owning the world, we are owned by it. Responding to its multiple claims, we have to negotiate between them. In particular, the essential plurality of the human condition signifies that we always have to balance the claims of our own and our others' embodied being-in-the-world. The special sense of responsibility, taken as a responding, that follows from the above is, in fact, that of negotiation. Negotiation is the way we respond to the plural nature of our human condition. It is our being responsible to this condition.

Freedom and responsibility form the parameters of ethics. Freedom, as Kant showed, is the ground of ethics understood as self-limitation. The imperative of ethics follows from the fact that as free, we alone can bind ourselves to follow the moral rule (see above, pp. 6, 148). Freedom as self-alterity is, however, itself founded. Each of us, in our conscious lives, is a place where the world comes to presence. By virtue of our being in and through others, this presence involves the self-alterity that makes freedom possible. Thus, freedom begins with our being called into question by our others. The imperative of ethics in this case is that of being open to them, of responding to their presence.

To think these two imperatives together is the task of ethics. Ethics is both freedom and responding, both self-limitation and openness. If it is faithful to this task, it will not collapse their duality in pursuit of some imagined autonomy—the autonomy, for example, of a noumenal self outside of or "otherwise than" the world. It will rather continue to negotiate the demands that come from our being in and through the world. Negotiation is the presence of responsible freedom. In keeping open the alternatives whose demands it mediates, it is the self-limitation that opens up rather than closes off the range of our human possibilities. As such, it is our responsibility to our humanity.

Notes

Introduction

1. This was particularly the case in Eastern Europe, where the violence of the Nazi occupation was unrestrained.

2. It is on this that she bases her verdict on Eichmann. She writes in the epilogue: "And just as you supported and carried out a policy of not wanting to share the earth with the Jewish people and the people of a number of other nations—as though you and your superiors had any right to determine who should and who should not inhabit the world—we find that no one, that is, no member of the human race, can be expected to want to share the earth with you. This is the reason, and the only reason, you must hang" (Arendt 1977, p. 279).

3. Emile Fackenheim writes that "to confront the Holocaust . . . is to face the fact that the precise point which marks the limits of penultimate rational intelligibility marks the end also of ultimate or philosophical rationality" (Fackenheim 1988, 65). His claim is that in its very senselessness, the Holocaust escapes any ultimate philosophical explanation. This is because "the evil [of the Holocaust] systematically eludes [thought]" (69). What is required, according to Fackenheim, is "resistance that is beyond the sphere of thought altogether and in the sphere of life" (69). This resistance will be the subject of chapter 4.

4. We also have no ready answers for how long we should prolong life through artificial means using our current technologies. The replacement of biological functions with technological analogues—dialysis for kidneys, catheters for urea, heart and lung machines for cardiac and pulmonary functions—poses the question of the voluntary termination of life. When should we let the patient die? The difficulty in answering this comes from the fact that the framework for thinking of "life" as a natural function has already been exceeded by the technologies in question.

5. Martha Nussbaum makes the same point in an Aristotelian context by noting with Aristotle that "the ethical virtues . . . will seem pointless in the god's life; and yet each has a claim to be an end in itself for a human life." Thus, courage is not attributable to the gods, "since there is nothing grave for them to risk. On the other hand courageous action seems to be a fine *human* achievement" (Nussbaum 1990, 374). For Nussbaum, then, "human limits structure the human excellence and give excellent action its significance. The preservation of

185

the limits in some form . . . is a necessary condition of excellent activity's excellence" (378). She adds, "[W]hat my argument urges us to reject as incoherent is the aspiration to leave behind altogether the constitutive condition of our humanity, and to seek for a life that is really the life of another sort of being—as if it were a higher and better life for us. It asks us to bound our aspirations by recalling that there are some very general conditions of human existence that are also necessary conditions for the values that we know, love, and appropriately pursue" (379).

6. References to Paton's translation (Kant 1964) are followed by the corresponding page number in vol. 4 of *Kants gesammelte Schriften* (Kant 1955a).

7. Such results, Kant repeatedly emphasizes, have no bearing on the moral worth of the act. He writes, for example, "That the purposes we may have in our actions and also their effects considered as ends and motives of the will can give to actions no unconditioned and moral worth is clear. . . . Thus the moral worth of an action does not depend on the result expected from it . . ." (Kant 1964, 68, 69; 1995a, 400, 401).

8. Failure to recognize this fact is why "all the previous efforts that have been made to discover the principle of morality . . . have one and all been bound to fail." It never occurred to their authors that man "is subject only to laws which are made by himself and yet are universal" (Kant 1964, 100; 1995a, 432).

9. Leibniz puts this in terms of an analogy with a mill: "Supposing that there were a machine whose structure produced thought, sensation, and perception, we could conceive of it as increased in size with the same proportions until one was able to enter into its interior, as he would into a mill. Now, on going into it he would find only pieces working upon one another, but never would he find anything to explain perception" (Leibniz 1962, 254).

10. The modern version of this position occurs in Nagel 1974.

11. The etymological sense is from the Greek, *pathein*, "to suffer or undergo," and *en*, signifying "in."

Chapter 1. Selfhood and Certainty

1. This assumption is implicit in Socrates' answer to Meno about the possibility of inquiry. See *Meno* 81d.

2. Husserl explores the same theme in the late manuscripts in his discussions of the "anonymity of the ego." He writes, for example: "The ego which is the counterpart (*gegenüber*) to everything is anonymous. It is not its own counterpart. The house is my counterpart, not vice versa. And yet I can turn my attention to myself. But then this counterpart in which the ego comes forward along with everything which was its counterpart is again split. The ego which

comes forward as a counterpart and its counterpart [e.g., the house it was perceiving] are both counterparts to me. Forthwith, I—the subject of this new counterpart—am anonymous" (MS. C 2 I, p. 2, Aug. 1931).

3. The phrase is used by Descartes to describe the apprehension of a piece of wax all of whose sensuous qualities change as it is heated. See Descartes 1990, 30–31.

4. The necessity for my doing so is derived in Kant's "Transcendental Deduction." Its essential point is that were I to violate these rules, not just the unity of the multiplicity of my intuitions would go, but my own unity of consciousness—my identity as an apperceiving being—would also be undermined. In Kant's words, "The synthetic unity of the multiplicity of intuitions as apriori given is thus the ground of the identity of apperception itself, the identity that apriori precedes all my determinate thoughts . . ." (Kant 1955c, 110; B 134). Were I to violate the categories in putting together my intuitions, then, rather than having a unified experiencing self, "I would have as colorful and motley a self as the representations I consciously possess" (110). Since the latter makes experience impossible, it is a priori excluded.

5. See Mensch 1996b, which develops these implications.

Chapter 2. Empathy and Self-Presence

1. John Hull in his remarkable book, *Touching the Rock*, describes how he "sees" an altar by touch. He writes, "Pushing myself up on it, my feet hanging out over the front, I could reach the back. I did this again and again, measuring it with my body, till at last I began to have some idea of its proportions" (Hull 1991, 216). In the postscript to this work, he states: "Increasingly, I do not think of myself so much as a blind person, which would define me with reference to sighted people and as lacking something, but simply as a whole-body-seer [WBS]. A blind person is simply someone in whom the specialist function of sight is now devolved upon the whole body, and no longer specialized in a particular organ. Being WBS is to be in one of the concentrated human conditions. It is a state, like the state of being young, or being old, of being male or female; it is one of the orders of human being" (217). His book is a remarkable example of making available to us "the experience of someone who has crossed over the border" into blindness (217)

2. Such situatedness is a theme that appears in other philosophers, most notably Husserl and Sartre. For Husserl, "the ego is only possible as a subject of an 'environment,' only possible as a subject who has facing it things, objects, especially temporal objects, realities in the widest sense . . ." (MS. E III 2, p. 46). By determining its situation, these objects particularize the ego. Apart from them, it has no "material content" of its own. "It is quite empty as such." It is, in itself, "an empty form which is only 'individualized' through the stream [of its

experiences]: this, in the sense of its uniqueness" (18). Sartre ties the self's uniqueness directly to the body. The body is "our original relation to the world . . ." (Sartre 1966, 428). It gives us a situated, contingent perspective. In Sartre's words, "The necessity of a point of view . . . is the body . . ." (431). We can, in fact, "define the body as a contingent point of view on the world" (433).

Chapter 3. The Divided Self

1. These include the differences between men and women, as the *Republic* indicates.

2. That pleasure is conceived as a bodily condition is obvious from the argument that pleasure and pain end at the same time. This holds only for bodily conditions such as the pain of thirst and the pleasure of drinking. See Plato 1971, 100, *Gorgias* 497, c–d.

3. See, e.g., the critique of democracy in the *Republic* 556e–61e. *Republic* 556e–57a describes the coming of democracy as the onslaught of an illness.

4. As opposed to the legitimate ruler who rules from within, i.e., by virtue of his position within the community.

5. As Merleau-Ponty puts this, "The absolute positing of a single object is the death of consciousness, since it congeals the whole of existence, as a crystal placed in a solution suddenly crystallizes it" (Merleau-Ponty 1967, 72). The congealing is the eliminating of its foreground-background structure.

6. Plato writes that "the very being of to be (αὐτὴ ἡ οὐσία τοῦ εἶναι) is to be "always in the same manner in relation to the same things." This is to be "unchanging" and, thus, to remain the same with oneself. The ideas "beauty itself, equality itself, and every itself" are called "being" (τὸ ὄν) because, in their unchanging self-identity, they "do not admit of any change whatsoever" (*Phaedo* 78d).

7. The Platonic term for the idea, εἶδος, is taken from εἴδω, which means to look at or perceive. The second aorist of εἴδω is εἶδον. Our word "look" conveys its one time, aoristic sense.

8. Frege makes a parallel point about the relation between objects and the concepts that define them. In Frege's words, "The concept *square* is not a rectangle; only the objects which fall under this concept are rectangles; similarly the concept *black cloth* is neither black nor a cloth. Whether such objects exist is not immediately known by means of their definitions. . . . Neither has the concept defined got this property [of the object], nor is a definition a guarantee that the concept is realized [in the object]" (Frege 1970, 145).

9. In Kant's words, a person "has therefore two points of view from which he can regard himself. . . . He can consider himself *first*—so far as he belongs to

the sensible world—to be under laws of nature (heteronomy); and *secondly*—so far as he belongs to the intelligible word—to be under laws which . . . have their ground in reason alone" (Kant 1964, 120; 1995a, 452).

10. This determines the "specific function" (ἔργον) of man according to Aristotle. See *Nicomachean Ethics* 1098a. 6–7.

11. See Darwin 1967a, 453, p. 471.

12. This random distribution can be represented by a bell curve, with its inverse correlation of frequency and distance from the mean. The further some feature—say, the length of the index finger—is from the mean, the less frequent is its occurrence.

13. This destructive element, of course, must be kept within bounds for the normal functioning of appetite. As Freud writes: "Modifications in the proportions of the fusion between the instincts have the most tangible results. A surplus of sexual aggressiveness will turn a lover into a sex-murderer, while a sharp diminution in the aggressive factor will make him bashful or impotent" (Freud 1989, 19).

14. In Freud's words, it is "only when the authority is internalized through the establishment of a super-ego . . . that we should speak of conscience or a sense of guilt" (Freud 1962, 72).

15. "The symptoms of neuroses are . . . either a substitutive satisfaction of some sexual urge or measures to prevent such satisfaction; and as a rule they are compromises between the two" (Freud 1989, 67). This substitution can take on highly symbolic forms. Freud gives the account of a lady who repeatedly perplexed her maid by calling her and pointing to "a great mark on the dining table cover" (Freud 1965, 273). Ten years earlier, she had married a much older man who proved impotent on their wedding night. He covered the fact of his failure from the maid by pouring red ink on the bed in a place corresponding to the mark on the tablecloth. As Freud remarks, "It is clear, first of all, that the patient identified herself with her husband" (273). Her action symbolically satisfies his wish to hide his "disgrace . . . in the eyes of the maid who does the beds" (273). Beyond this, the "sexual urge" that receives symbolic fashion is that involved in his overcoming his impotency—a wish she would, presumably, have shared.

16. In addition, "a wasteful expenditure of energy [expended in repressing the demand] has been made unnecessary," since one now consciously rejects or accepts it (Freud 1989, 58).

17. In Socrates' formulation, "A man who has learnt about right will be righteous . . . and a righteous man . . . will in fact of necessity always will to perform right actions" (Plato 1971, 39–40; *Gorgias* 460b).

18. No such transformation, for example, happens in the *Meno*.

19. The same holds for desire, which becomes the erotic appetite for the ideas.

20. The word for character, *hexis* (ἕξις), is related to *echein* (ἔχειν), to have or to hold as a possession. The Latin translation of hexis, *habitus*, has a similar relation to *habere*. In English we find a parallel relation between habitude, habit, and have.

21. "Pleasure . . . accompanies all objects of choice" (Aristotle 1962, 38; *Nic. Eth.* 1104b. 35).

22. The major reason for this is the fact that the properties of Plato's ideas are not those of things for which they are ideas (*Parmenides* 131d). Given this, we cannot realize such things as justice itself in our actions.

23. This argument does not, of course, apply to all knowledge. For example, "our conviction that a triangle has or does not have the sum of its angles equal to two right angles" is unaffected by our relation to "pleasure and pain." What is affected are "the convictions we hold concerning how we should act" (Aristotle 1962, 153; *Nic. Eth.* 1140b. 15–16). It is in the area of action and practical reason that our interests determine our perception and hence our reasoning process. This, however, is the area delimited by the moral "ought."

24. Suppose, for example, my deliberation concerns whether I should marry a particular person. To deliberate I have to know what marriage in general is—i.e., the kind of commitments it involves. I also must know both myself and the person I am marrying—i.e., the particulars of our characters. Only then can I begin to reason out whether we can undertake these commitments.

25. What they do is, rather, shape the pleasure I do follow.

28. In Mill's words, "It is by associating the doing right with pleasure, or the wrong with pain, or by eliciting and impressing and bringing home to the person's experience the pleasure naturally involved in the one or the pain in the other, that it is possible to call forth that will to be virtuous which, when confirmed, acts without any thought of either pleasure or pain." Such a will, though not consciously directed by pleasure, still continues the habit formed by pursuing it (Mill 1979, 39; *Util.* IV).

27. This is why Kant, for example, disassociates ethics from subjective feelings. See Kant 1964, 93.

28. We do so to justify punishment. See Mill 1979, 55; *Util.* V;).

Chapter 4. Rescue and the Origin of Responsibility

1. The networks set up to rescue Jews were mostly in the Netherlands and in France. In Eastern Europe, where the occupation was particularly brutal and anti-Semitism widespread, rescue remained overwhelmingly a matter of the "face-to-face" encounter. Dr. Paldiel, the director of the Archives for the

Righteous, writes, "The record here with regard to the 'righteous Among the Nations' testifies that most (but certainly not all) rescue operations were initiated between the potential rescuer and a Jewish person on the run. This face-to-face encounter, against the terrible setting of the Holocaust, had a near cataclysmic effect on the rescuer, who decided to do his best and save the distraught and totally helpless person standing in front of him. This scenario is especially true for rescue operations in Eastern Europe. Other rescue operations were initiated, not necessarily as a result of such a direct, face-to-face encounter, but as a result of the rescuer witnessing the unprecedented Nazi terror unleashed, especially against Jews. This made him determined to try to do something to help. Many rescue operations in Western Europe were the result of such a realization. Here too, 'the face of the other person' is what led most rescuers to get involved" (letter dated "Jerusalem, May 18, 1998").

2. These cases are on file at the Archives at Yad Vashem in Jerusalem. I wish to express my gratitude to Dr. Mordecai Paldiel, the director of the Department for the Righteous, for permission to quote from this material. Without Dr. Paldiel's assistance and encouragement, this chapter could not have been written.

3. The doctor's name is Yelina Kutogiene; the woman she rescued is Shulamit Lirov. Ms. Lirov told her story to me and Dr. Paldiel at Yad Vashem in August 1998. With her was the son of the doctor who rescued her, Victor Kutorgas.

4. Quoted from the testimony of Neeltje Fischer-Lust and Maartje Bruna-Lust, 8 May 1997, Yad Vashem. The rescuers are Trijntje Lust-Heijnis and her husband, Hermanus Lust.

5. "A la nuit tombante, les 9 personnes composant notre famille ont frappé à la porte de M. and Mme. Astier. Ils nous ont ouvert et sans nous posé des questions, nous ont fait asseoir à la table famille et nous ont offert à diner. Des lits ont été préparé et ils ont même donné leur propre chambre à mes parents" (Testimony of Mme. Raymond Zarcate, 24 July, 1994, case #6961, Yad Vashem).

6. "The woman of the house warned me to go away, that someone was there who would kill me. She must have realized I had nowhere to go and she grabbed my hand and led me down to a bunker under the barn, where I met two other Jews that this family was hiding . . ." (Testimony of Sidney Olmer, 25 June 1986, Yad Vashem Archives).

7. According to the Oliners's study, "most rescuers reported rarely reflecting before acting" (Oliner and Oliner 1988, 169).

8. The rescuer, moreover, can always turn back. He can ask the Jew he is sheltering to leave. In this sense the rescuer has to continually renew his commitment.

9. Yad Vashem Archives, case #5482. Jan Tulwinski and his wife, Paulina, hid the Jew, Eliahu Rosenberg, while Jan's brother, Stanislaw, was the anti-Semitic member of the Home Army.

10. "As soon as we were liberated, we had additional troubles. We couldn't buy food. The Polish anti-Semites wouldn't return our houses to us. They were inhabited by Poles. We had to live in an attic which had broken walls. . . . At night the low temperatures were unbearable, and we were suffering from hunger. A short time later, the A.K. (Polish Army Underground) penetrated a house nearby which was inhabited by ten Jews who had returned from the work camps. Four people were shot to death. Others were wounded. . . . The Poles caught the killers and they were later let loose unpunished" (testimony of Mr. Ira Crandell, 29 April, 1985, Yad Vashem Archives).

11. "The two soldiers that were our guardians were advised to escort us back to my parents' house. The night that the Russians helped us go back to the house we found the Polish gentiles of the community gathered around the house screaming that they had found Jews to kill" (Testimony of Sol Gersten, Samuel Gersten, and Esther Scheinman Krulik, 20 October, 1985, Yad Vashem Archives).

12. This was for their own safety. As the members of the Szoors family report: "We left the Kaszuba home two at a time because he was justifiably afraid to let anyone know that he had hidden us. Even after the war he and his family's lives were in danger for hiding us." (Testimony of Philip Shore, Nachum Shore, Abe Shore, and Sara Goldlist, 11 May, 1993, Yad Vashem Archives).

13. This is his distinction from the tragic hero. As Kierkegaard writes: "Abraham is therefore at no instant the tragic hero, but something quite different, either a murderer or a man of faith" (Kierkegaard 1985, 85).

14. *Universalia ante rem* as opposed to concepts which are *universalia post rem*, that is, universals that are after the fact of the things being given. See Nietzsche 1967, 103.

15. Some versions do not have "of Israel," which may be a later addition.

16. This seems to be the wonder that the Mishnah expresses in speaking of God's creation of human life. God creates it as absolute in this sense.

17. Still less do I gain an experience of the absence of all experience, which is death itself. As Levinas asks, "If, in the face of death, one is no longer able to be able, how can one still remain a self before the event it announces?" (Levinas 1994b, 78). In other words, the actual experience of death is the end of the experiencing self and cannot as such be experienced. Given this, it is through the other, in particular through the face-to-face encounter, that I experience death. In Levinas's words, "Everything we can say and think about death" actually

"comes from the experience and observation of others . . ." (Levinas 1993, 17, my translation).

18. "This mortality . . . is also an assignation and obligation that concerns the ego" (Levinas 1994a, 107).

19. It is in fact my absence. Levinas quotes Epicurus: "If you are, it is not; if it is, you are not" (Levinas 1994b, 71).

20. It is not, then, the case that my mortality and that of the Other are on par with each other. For Levinas, there is an essential asymmetry between the self and its Other in which the Other has priority.

21. In this emendation, it does not point to the "beyond being" that Levinas speaks of. For an extended critique of Levinas's sense of alterity, see the chapter "Presence and Ethics" in Mensch 2001.

22. *Miami Herald*, 8 November, 1988, 1B; see case #1381, Yad Vashem Archives, Jerusalem.

23. The very fact that the other's need interrupts my enjoyment can be seen as a factor motivating me to meet this need. Equally, however, the motivation can be to turn away and thus avoid the interruption of enjoyment. In neither case does the motivation amount to an "ought."

24. The space, one can say, is a break in the necessity of being. It is the experience of contingency.

25. This origin is, then, something more than the freedom Heidegger points to in asserting that "freedom is the origin of the principle of reason" (Heidegger 1967b, 68). This "principle" (*Satz*) is the proposition that everything must have a reason, i.e., that one can always ask why something is as it is. Freedom is not the origin of the contingency that raises this question, our inner alterity is. Without this alterity, i.e., without others, there is, in fact, no freedom. Freedom, in other words, is an intersubjective, not a monadological, condition.

26. This is the assumption of the *Phaedo*, which describes the philosopher as desiring above all to be separated from his body, because the body "fills us with wants, desires, fears, [and] all sorts of illusions . . ." (*Phaedo* 66c). See also, *Phaedo* 64a–67b).

27. Sartre expresses this sense when he writes, "Descartes, following the Stoics, has given a name to this possibility, which human reality has, to secrete a nothingness which isolates it—it is *freedom*" (Sartre 1966, 60).

28. See, for example, the excellent work of Fogelman 1994, Gross 1994, Monroe and Epperson 1994, and Oliner and Oliner 1988.

29. An additional difficulty with the attempt to reduce the rescuers' actions to the circumstances of their upbringing is the fact that many of the perpetrators

came from similar homes. Members of the same family sometimes split on the issue, some favoring, others actively opposing, the elimination of the Jews.

30. "Stretching out," "straining," and "tension" are the three basic meanings listed by Lewis and Short for *intentio*. From thence its meaning comes to be "a directing of the mind towards anything." See Lewis and Short 1966, 976.

31. This holds especially in conditions where parental attention is essential—i.e., those involving limited resources and the danger of accidents and infections. Such conditions, were, of course, quite general until recent times. The attachment theory that Bowlby developed grows out of the insight that the child's chances of survival are increased with its ability to attach its caregivers to it. In Robert Karen's words, "Each of the instinctual responses Bowlby describes is present because of its survival value. Without them the child would die, especially the child that was born on the primitive savannas where people first evolved" (Karen 1994, 102). See Bowlby 1982 for a summary of his position.

32. Soffer writes, "[A]t the first stage there is differentiation between the other and the background environment, but little or no differentiation between the self and the other" (Soffer 1999, 157). Some differentiation, however, must occur if there is to be the original intentionality of the child's attaching the parent to itself.

33. As she also put this: "Thus, it is through repeated over-extensions and experiences of the 'breaking-up' of over-extensions, that the infant gradually realizes that there are two relatively distinct living bodies, one in which there is sensation and holding sway, and another in which there is not (first-person) sensation and only a partial and mediated kind of holding sway" (Soffer 1999, 159–60).

34. This, however, does not mean, as Soffer seems to imply, that no trace of the original identity remains. Were this the case, any talk of "empathy" would lose all its original content.

35. The comparison is, of course, with Heidegger. For Heidegger, "death is essentially, in every case, mine" (Heidegger 1967a, 240). It "lays claim to me as an individual." Because it cannot be shared, "the nonrelational character of death individualizes Dasein down to itself" (263). The point here is that all our organic functions have this "nonrelational character." Just as no one can die for me, so no one can eat for me.

36. This was the reaction of Eichmann to the gas chamber: "I still remember how I pictured the thing to myself, and then I became physically weak, as though I had lived through some great agitation. Such things happen to everybody, and it left behind a certain inner trembling" (Arendt 1977, 87). Each time he encountered extermination, he "could not [look]." He turned away and busied himself with his bureaucratic concerns. See Arendt 1977, 87–95.

37. I am speaking of "motives" here in Husserl's sense. The phenomenological concept of motivation is, he writes, "a generalization of that concept of moti-

vation according to which we can say, e.g., that the willing of the end motivates the willing of the means." The concept exists "as a contrast to the concept of causality" at work in the natural sciences (Husserl 1976, 101 n. 1). Such causality is blind. Motivations exist in the framework of some goal we wish to reach. They are the means we are motivated to use in reaching these goals. Thus, to ask for the motivations for turning away is to ask what are the means this goal motivates us to use. The Nazis, for example, made use of a number of means to motivate people to turn away from the Jews.

38. This stereotype meant that the "Schmalzniks" who searched out Jews to blackmail them could justify themselves by assuming that they were just getting back what was stolen from Poland.

39. Case #421, Yad Vashem Archives.

40. For primitive man, however, it usually does not extend beyond the group. As Darwin said with regard to our "social instincts": "It is no argument against savage man being a social animal, that the tribes inhabiting adjacent districts are almost always at war with each other; for the social instincts never extend to all the individuals of the same species" (Darwin 1967a, 480). It is, in fact, only within the tribe that the social instincts are informed by Eros. Outside of it, the death instinct predominates.

41. Thus, initially, "the total available energy of Eros . . . serves to neutralize the destructive tendencies which are simultaneously present" through the death instinct (Freud 1989, 19). Afterward, however, disturbances can occur as one or the other instinct becomes weakened in the individual. See e.g., Freud 1989, 59–60.

42. The danger of such stereotyping does not just hold for negative stereotypes. It includes positive ones insofar as they overcome alterity. The admiration for the "outsider" does not disarm the action of the death instinct. The Nazis, for example, entertained a number of positive stereotypes regarding the abilities of the Jews. This, however, just increased their "danger" in the eyes of the Nazis.

43. The rescuer Johanna Eck expressed this demand as follows: "The motive for my helping [the Jews]? There were no special motives in the particular cases. Basically, I thought as follows: If I don't help, I don't fulfill the task that life (or, perhaps, God) demands of me. It seems to me that humans form a great unity; and when they act unjustly to each other, they are striking themselves and everyone in the face. This [was] my motive" (Testimony of Johanna Eck, 2 August, 1956, Yad Vashem Archives). A similar sentiment regarding the unity of life was expressed by Michael Erlich: "We had nothing tangible that we could have given them [the rescuers]. Their philosophy was that they and we all together would live or die" (Testimony of Michael Erlich, 20 December, 1973, Yad Vashem Archives). Ira Pozdnjakoff wrote of the Danguvietytes with whom he stayed, "All [the] 'rescuers' in this family believed deeply that human life was sacred." (Testimony of Ira Pozdnjakoff, given on 9 January, 1984, Yad Vashem Archives, case #3872).

44. Classical Greek nicely captures this sense of externality in the root meaning of "category" (κατηγορία), which is that of an "accusation" or "charge."

Chapter 5. An Ethics of Framing

1. "*Being* good," in other words, becomes invisible in this view. The result, Arendt writes, is that "the 'valuable' things themselves become mere means, losing thereby their own intrinsic 'value'" (Arendt 1958, 155).

2. For an extensive phenomenological discussion of "place," see Edward Casey's excellent study, *Getting Back into Place*. Casey's focus is on being in place as a particularization of Heidegger's category of 'being-in-the-world.' He writes: "Place is the phenomenal particularization of 'being-in-the-world,' a phrase that in Heidegger's hands retains a certain formality and abstractness which only the concreteness of *being-in-place*, i.e., being in the *place-world* itself can mitigate." The aim of his book is to "rediscover and redescribe that concreteness," thereby restoring "a sense of the full significance of place" (Casey 1993, xv). Our own focus, which is limited to its ethical implications, is much narrower. Darwin, rather than Heidegger, forms its basis.

3. See section 2 of book 1, "The Determination of Centripetal Forces" in Newton's *Mathematical Principles of Natural Philosophy* .

4. The naturalist Lyall Watson schematizes this process through his three principles of "pathetics" or environmental "suffering." They are: "Order is disturbed by loss of place"; "Order is disrupted by loss of balance" (33); and "Order is destroyed by loss of diversity" (Watson 1995, 30, 33, 42). My account of environmental evil is largely determined by his and Darwin's descriptions.

5. The same holds "in the beautifully plumed seed of the dandelion, and in the flattened and fringed legs of the water-beetle." The first has reference "to the land being already thickly clothed with other plants, so that the seeds may be widely distributed and fall on unoccupied ground." The second, in adapting the beetle for diving, "allows it to compete with other aquatic insects, to hunt for its own prey, and to escape serving as prey to other animals" (Darwin 1967b, 61).

6. As Watson notes, "Rabbits reached Australia with the first European settlers as early as 1788, and repeated introductions took place with every new wave of colonists. By the beginning of the 1800's rabbits were common in every village and were liberated, both accidentally and deliberately, many times" (Watson 1995, 29). It was only in 1862, however, that the rabbits got lucky—i.e., managed to find sufficient food and water to establish a breeding colony.

7. These facts explain why evolution has a tendency towards diversity. The "principle of divergence" is inherent in it "from the simple circumstance

that the more diversified the descendants from any one species become in structure, constitution, and habits, by so much will they be better enabled to seize on many and widely diversified places in the polity of nature, and so be enabled to increase in numbers" (Darwin 1967b, 84). From a modern perspective, we can say that those genes that promote diversity and hence greater numbers of descendants increase the chance of leaving copies of themselves behind. Since such copies would have the same tendency, the process of divergence would naturally continue.

8. As Freud writes of the disruptions that can result: "The whole process seems so strange to us because we take for granted the synthetic nature of the workings of the ego. But we are clearly at fault in this. The synthetic function of the ego, though it is of such extraordinary importance, is subject to particular conditions and is liable to a whole series of disturbances" (Freud 1959, 373). Amongst these is the fact that the function itself can be split, resulting in the splitting of the ego. In such an instance two separate interpretative stances can develop, each with its corresponding ego. For an account of this, see Mensch 1996a, 205–220.

9. When he finally did, Kurtz could only exclaim in "a cry that was no more than a breath—'The horror! The horror!'" (Conrad 1989, 111). This moment of recognition is both complete and too late.

10. That Kurtz thinks of himself as a deity is apparent in the adoration of the tribes, which he enforced by coming to them "with thunder and lightning, you know—and they had never seen anything like it" (Conrad 1989, 94), in his making their chiefs "crawl" to him (96), and in his presiding "at certain midnight dances ending with unspeakable rites, which . . . were offered up to him," certain sacrifices that Marlow hints at but does not describe (86).

11. As Fackenheim asks, "[W]hen all came crashing down, why was it more important to annihilate the few remaining Jews than to save all the Germans?" (Fackenheim 1988, 63).

12. According to John Cornwell, the price Pius XII had to pay for this Concordat was the disbandment of the Catholic Center Party, the last remaining opposition to Hitler. See Cornwell 1999, 149–51.

13. Fackenheim, in this regard, mirrors the common judgment in writing: "[N]o thoughtful reader can have any doubt as to the 'almost inconceivable spiritual, moral and human inferiority' of Adolph Hitler. . . . His ideas . . . are unoriginal and trite." His "passion . . . is for the most part fed by long-nursed, petty resentments, by a mean thirst for vengeance for old but never forgotten slights" (Fackenheim 1988, 65).

14. David Jones expresses this in terms of the notion of the "active construction of the self." Against the argument that the Germans were socialized to the extent that they could no longer form moral judgments or, at least, had a "diminished capacity" for doing so, he argues that "socialization is never an

entirely one-way relation of active socializers to passive learners." What we find, in fact, is "the active learner engaged in a process that includes selective adaptation to the prevailing culture as presented through socialization" (Jones 1999, 113). What opens the way for this is the fact that the messages experience affords us are never uniform. For example, a child growing up in a household with "anti-Semitic, authoritarian, and nationalistic beliefs and values" cannot avoid a certain "cognitive dissonance caused by new experiences and information that conflicts with his or her anti-Semitic beliefs and values. For example, Jewish friends at school seem nice and have ordinary human qualities, hatred of Jews is inconsistent with basic Christian teachings (love your enemy; do good to those that hate you), with moral precepts such as the wrongfulness of harming others, and with the fact that scientific evidence does not support racist ideology." If the person chooses to overcome such dissonance, he or she must engage "in various tactics of purposeful self-deception—a species of motivated irrationality." Jones's point is that this choice is not itself predetermined by society. In his words, "There is nothing inevitable about choosing to engage in self-deception in order to avoid the psychological stress of calling into question one's culturally defined identity." Given that "the individual can choose what kind of person he or she wants to be," we thus have to say that "engaging in self-deception in order to evade acknowledging morally relevant facts or to avoid making a difficult moral choice is both irrational and blameworthy . . ." (114). The result of such habitual self-deception may be his or her "diminished capacity," but since this is the result of his or her own repeated actions, the person is "to some extent blameworthy for having the deficiency" (115).

15. As Levinas observes, these limits also apply to the nothingness of death, which for philosophy is a "néant impossible à penser." He adds, "On ne peut méconnaître le néant de la morte, mais on ne peut non plus le connaître" (Levinas 1993, 80–81).

16. "Dasein's Being is care (*Sorge*)" (Heidegger 1967a, 284).

17. In Heidegger's words: "'The Dasein is occupied with its own being' means more precisely: it is occupied with its ability to be. As existent, the Dasein is free for specific possibilities of its own self. It is its own most peculiar able-to-be. . . . it is these possibilities themselves" (Heidegger 1988, 276).

18. There is here an echo of Kant's positioning of the person as an "end in himself." It may well be that Arendt in her criticism of Kant's "utilitarianism" also had Heidegger in mind. See Arendt 1958, 154–55.

19. As such, they appear as "equipment." "Equipment," Heidegger writes, "is 'in order to.'" He adds, "[A] being is not what and how it is, for example, a hammer, and then in addition something 'with which to hammer.' Rather, what and how it is as this entity, its whatness and howness, is constituted by this in-order-to as such, by its functionality" (Heidegger 1988, 293).

20. Thus, I disclose both it and myself through my project. In the latter, the Dasein "is unveiling itself as this can-be, in this specific being" (Heidegger 1988, 277).

21. Heidegger, thus, writes: "If circumspective letting-function were not from the very outset an expectance . . ."—i.e., an expecting that an item I need will be present when I need it— "then the Dasein could never find that something is missing" (Heidegger 1988, 311).

22. See Heidegger 1988, 276. The understanding of being that underlies my projects depends on this. Such understanding is through the original temporality of Dasein, which is composed of its having-been, its making-present, and its being-ahead-of-itself. These three temporal modes form the horizon of all possible understanding of being. They themselves, however, are grounded in our projective, purposeful existence. Thus, in this framework, being is what is disclosed through such purposive existence. See Heidegger 1988, 325.

23. See Fackenheim 1988, 63.

24. The silence on this was first broken in Ferías 1987.

25. Gilson writes, summing up his position, "Evil is the privation of a good which the subject should possess, a failure to be what it should be and hence, a pure nothingness" (Gilson 1961 144).

26. As Heidegger points out, our modern notion of correspondence is based on this conception. The intellect corresponds with reality when it accords with its exemplar—i.e., with the form specifying what a human is. In the Middle Ages, this form is God's creative idea of the human intellect. See Heidegger 1967b, 76–7.

27. Theologically, one can express this by noting that the goodness that is defined in relation to God cannot be defined in terms of being "good for" something. God does not need his creations. While they may be useful to each other, he does not depend on them for the achievement of his purposes. His omnipotence includes his independence from his creations.

28. Here, of course, the position reveals its Parmenidean ancestry. Its inability to grasp evil follows from the inconceivability of the "is-not."

29. Such self-concealment can be expressed in terms of a fifth transcendent quality of being that is sometimes added: beauty. Here the lack of goodness also expresses itself in a certain ugliness or disproportion. Subjectively, it is experienced in the desire to turn away. This turning away is also part of evil's occasioning its own concealment. In Conrad's tale, this aspect of evil appears in Marlow's inability to actually repeat Kurtz's last words to his fiancée. The substitution of her name for "the horror, the horror" appears to be the final covering up or nonrecognition generated by Kurtz. See Conrad 1989, 121.

30. Such thoughts may well be behind Levinas's position that the possibility of ethics is rooted in the "beyond being." This means that its basis is not being (in its essential finitude), but rather the infinite; the basis is not phenomenological givenness, but rather its "rupture," not knowledge, but, instead, what unsettles this. For an account of this position, see Mensch 2001, 195–220.

31. Fackenheim 1988, 66. Fackenheim himself takes this incident as a refutation of Hannah Arendt's idea that "evil [of the Holocaust] is 'only extreme' and not 'radical,' spreading 'like a fungus on the surface.' It is 'thought-defying' in the sense that thought, 'trying to reach some depth,' is 'frustrated because there is nothing'" (66; the referenced passage is Arendt 1978, 250ff.). The position of my book is that this "nothing" is itself revealed by this smirk.

32. Such blindness recalls Conrad's description of the Romans in their conquest of Britain as "men going at it blind." An equal blindness is present in the men at the Company station.

33. In a certain sense, this phenomenology of evil recalls Derrida's description of the "trace": "The trace is not a presence, but is rather the simulacrum of a presence that dislocates, displaces and refers beyond itself." This reference to what lies beyond itself is inherent in it. In fact, as Derrida immediately adds, "The trace has, properly speaking, no place, for effacement belongs to the very structure of the trace." This is because "from the start, effacement constitutes [the trace] as a trace—makes it disappear in its appearing, makes it issue forth from itself in its very position" (Derrida 1973, 156).

34. An essential part of literature's moral dimension may be to afford us this education of our sensibility. Martha Nussbaum writes in this regard: "Situations are all highly concrete, and they do not present themselves with duty labels on them. Without the abilities of perception, duty is blind and therefore powerless. . . . Obtuseness is a moral failing; its opposite can be cultivated" (Nussbaum 1990, 156). Good literature promotes such cultivation. Our attention to its characters "will itself, if we read well, be a high case of moral attention." As she explains this: "A novel, just because it is not our life, places us in a moral position that is favorable for perception and it shows us what it would be like to take up that position in life. We find here love without possessiveness, attention without bias, involvement without panic" (162).

35. See the *Shorter Oxford English Dictionary*, 3d ed. s.v. "*Tolerance.*"

36. See Lewis and Short 1966, 1876.

37. The development of flying insects, for example, opened a niche that can be thought of as an intention towards the birds and bats that would one day prey upon them.

38. For an account of tolerance from the perspective of Husserl's theory of intersubjectivity, see Mensch 1988, 380–93.

Chapter 6. Freedom and Alterity

1. In terms of our previous chapters, this implies that whatever alterity nature (and natural "life") in its nonfoundational wholeness may possess, it is insufficient to establish our own inner alterity.

2. Ferry also remarks, "It is because he is capable of taking his distances not only from the cycle of his biological life but also from his particular language, nature, and culture that man can enter into communication with others. His capacity for universality is a direct function of this distancing" (Ferry 1995, 15–16).

3. It was the failure to recognize this that, according to Kant, caused "all the previous efforts to discover the principle of morality . . . to fail." It never occurred to their authors that man "is subject only to laws which are made by himself and yet are universal, and that he is bound only to act in conformity with a will which is his own. . . ." Instead they thought that "the law had to carry with it some interest in order to attract or compel." This reduction of ethics to interest "meant that all the labor spent in trying to find a supreme principle of duty was lost beyond recall" (Kant 1964, 100; 1955a, 432–33).

4. In Kant's words, "[T]o be independent of determination by causes in the sensible world [the world in which the subject appears] . . . is to be free" (Kant 1964, 120; 1955a, 452).

5. In Kant's words: "I render my subjective synthesis of apprehension [of the house] objective only by reference to a rule in accordance with which the appearances in their succession are determined by the preceding state. The experience of an event is itself possible only on this assumption" (Kant 1955c, 171; B240).

6. Put in terms of validity, the assumption is that objective validity and universal validity (validity for everyone) are equivalent. In Kant's words, the first implies the second, "for when a judgment agrees with an object, all judgments concerning the same object must agree with each other." The second implies the first, for otherwise "there would be no reason why other judgments would necessarily have to agree with mine, if it were not the unity of the object to which they all refer and with which they all agree, and for that reason must agree amongst themselves" (Kant 1955d, 298; §18).

7. This is why, as Merleau-Ponty notes, "Perception is precisely that kind of act in which there can be no question of setting the act itself apart from the end to which it is directed" (Merleau-Ponty 1967, 374).

8. To posit an object "absolutely" without this structure is, then, to posit it in a way that it can never be grasped by consciousness. In fact, as Merleau-Ponty writes, "the absolute positing of a single object is the death of consciousness . . ." since it dispenses with this structure (Merleau-Ponty 1967, 71).

9. Lacan believes this occurs with the child's recognizing "his own image in the mirror." For Lacan, this stage, in which "the I is precipitated in a primordial form," occurs "before it [the I] is objectified in the dialectic of identification with the other, and before language restores to it, in the universal, its function as subject" (Lacan 1977, 2). My position is that the original "mirror" is the bodily presence of the caregiver.

10. As Husserl puts this, when I anticipate, "the style of the past becomes projected into the future" (MS. L I 15, p. 32b).

11. Sense here signifies being one in many. The object is the one central referent of the many perceptions. It is the point of their unification.

12. For Levinas, consequently, "the other is the future" (Levinas 1994b, 77).

13. If this were not the case, then the alterity of animals would have as much a claim on us as that of animals. Todd May writes, arguing against Levinas: "Being a bat is infinitely other in the precise sense Levinas articulates. But that the experience of the bat transcends my own experience does not imply that there is some responsibility I have towards bats" (May 1997, 143).

14. See William James, "Reasoning," in James, 1948, 354–57.

15. This is why, as he writes, "World is only, if, and as long as Dasein exists" (Heidegger 1988, 170). As an "equipmental totality," which is uncovered by our projects, it depends on us. See Heidegger 1988, 163–64. Such a world, of course, is not "nature," which "always already is." The elements of nature become objects in our "world" when through our projects we disclose them (169).

16. Such newness, of course, ultimately depends on others, since they are the ones that introduced me to the different uses of objects.

Chapter 7. Alterity and Society

1. As Levinas expresses this in his essay "Substitution:" "In the relationship with beings which is called consciousness, we identify these beings through the dispersion of 'adumbrations' in which they appear. Similarly, in self-consciousness, we identify ourselves through a multiplicity of temporal phrases." In each case "an ideality corresponds with the dispersion of aspects and images, adumbrations or phrases," the ideality being the object as the same, i.e., the same thing showing itself through such aspects (Levinas 1996, 80).

2. As Levinas puts this conclusion: "I am trying to show that man's ethical relation to the other is ultimately prior to his ontological relation to himself

(egology) or to the totality of things which we call the world (cosmology)" (Levinas 1984, 57).

3. Other negative formulations of the rule are: "This is the sum of duty: do naught to others which if done to thee would cause thee pain" (from the *Mahabharata*); "What is hateful to you, do not do to your neighbor: that is the whole Torah, all the rest of it is commentary" (from the Talmud, *Shabbat* 31a); "Whatever is disagreeable to yourself do not do unto others" (from the Zoroastrian *Shayast-na-Shayast* 13:29); "Hurt not others with that which pains yourself" (from the Buddhist *Udana*). See http://www.fragrant.demon.co.uk/golden.html for an extended list of quotations on the Golden Rule.

4. This mirrors the Christian precept to do unto others what you would have them do unto you. Christianity's command to love your neighbor as you love yourself can be taken as an injunction to engage in the empathy that takes up the standpoints of self and neighbor.

5. *Shorter Oxford English Dictionary*, 3d ed., s.v. *Conscience*.

6. Childhood, for example, can lay claim to be a natural human state. Yet for long periods it was neither recognized nor constituted as such.

7. Since humans labor together at tasks they set for one another, this analogue is collective. Even solitary occupations such as housework imply others in, say, cleaning up after (or for) them.

8. "The common characteristic of both, the biological process in man and the process of growth and decay in the world, is that they are part of the cyclical movement of nature and therefore endlessly repetitive; all human activities which arise out of the necessity to cope with them are bound to the recurring cycles of nature and have in themselves no beginning and no end, properly speaking, unlike working, whose end has come when the object is finished, . . . laboring always moves in the same circle, which is prescribed by the biological process of the living organism . . ." (Arendt 1958, 98).

9. Thus, when labor becomes the dominant mode of our self-presence, we have, according to Arendt, the consumer society, whose dominant mode "consists in treating all use objects as though they were consumer goods, so that a chair or a table is now consumed as rapidly as a dress and a dress used up almost as quickly as food. . . . [T]he industrial revolution has replaced all workmanship with labor, and the result has been that the things of the modern world have become labor products whose natural fate is to be consumed, instead of work products which are there to be used" (Arendt 1958, 124).

10. "The trouble with the utility standard inherent in the very activity of fabrication is that the relationship between means and end on which it relies is very much like a chain whose every end can serve again as a means in some other context" (Arendt 1958, 153–54).

11. On the one hand, then, others make possible our freedom by grounding our self-separation. On the other, they limit this through their own free acts. Such acts weave a web that entangles us. The thought of being so enmeshed that all outcomes but one are impossible is behind the Greek concepts of fate and tragedy. Fate is not opposed to freedom, but rather woven from the strands of individual acts of relatively free individuals. The net that Clytaemestra throws over Agamemnon when she kills him symbolizes for Aeschylus this interweaving (see Aeschylus, *Agamemnon*, 1375ff.).

12. Arendt here draws a parallel with Aristotle's notion of *energeia*. She writes, "It is this insistence on the living deed and the spoken word as the greatest achievements of which human beings are capable that was conceptualized in Aristotle's notion of *energeia* ('actuality') . . . in these instances of action and speech the end (telos) is not pursued but lies in the activity itself which therefore becomes an *entelecheia*, and the work is not what follows and extinguishes the process but is imbedded in it; the performance is the work, is *energeia*" (Arendt 1958, 206).

13. Arendt writes that in contrast to the productive process, "the means to achieve the end would already be the end; and this 'end' conversely cannot be considered a means in some other respect, because there is nothing higher to attain than this actuality itself" (Arendt 1958, 207).

14. As Ricoeur points out, the subject, thus conceived, has an identity that is conferred on him by the "plot" of his life. For a description of this "narrative identity," see Ricoeur 1993, 114–15.

15. In this they express the fundamental human condition, which, according to Arendt, is to be conditioned. In Arendt's words, "Men are conditioned beings because everything they come into contact with turns immediately into a condition of their existence." This includes "the things that owe their existence exclusively to men." They too "constantly condition their human makers" (Arendt 1958, 9).

16. These criticisms of action are my own. Arendt's book *The Human Condition* is largely insensitive to the plight of women in ancient societies.

17. In Arendt's words: "[I]n action and speech generally, we are dependent upon others, to whom we appear in a distinctness which we ourselves are unable to perceive" (Arendt 1958, 243).

Bibliography

Arendt, Hannah. 1958. *The Human Condition.* Chicago: University of Chicago Press.

————. 1977. *Eichmann in Jerusalem: A Report on the Banality of Evil.* New York: Penguin Books.

———— 1978. *The Jew as Pariah.* New York: Grove Press.

Aristotle. 1962. *Nicomachean Ethics.* Trans. Martin Ostwald. New York: Macmillan.

————. 1964. *De Anima.* (Greek text). In *On the Soul, Parva Naturalia, On Breath*, trans. W. S. Hett. Cambridge: Harvard University Press. The translation into English is my own.

Augustine, Aurelius. 1961. *Saint Augustine Confessions.* Trans. R. S. Pine-Coffin. London: Penguin Books.

Bowlby, John. 1982. "Attachment and Loss: Retrospect and Prospect." *American Journal of Orthopsychiatry*, 52, no. 4: 664–678.

Casey, Edward. 1993. *Getting Back into Place: Towards a Renewed Understanding of the Place World.* Bloomington: Indiana University Press.

Cervantes, Miguel de. 1949. *Don Quixote.* Trans. S. Putnam. New York: Random House.

Clemens, Samuel. 1977. *Huckleberry Finn.* New York: Signet Classics.

Conrad, Joseph. 1989. *Heart of Darkness.* Ed. Paul O'Prey. London: Penguin Books.

Cornwell, John. 1999. *Hitler's Pope: The Secret History of Pius XII.* New York: Viking.

Darwin, Charles. 1967a. "The Descent of Man." In *"The Origin of Species" and "The Descent of Man."* New York: Random House.

———. 1967b. "The Origin of Species." In *"The Origin of Species" and "The Descent of Man."* New York: Random House.

Dawkins, Richard. 1995. *River Out of Eden*. New York: Basic Books.

Dennett, Donald. 1991. *Consciousness Explained*. Boston: Little, Brown.

Derrida, Jacques. 1973. "Differance." in *Speech and Phenomena and Other Essays*, trans. David Allison. Evanston, Ill.: Northwestern University Press.

Descartes, René. 1955a. "Discourse on the Method." In vol. 1 of *Philosophical Works of Descartes*, trans. E. Haldane and G. Ross. New York: Dover.

———. 1955b. "The Passions of the Soul." In vol. 1 of *Philosophical Works of Descartes*, trans. E. Haldane and G. Ross. New York: Dover.

———. 1990. *Meditations on First Philosophy*. Trans. L. LaFleur. Vol. 1. New York: Macmillan.

Epstein, Rabbi Dr. I., ed. 1935. *The Babylonian Talmud*. London: Soncino Press.

Fackenheim, Emil. 1988. "The Holocaust and Philosophy: Reflections on the Banality of Evil." *Independent Journal of Philosophy* 5/6: 63–69.

Ferías, Victor. 1987. *Heidegger et le nazisme*. Paris: Editions Verdier. Translated under the title *Heidegger and Nazism*, trans. Paul Burrell. Philadelphia: Temple University Press, 1989.

Ferry, Luc. 1995. *The New Ecological Order*. Trans. Carol Volk. Chicago: University of Chicago Press, 1995.

Fogelman, Eva. 1994. *Conscience and Courage: Rescuers of Jews During the Holocaust*. New York: Doubleday.

Frege, Gottlob. 1970. *Translations from the Philosophical Writings of Gottlob Frege*. Ed. and trans. Peter Geach and Max Black. Oxford: Basil Blackwell.

Freud, Sigmund. 1959. "Splitting of the Ego in the Defensive Process." In vol. 5 of *Collected Papers*, trans. and ed. James Strachey. New York: Basic Books 1959.

———. 1962. *Civilization and its Discontents*. Trans. James Strachey. New York: W. W. Norton and Company.

————. (1965). *A General Introduction to Psychoanalysis.* Trans. Joan Riviere. New York: Washington Square Press.

————. 1989. *An Outline of Psycho-Analysis.* Trans. James Strachey. New York: W. W. Norton and Company.

Gilson, Etienne. 1967. *The Christian Philosophy of Saint Augustine.* Trans. L. E. M. Lynch. New York: Vintage Books.

Gross, Michael. 1994. "Jewish Rescue in Holland and France during the Second World War: Moral Cognition and Collective Action." *Social Forces* 73, no. 2: 463–95.

Heidegger, Martin. 1967a. *Sein und Zeit.* Tübingen: Max Niemeyer.

————. 1967b. "Von Wesen des Grundes." In *Wegmarken.* Frankfurt am Main: Vittorio Klostermann.

————. 1988. *The Basic Problems of Phenomenology.* Trans. Albert Hofstadter. Rev. ed. Bloomington: Indiana University Press.

Hull, John. 1991. *Touching the Rock.* New York: Vantage Books.

Hume, David. 1973. *A Treatise of Human Nature.* Ed. L. A. Selby-Bigge. Oxford: Clarendon Press.

Husserl, Edmund. 1976. *Ideen zu einer reinen Phänomenologie und phänomenologischen Philosophie.* Ed. R. Schuhmann. Vol. 1 Husserliana III, 1. The Hague: Martinus Nijhoff.

————. Unpublished manuscripts, courtesy of the Director of the Husserl Archives, Louvain, Belgium.

James, William. 1948. *Psychology: Briefer Course.* Cleveland, Ohio: World Publishing Company.

Jones, David. 1999. *Moral Responsibility and the Holocaust.* Lanham, Md.: Rowman & Littlefield.

Kant, Immanuel. 1955a. "Grundlegung zur Metaphysik der Sitten." Reprinted in vol. 4 of *Kants gesammelte Schriften*, ed. Königlich Preussische Akademie der Wissenschaften, 386–463. 23 vols. Berlin: Georg Reiner.

————. 1955b. "Kritik der reinen Vernunft." 1st ed. Reprinted in vol. 4 of *Kants gesammelte Schriften*, ed. Königliche Preussische Akademie der Wissenschaften, 1–252. 23 vols. Berlin: Georg Reiner.

————. 1955c. "Kritik der reinen Vernunft." 2d ed. Reprinted in vol. 3 of *Kants gesammelte Schriften.* Ed. Königliche Preussische

Akademie der Wissenschaften, 1–594. 23 vols. Berlin: Georg
Reiner.

———. 1955d. "Prolegomena." Reprinted in vol. 4 of *Kants gesammelte
Schriften*, ed. Königliche Preussische Akademie der Wissenschaften, 253–383. 23 vols. Berlin: Georg Reiner.

———. 1964. *Groundwork of the Metaphysics of Morals*. Trans. H. J.
Paton. New York: Harper and Row.

Karen, Robert. 1994. *Becoming Attached: Unfolding the Mystery of the
Infant-Mother Bond and Its Impact on Later Life*. New York:
Warner Books.

Kawabata, Yasunari. 1970. *The Sound of a Mountain*. Trans. E. M.
Seidensticker. New York: Perigee Books.

Kierkegaard, Søren. 1985. *Fear and Trembling*. Trans. Alastair Hannay.
London: Penguin Books.

Klemperer, Victor. 1998. *I Will Bear Witness: A Diary of the Nazi Years,
1933–1941*. Trans. Martin Chalmers. New York: Random
House.

Lacan, Jacques. 1977. *Écrits: A Selection*. Trans. Alan Sheridan. New
York: W. W. Norton & Company.

Leibniz, Gottfried Wilhelm. 1962. "Monadology." In *Basic Writings*,
trans. George Montgomery. La Salle, Ill.: Open Court.

Levinas, Emmanuel. 1984. "Dialogue with Emmanuel Lévinas." In
Dialogues with Contemporary Continental Thinkers, ed.
Richard Kearney. Manchester: Manchester University Press.

———. 1985. *Ethics and Infinity*. Trans. Richard Cohen. Pittsburgh,
Pa.: Duquesne University Press.

———. 1988. "The Paradox of Morality: An Interview with Emmanuel
Levinas." Interview by T. Wright, P. Hughes, and A. Ainsley.
Trans. A. Benjamin and T. Wright. In *The Provocation of
Levinas: Rethinking the Other*, ed. R. Bernasconi and D. Wood.
London: Routledge, 1988.

———. 1993. *Dieu, La Mort, et le Temps*. Ed. Jacques Rolland. Paris:
Bernard Grasset.

———. 1994a. "Diachrony and Representation." In *Time and the
Other, and Additional Essays*, trans. Richard Cohen, 97–120.
Pittsburgh, Pa.: Duquesne University Press.

———. 1994b. "Time and the Other." In *Time and the Other, and Additional Essays*, trans. Richard Cohen, 29–94. Pittsburgh, Pa.: Duquesne University Press.

———. 1996. "Substitution." In *Basic Philosophical Writings*, ed. A. Peperzak, S. Critchley, and R. Bernasconi, 79–96. Bloomington: Indiana University Press.

———. 1998. "Transcendence and Evil." In *Of God Who Comes to Mind*, trans. Bettina Bergo, 122–36. Stanford, Calif.: Stanford University Press.

Lewis, Charlton, and Charles Short, eds. 1966. *A Latin Dictionary*. London: Oxford University Press.

Locke, John. 1995. *An Essay Concerning Human Understanding*. Amherst, NY: Prometheus Books.

May, Todd. 1997. *Reconsidering Difference*. University Park: Pennsylvania State University Press.

Mensch, James. 1996a. *After Modernity*. Albany: State University of New York Press.

———. 1996b. *Knowing and Being*. University Park: Pennsylvania State University.

———. 1988. *Intersubjectivity and Transcendental Idealism*. Albany: State University of New York Press.

———. 2001. *Post-foundational Phenomenology: Husserlian Reflections on Embodiment*. University Park: Pennsylvania State University Press.

Merleau-Ponty, Maurice. 1967. *Phenomenology of Perception*. Trans. Colin Smith. London: Routledge & Kegan Paul.

———. 1968. *The Visible and the Invisible*. Trans. Alphonso Lingis. Evanston, Ill.: Northwestern University Press.

Mill, John Stuart. 1979. *Utilitarianism*. Ed. George Sher. Indianapolis, Ind.: Hackett Publishing Company.

Monroe, Kristen, and Epperson, Connie. 1994. "'But What Else Could I Do?' Choice, Identity and a Cognitive-Perceptual Theory of Ethical Political Behavior." *Political Psychology* 15, no. 2: 201–26.

Montaigne, Michel de. 1949. *Selected Essays*. Trans. William Hazlitt. New York: Random House.

Nagel, Thomas. 1974. "What Is It Like to Be a Bat?" *Philosophical Review* 4:435–50.

Newton, Isaac. 1960. *Newton's "Principia."* Trans. Andrew Motte, revised by Florian Cajori. Berkeley: University of California Press.

Nietzsche, Friedrich. 1967. *"The Birth of Tragedy" and "The Case of Wagner."* Trans. W. Kaufmann. Toronto: Random House of Canada Limited.

Nussbaum, Martha. 1990. *Love's Knowledge: Essays on Philosophy and Literature.* New York: Oxford University Press.

Oliner, Samuel, and Pearl Oliner. 1988. *The Altruistic Personality: Rescuers of Jews in Nazi Europe.* New York: The Free Press.

Parmenides. 1966. "The Way of Truth." In *The Presocratic Philosophers: A Critical History with a Selection of Texts,* by G. S Kirk. and J. E. Raven. Cambridge: Cambridge University Press.

Pascal, Blaise. 1960. *Pensées.* Trans. John Warrington. London: J. M. Dent.

Plato. 1957. *Platonis Opera.* Ed. John Burnet. 5 vols. Oxford: Clarendon Press.

———. 1971. *Gorgias.* Trans. W. Hamilton. London: Penguin Books.

Ricoeur, Paul. 1993. "Self as Ipse." In *Freedom and Interpretation,* ed. Barbara Johnson, 103–20. New York: Basic Books.

Robinson, Hoke. 1989. "Inner Sense and the Leningrad Reflection." *International Philosophical Quarterly* 3:271–79.

Sinclair, W. A. 1950. *The Traditional Formal Logic.* London: Methuen.

Singer, Wolf. 1996. "Wissenschaft und Ethik." In *Die Zeit* (overseas edition) 27, no. 5 (July): 19.

Sartre, Jean-Paul. 1966. *Being and Nothingness.* Trans. Hazel Barnes. New York: Washington Square Press.

Soffer, Gail. 1999. "The Other as an Alter Ego: A Genetic Approach." *Husserl Studies* 15:151–66.

Testimonies registered in the Archives of Yad Vashem, Jerusalem (quoted with the permission of Dr. Mordicai Paldiel, the Director, Department for the Righteous).

Watson, Lyall. 1995. *Dark Nature: A Natural History of Evil.* New York: Harper Collins.

Name Index

Subject Index